The Enemy Within
The Impact of Overseas Players on English Cricket

The Enemy Within

The Impact of Overseas Players
on English Cricket

Alastair McLellan

BLANDFORD

A Blandford Book

First published in the UK by Blandford
A Cassell Imprint
Cassell PLC, Villiers House,
41/47 Strand, London WC2N 5JE

Distributed in the United States by Sterling Publishing Co., Inc.,
387 Park Avenue South, New York, NY 10016-8810

Distributed in Australia by Capricorn Link (Australia) Pty Ltd
2/13 Carrington Road, Castle Hill, NSW 2154

British Library Cataloguing-in-Publication Data
A catalogue entry for this title is available from the British Library

ISBN 0-7137-2435-8

Typeset by Method Limited, Epping, Essex

Printed and Bound in Great Britain by
Hartnolls Limited, Bodmin, Cornwall.

For Amanda
and
C. J. Tavare
(Kent, Somerset and England)

Contents

Acknowledgements

A book like this does not get written, certainly by a first-time author, without a considerable amount of help from a lot of people. My research took me all over the UK and put me in touch with players, officials and supporters from most counties – the great majority of whom treated my often intrusive questioning with patience and courtesy. Due to the sensitivity of some of the issues dealt with in the following pages many, including one former English captain, preferred to speak 'non-attributably'. But, as the saying goes, 'they know who they are', and I thank them all for their time and hope I have represented their views accurately. Two leading county cricketers did speak to me on the record and at length, and it was the well-argued opinions of Tim Curtis and Alastair Hignell that sparked much of what follows.

Assembling the playing records for all overseas players since 1968 was a complicated and time-consuming task, and would have been impossible without the help of many county statisticians. My thanks go to Andrew Hignell (Glamorgan), Vic Isaac (Hampshire), Malcolm Lorimer (Lancashire), Jeremy Barlow (Leicestershire), Laurie Newell (Northamptonshire), Peter Wynne-Thomas (Nottinghamshire), David Oldham (Somerset), Robert Brooke (Warwickshire), Les Hatton (Worcestershire) and Sussex librarian Ossie Osborne.

Thanks must also go to Delroy Alexander and my brother Ian who kindly agreed to read the manuscript, and made a number of highly perceptive suggestions. My publisher Rod Dymott suggested that I write this book and showed an amazing amount of trust in such an inexperienced writer. Adrian Murrell and Abigail Sims of Allsport treated me with equal consideration. But two people above all others have contributed most to the writing of this book, namely Michele Savidge and my wife Amanda Brewer. Michele, ever since her time as deputy editor of *Cricket Life International*, has been my mentor as a cricket writer. I have been inspired by her talent and her encouragement. Amanda has committed so much of her own time to aiding the completion of this book, that her name should really share equal billing with my own.

Preface

'English cricket is dying and may take decades to recover unless overseas internationals are immediately banned from county ranks. England must wake up before it's too late.' Former Australian captain Bill Lawry, 1983

'It's the overseas players who have made the county game the commodity it is today; without those players, I dread to think what the standard would be like.' Richard Hadlee, Nottinghamshire and New Zealand, 1989

When Margaret Thatcher described Britain's striking miners as the 'enemy within', she was expressing her belief that the coalmen of Yorkshire and South Wales were attempting to overthrow British democracy, while still enjoying the benefits that this system of government bestowed on them. The foreign cricketers who have played county cricket since the late 1960s have not plotted to damage or destroy the English game, indeed many have arrived (at the invitation of the English cricketing authorities) sincerely thinking and hoping they would be in a position to make it stronger. But, despite all this, the overseas player is, in the eyes of many, the cricketing equivalent of Thatcher's demonized miner. As England lost test match after test match during the 1980s, the perception of the overseas player as a 'mercenary' who was paid relatively large sums to play for an English county, while all the time gaining experience and 'spying' on present and potential English internationals, intensified. This book is an attempt to get away from such gross stereotypes and to examine, without prejudice, the impact of overseas players on English test and county cricket.

Along with the spread of one-day cricket, the wholesale importation of overseas players by the first-class counties has been the most significant change in the English game over the last three decades. During the late 1970s, over 40 overseas players were employed by the county clubs. A game between the first-choice XIs of two English counties in those days would probably have seen up to 6 overseas players taking the field with their 16 English colleagues and rivals.

Much has been written about the overseas players themselves and the odd article has discussed the effect that their presence in county cricket has had on England's performance at test level. But these observations, however perceptive, have usually been made from a position of ignorance. Amazingly, over the 25 years since the rule changes which facilitated the flood of foreign cricketers into the UK, there has not been one comprehensive attempt to examine the phenomenon or the end result of English cricket's employment of overseas players. The sheer number of players involved always meant that overseas players were going to have some effect on the English game, but most observers (sniping from entrenched positions) could not be bothered to do the leg-work to determine exactly what that effect might be.

This book tries to remedy this situation. It contains much statistical analysis, but also tries to balance the tendentious conclusions, which can often be drawn from figures, with anecdotal evidence from players, officials and commentators. In this way I have attempted to answer once and for all the $64,000 question, 'Have overseas players been good or bad for English cricket?'

But what exactly is an overseas player? From the early 1980s onwards there has been much discussion of players born or raised overseas who manage to qualify to play test cricket for England. This book is not about these players. It is about those players from other test-playing nations who decided to join an English county without surrendering their allegiance to the country of their birth.

Of course, there are players who fit neither of these two neat descriptions. Gordon Greenidge and Glamorgan fast bowler Tony Cordle both arrived in England in their mid-teens, and while one went on to enjoy a lengthy test career with the West Indies, the other only ever played first-class cricket once outside the UK. Both, however, are considered overseas players in this book, as Cordle, in a period when the West Indies were less blessed with fast bowlers, would have certainly played test cricket. Likewise, Graeme Hick and Allan Lamb are considered as overseas players until they qualified to play for England, as they would have certainly both been picked by South Africa or Zimbabwe, respectively, had either side been eligible to take part in test matches.

In short, a cricketer is defined as an overseas player in this book if he played test cricket for any other nation apart from England, was eligible at any time to play test cricket for another nation but was never picked or was prevented from playing because the nation of his birth was unable to take part in international competition. Players from Zimbabwe are considered overseas players because many of those taking part in county cricket during the 1960s and 1970s would have found themselves playing test cricket for South Africa had that nation not been banned from international competition. It is also the case that had players such as Kevin Curran and Hick not decided to concentrate on their county careers, Zimbabwe might have made a much earlier entry into test cricket.

This definition owes little to the ever-changing 'official' version of what constitutes an overseas player. But it does, I believe, reflect the true nature of the phenomenon – that ever since 1968, English domestic cricket has played host to nearly 200 players whose natural allegiance was to rival test sides. The domestic game which was and is the well-spring of the English test team's strength was, for the first time, providing widespread employment for those players who would challenge that strength.

Although most of the debate surrounding overseas cricketers has concerned their effect on England's test team, the mass migration of foreign talent has also had a massive impact on the county game. This book attempts to gauge that impact and to puncture some of the myths about what type of overseas player is the most effective in county cricket.

The concentration on county cricket means that, apart from in Chapter 2, the well-established employment of overseas players in club and league cricket has only been touched on. In any case, since the late 1960s the majority of test-class overseas players have chosen to play county rather than league cricket.

That situation, however, may change in the coming years as restrictions on overseas players in county cricket mean that once again they seek employment in the leagues. Already there are signs of the better overseas players pushing existing league professionals down into club cricket and most team's second XIs usually now include one or two young overseas players hoping to pick up the knowledge and experience that will allow them to break into the first-class game at home.

The conclusions reached at the end of this book might lead some to believe that it constitutes an attack on overseas players. This is not the case, since there is much to say in their favour and this book does not seek to blame the overseas players themselves for anything. Instead, it attempts to analyse the allegations which underpin the tag of an 'enemy within', and to show how the unquestionably attractive idea of having the world's leading players take part in English county cricket can contribute to improved playing standards at county level and help reverse a decade of decline in English test cricket.

1 The entertainers arrive

In the late 1960s English county cricket was on its deathbed. Falling revenues were perhaps less important than the way the game was being sidelined as part of English social and sporting life. Cricket was still played and watched on a relatively wide scale, but, compared with the upheaval taking place in the arts, popular music and entertainment, as well as in rival sports, cricket simply seemed to be going through the motions.

In 1966, England hosted the football World Cup and achieved a deathless victory over Germany in the final. England's play was enlivened by sporting individualists like Geoff Hurst and Bobby Charlton and the nation rejoiced. During the same year the West Indies took on England's cricketers in a five-match series and beat them 3–1. Gary Sobers scored 722 runs, with three centuries, at an average of 103.14, took 20 wickets and 10 catches.

While Sobers was the star, batsmen like Hunte, Kanhai, Butcher, Nurse and Holford all at times displayed an exuberance that seemed much in tune with the times. The bowling attack of Hall, Griffith, Sobers, Gibbs and Holford was varied and effective, but most important of all it contained the excitement of uninhibited pace, backed up by glorious close to the wicket and out-fielding. England, despite the efforts of Milburn, Graveney, D'Oliveira and Snow, appeared workmanlike in contrast. The England team seemed, unfairly, to be packed with dour 'Roundheads' whose lack of imagination had found them decidedly wanting when tested against the Windies' at-the-limits attack. English cricket was simply not 'where it was at'.

But the Rothmans' International Cavaliers definitely were. A marketing man's dream of the pick of the world's cricketers, packaged in limited overs games on a Sunday afternoon and given national TV coverage, the Cavaliers gave the English sporting public a taste of the exotic that they have not lost to this day.

The Cavaliers first appeared in 1963, the brainchild of entrepreneur Bagnal Harvey, and before long had secured a regular place on the county circuit. Each year their squads would consist of leading test cricketers from overseas, retired and established English internationals, as well as young hopefuls from both the UK and abroad. One-day matches of 40 overs a side were arranged with most counties and the games were slotted into the crowded domestic schedule on a Sunday, then left sacrosanct by the first-class programme and one-day competitions. A careful choice of players, the title of Cavaliers being no accident, attracted lucrative sponsorship from Rothmans and eventually regular coverage on BBC2.

It was through this coverage that the bulk of England's sports enthusiasts rediscovered domestic cricket. While test matches remained relatively well supported, attendances at county games had dwindled alarmingly, leaving the public out of touch with the state of the domestic game. The Cavaliers, with average gates of 10,000 each Sunday, helped re-establish that contact as county players had their 15 minutes in the spotlight, facing down the world's best, who, during the short history of the Cavaliers, included English players such as Jim Laker, Dennis Compton, Tom Graveney, the South African Dennis Lindsay, and West Indians Gary Sobers, Clive Lloyd and Lance Gibbs.

The side of 1969 was weaker than many before it, but nevertheless typical of the Cavaliers' approach. The 12-man squad was captained by Ted Dexter, who had ended his test career a year before. He was joined by two current test captains, Australia's Bobby Simpson and Pakistan's Saeed Ahmed, and the jewel of the side, widely regarded as the best batsman in the world, South African Graeme Pollock. This fund of experience was topped by the 39-year old Freddie Trueman and wicket-keeper Godfrey Evans, 10 years his senior.

The remainder of the squad were six young West Indians, recommended to the Cavaliers by their Board of Control. Only one, Lawrence Rowe, was to go on to establish himself as a test player, but fast bowler Hallam Moseley played for Somerset for ten years, and in days when the Windies did not have world-class fast bowlers lurking under every palm tree, he would certainly have played test cricket. The other four players were Colin Blades, a hugely talented attacking batsman who often outshone Pollock in Cavaliers' matches and who moved to Bermuda before representing them in the 1975 World Cup, fast bowler Castell Folkes, off-spinner Lawrence Maxwell and opening batsman Alvin Corneal.

At the end of the season, the side was split into two as the Cavaliers took on Barbados during the Scarborough festival. It was a match played with a typical exuberance by both sides and took place in an almost unbelievably heady atmosphere.

The Cavaliers' side for this match included young West Indian Roy Fredericks, Australian fast bowler Neil Hawke, Sussex opener David Green, Rhodesian Peter Swart, South African fast bowler Patrick Trimborn and Gloucestershire spin bowler John Mortimore, as well as Pollock, Rowe, Trueman and Evans. The Barbados side, though, were worthy opponents, fielding seven test players, including Holford, Nurse and Hall.

The Cavaliers batted first and straight away Fredericks and Green attacked the Barbadian pace attack of Hall and Edwards. By the time Pollock came to the wicket, the Cavaliers were a healthy 113 for 2. The South African master took this as his cue to slaughter the opposition attack. Sparing no bowler he reached his first 50 in just 26 minutes and maintained this breathless pace to reach 100 in 52 minutes. He faced only 67 deliveries and hit a 6 and 19 4s to record the second fastest century for 60 years.

Dismissed for 340 in 75 overs, the Cavaliers threw down the gauntlet to Barbados who responded by striking 271 in 89 overs. Five batsmen passed 30 and the scoring rate might have equalled the Cavaliers if it were not for a marathon spell of 38-15-83-3 from the highly experienced Mortimore. Going in again the Cavaliers battled against Holford and the slow left arm of Brancker who between them bowled 44 of the 63 overs. In that time the Cavaliers scored 231 for 9, Pollock leading the way with 61 in 65 minutes with 2 6s and 6 4s.

Barbados needed 301 to win in just 4 hours, a stiff task on a wicket with 3 days' wear and tear, and against an attack containing 4 test bowlers. But Bynoe and Lashley attacked from the beginning; Trueman and Hawke being driven out of the attack. The first wicket fell at 110 and then as Blades, Holford and Nurse all pitched in, the score rose to 233 for 3. The game gave its final twist with a tight spell of bowling by Trimborn, and the inability of the tail to cope with a combination of Trueman and Hawke while maintaining the run chase. Yet, when the final wicket fell at 289, after just 67 overs, the Bajans were just 11 runs short of their target.

As the 1969 Barbados game demonstrated, there was something markedly different about the Cavaliers' matches and the way in which the players involved approached them. In the case of each Cavalier, whether it arose from the natural exuberance of youth or the knowledge of complete mastery without the responsibility of playing for club or country, there was a zest for the game that marked them out from the county pros against which they were set. And the county players began to recognize this and to realize that if they were not to appear as bit part players in the Cavaliers' drama then they would have to raise their game. Freed from the constraints of the county circuit, this is precisely what they began to do and the public watching by their millions every Sunday afternoon liked it and wanted more. A young Tim Curtis was typical of the players of the current generation who had their first experience of top-class cricket through the BBC's coverage of the Cavaliers' matches and as a result developed a strong desire to take up the game as a profession.

In the end the Cavaliers were victims of their own success. The Marylebone Cricket Club (MCC), searching desperately for a cure to the ailing finances of the game which had seen attendances at county games fall by 146,000 in 1966 alone, decided to copy the Cavaliers' idea and organize a Sunday-based one-day competition starting in 1969. The counties agreed to the new league and the sponsorship of £80,000 offered by John Player was twice that of Rothmans' support for the Cavaliers. Both the BBC and ITV, headed by London Weekend Television's Jimmy Hill, bid for the TV rights and, after a protracted court battle, the BBC won. ITV did televise a few Cavaliers games, but the counties withdrew the availability of their players who were needed to contest the John Player League (JPL) and at the end of the 1969 season Rothmans cancelled its sponsorship.

But by that time the mould had been broken. Counties, reacting to the amount of interest shown in the Cavaliers and overseas test teams, had begun recruiting foreign stars and the pattern for modern domestic cricket in England had been set.

It would be wrong to think, however, that the Cavaliers were solely responsible for establishing the overseas player as an integral part of English county cricket. The Cavaliers had in fact been the unwitting front-men for a campaign by a number of counties to change the registration rules governing the domestic game.

With some minor tinkering on the edges, the registration rules setting down who could play for each county had remained relatively the same, as far as overseas cricketers went, for most of the modern game's history. Essentially a player had to live continuously within the county boundaries for two years before he could play in its cricket team.

Prior to the late 1960s some overseas players had carved out long and impressive county careers, but most had done so at the expense of their international careers. A way was needed, thought many, to attract overseas stars without them having to make a choice between English county and home country.

The obvious answer was immediate registration as practised in the Lancashire Leagues which were packed with overseas professionals. With immediate registration the need to serve a qualification period was removed and a county career could be effortlessly segued into an overseas player's test and domestic responsibilities. The demand was obviously there: an opinion poll carried out for the *Daily Mail* by NOP in 1966 showed that Sobers was the most popular cricketer in the UK, capturing 27 per cent of the poll, Kanhai was eighth and, surprisingly, that difficult character Charlie Griffith was ninth.

Events began to move slowly in the direction of immediate registration during the early 1960s. In 1963 the MCC ruled that if an overseas player had lived anywhere in the UK for more than five years, he need serve only a one-year registration period. Overseas county players were also allowed for the first time to play abroad in the off-season provided they had the permission of their English employers. However overseas players were still banned from taking part in any tour of the UK by their national side and counties could only employ two cricketers born outside the UK in any one season.

These rule changes of 1963 were followed two years later by a proposal from Nottinghamshire that each county be allowed to register one overseas player without any qualification period on top of any two that might qualify under the existing residential rules.

The proposal had some support among the cricketing establishment. Alex Bannister addressed the issue in *The Cricketer* and wrote: 'To my mind to hamper the inflow of the world's best personalities into a competition (the County Championship) which sadly needs new life zest and skills, is a negation of common sense.' He put forward four possible objections to immediate registration, the first of which now seems rather ironic.

Would the overseas cricketing powers be 'drained of their talent' by becoming hunting grounds for the English counties, asked Bannister? No he claimed, making the obvious point that the overseas domestic competitions would not clash with the English game, therefore leaving the strength of the former unaffected. As for the second objection that the arrival of overseas players would restrict opportunities for English-born players, Bannister is dismissive: 'This argument produces a hollow laugh from the counties who would be only too thankful if there was any sort of competition for places by home-bred talent'. The third objection, that the existing wage structure within the game (based on a gentlemen's agreement between the counties not to go beyond a certain figure), would have to be changed, Bannister saw instead as an opportunity to modify an outdated system. As for the dangers of a 'football like' transfer system developing, Bannister puts his faith in 'the good faith and common sense of the clubs'.

Despite the support of *The Cricketer* the proposal was defeated. A year later Lancashire joined Nottinghamshire in proposing immediate registration. But again the idea was rejected, this time due to concern surrounding the proposed reduction in the number of games played during the county championship. The counties feared that with a smaller number of games to be played each season, they would have difficulty in getting 'full value' from an expensive overseas import. John Woodcock, again in *The Cricketer*, said that the decision displayed 'alarming complacency'.

But all the time support for the move was growing, with *The Cricketer* playing a leading role. A players' questionnaire put together by the magazine allowed Surrey captain Mickey Stewart to put forward his belief that overseas players were 'wanted' in English county cricket.

Stewart wrote that overseas players were needed 'to satisfy spectators that everything is being done to put the highest standard of cricket before them. I know that this will mean a higher wage bill for the counties, but it might be a risk that will have to be taken even if it means some of the less ambitious having to drop out of the competition (for overseas players)'. Although *The Cricketer*'s questionnaire did not specifically propose the introduction of overseas players as a solution to the game's ills, 30 per cent of the players suggested it anyway.

The campaign to introduce immediate registration was given further impetus by the findings of the 1966 Clark Report. The committee which produced the report was packed with some of cricket's most influential figures, including MCC treasurer Gubby Allen and chairman of the England test selectors Doug Insole. Chaired by Kent chairman David Clark, the committee was formed to determine how cricket should counter the decline in its popularity. Most of the Clark Report's wide-ranging recommendations were rejected by the counties, but many lent their whole-hearted support to the conclusion that: 'Overseas star players will not only raise the standard of county teams by their individual prowess, but they should also have a beneficial effect on the young men who play with them'.

The watershed came in 1967. In January the MCC's Advisory County Cricket Committee (ACCC) dropped the residential qualification period to just one year for a three-year trial period. But by now the bandwagon bearing the idea of immediate registration was really rolling, picking up speed as it went. In May the decision was described as a 'weak and senseless compromise', especially as far as established players went. Gloucestershire then proposed that the period of registration be restricted to one English season, but the supporters of immediate registration could sense success and pushed on. The final victory came when the autumn meeting of the ACCC finally gave the go-ahead to immediate registration, a report which *The Cricketer* marked with the exultant headline, 'Now higher standards are guaranteed'.

The author of the report, John Arlott, was fulsome in his praise of the decision to introduce immediate registration from the 1968 season onwards. Counties would now be able to contract an overseas player without a previous qualifying period once every three years. 'This relaxation' wrote Arlott, 'must be basically good for our cricket because . . . it puts 16 test class players in the place of the weakest member of each team.' Discussing the implications of the move, he says: 'The leading New Zealand, Indian and Pakistan players are not so good as our best, so not every county will be lifted sky high.' Arlott also attempted to soothe fears that deregulation would result in extortionate wage demands on the counties. He wrote: 'The employers are in a strong position, between May and September professional cricket is only available in England.' He concluded by hoping that the public would not expect too much of the overseas players and observing that most clubs were eager to sign West Indians, with Sobers and Gibbs being seen as 'the first choice' for most sides.

But for all the weight attached to the opinions of *The Cricketer* and its distinguished contributor, it was the verdict of *Wisden's Almanack*, the bell-wether of all cricketing change, which counted most. Editor Sydney Pardon, writing in the 1968 edition, gave his seal of approval by devoting a large section of 'Notes by the editor' to the issue. He claimed that the move was cricket's 'biggest step forward in recent years' and could prove to be 'the salvation of the three-day County Championship'. Flying in the face of modern opinion he says 'I am only surprised that the plunge was not taken sooner. The numerous provisos safeguard the welfare of English-born players and the very fact that a heavy responsibility will now rest upon the star cricketer should help the promising youngster to take his place in first-class company without the worry that any temporary failure will weigh heavily against his side.'

Pardon, however, praises Yorkshire for sticking to its insistence on only picking players born in the county and dismisses fears of a transfer system developing within the county circuit. 'Yet', he reasons, 'when one takes into account all the publicity and the interest that league football gains from the exchange of players is the time so very distant when cricket will be conducted in a similar fashion?'

A second proposal by Notts at the autumn meeting, that counties should only be allowed to have four overseas players on their books was also accepted, but the number was reduced to two, a stipulation which was soon widely ignored in practice.

The more forward-thinking counties had already begun to act before the immediate registration of overseas players became a reality. Overseas players were obviously going to be a major drawing card and those counties that waited for what was seen as the inevitable acceptance of the Notts' proposal were already going to be a season behind in only being able to field one overseas player.

In 1965 Northamptonshire had taken the bold step of signing a five-year contract with 22-year-old Pakistan all-rounder Mushtaq Mohammad. The youngest ever test player, having made his debut at the age of 15, he played with the county for 12 years.

During the English off-season of 1964–5 two unknown West Indians, Boyce and Shepherd, were spotted playing for Barbados by former Kent wicket-keeper Les Ames. He persuaded both to try their luck in England and they duly arrived in 1965, Boyce ending up at Essex thanks to Trevor Bailey's intervention and Shepherd becoming part of Kent's all-conquering XI of the 1970s. At the same time Lance Gibbs was qualifying by residence for Warwickshire, Younis Ahmed for Surrey, Deryck Murray for Nottinghamshire, Clive Lloyd for Lancashire, Glenn Turner for Worcestershire and South African Hylton Ackerman for Northants.

Despite this frenetic activity only 11 counties took advantage of the introduction of the immediate registration. Pakistan's two dazzling all-rounders, Asif Iqbal and Majid Khan, went to Kent and Glamorgan respectively, while the side's live-wire wicket-keeper Farokh Engineer was signed on by Lancashire. All three were established test players, and Kent had in fact had their eyes on Asif for a number of years. At the age of 20 Asif had been in a Pakistan Eaglets side which beat Kent by an innings and 84 runs. Asif's contribution was 74, batting at number 7, and 4 for 21 as the county was bowled out for 100 in the second innings.

Four South Africans were also signed up; Hampshire (Barry Richards) and Gloucestershire (Mike Procter) getting the best deals, and Essex (Lee Irvine) and Northamptonshire (Hylton Ackerman) picking up two solid performers. The sole Australian was batting tiro Greg Chappell who joined Somerset.

The real prizes, the West Indians, went to Nottinghamshire (Gary Sobers), Warwickshire (Rohan Kanhai) and Worcestershire (Vanburn Holder). Sussex's overseas recruit Geoff Greenidge, although another West Indian, was hardly of the same calibre.

Most of the other counties followed suit in 1969. Leicestershire signed Australia's leading fast bowler Graham McKenzie, while Middlesex picked up second prize by signing his opening partner Alan Connolly. Australia had in fact welcomed the change of the registration rules, giving, as it did, a chance for its 'amateur' players to earn a living during the winter. Alterations were made to the terms and conditions of Australian test players, allowing them to play without penalty in English county cricket.

At the end of the 1968 season the experiment was widely considered to have been a success. The effectiveness of the overseas players had been lessened by the bad weather which dogged the season, reducing opportunities for them to perform and unsettling those from warmer climes. But Warwickshire captain and England selector-to-be Alan Smith claimed that Sobers and Proctor had 'revitalized' Nottinghamshire and Gloucestershire respectively, while Warwickshire's batsmen and bowlers had 'learnt much' from Kanhai and Gibbs. Despite being in their 30s, Warwickshire's two West Indians also helped raise the county's fielding standards to a new high.

In general Smith believed that the enthusiastic approach of overseas recruits would have a beneficial effect on their county colleagues. Writing in *The Cricketer*, he claimed: 'I think their attitude will get through to English players and that in the end will be their major contribution to the English game. Rather than restrict the development of English talent, our imports will help home players to develop in the right way.' Smith, of course, had good reason for this optimism as the Warwickshire team – complete with Kanhai and Gibbs – won the Gillette Cup in 1968.

The changes in the registration rules, as well as being brought about by the need to resurrect the county championship, were also a reflection of the increasing influence of overseas players and the multi-ethnic nature of England in the 1960s. A survey carried out in 1969 revealed that between the years of 1963 and 1968, 57 players born outside the UK had played in English county cricket. There were a large number of red herrings, including Colin Cowdrey who was born in India, but the trend was clear. Kent and Warwickshire were the most widespread seekers of overseas talent during the six-year period, each having five apiece. In fact, 25 plus of the 30-odd players representing the two clubs during the mid-1970s were born outside the county boundaries. The West Indies provided most of the county cricketers to be born outside the UK with 22, while South Africa sent 14, India 7, Australia 4, and Pakistan, Ceylon and New Zealand 3 each.

In the summer of 1969 *The Cricketer* ran an article which claimed that immediate registration had been a 'great success'. It agreed with Smith's verdict on Sobers who, as well as instantly becoming the county's leading player, also took on the captaincy. The magazine praised his 'easy natural approach and his complete lack of dour safety first methods used by so many first-class players today'. This approach was a 'breath of fresh air', which had blown across the county championship scene and taken Nottinghamshire from sixteenth place in 1967, without a single victory, up to fourth the next year. According to *The Cricketer*, Sobers had had an inspirational effect on the Notts side: 'Slowly the players who had been struggling for years through general lack of confidence began to have faith in themselves and the team.'

In his 1968 editorial Pardon had agreed with Arlott that Sobers was 'the big prize'. Before the introduction of immediate registration Sobers had been approached by both Gloucestershire and Northants, but was not prepared to forgo his international career while serving the two-year qualifying period.

In the run-up to the 1968 season seven counties attempted to sign the West Indian captain, but Nottinghamshire, perhaps remembering the effect Australian leg-spinner Bruce Dooland had had on their fortunes in the early 1950s, were prepared to pay the highest price. Pardon speculated that Sobers' contract 'could be worth £7,000 a year, including a flat and car'. And the ever practical editor asked, 'Where is the money coming from to pay these expensive stars with county cricket in its present parlous state?'

The contract made Sobers the highest-paid cricketer in the world, but Notts had high hopes that the all-rounder would more than repay their investment. Sobers had already resurrected one overseas domestic club. A few years before moving to Nottinghamshire, and in between his commitment to the Lancashire League and the International Cavaliers, he had helped South Australia win the Sheffield Shield for only the second time in the previous 25 years. He played for South Australia for a total of three seasons, and in two of them he performed the Australian double of 1,000 runs and 50 wickets. Sponsored by Coca-Cola his cricket was some of the most exciting ever seen in Australia. In one match during his first season with South Australia he masterminded a victory over New South Wales by scoring 251, and taking 3-51 and 6-72 against a side including Bobby Simpson, Norman O'Neill, Neil Harvey, Alan Davidson, Richie Benaud and four other test players.

Sobers matched this performance in his first season for Notts, topping the county's batting averages with 1,590 runs at 42.97 and taking 83 wickets. Notts won seven more games than in 1967 and Sobers was able to collect the six bottles of champagne that Les Ames's wife had staked against Notts finishing in the top six. But the relative weakness of Notts' bowling attack still meant that many opportunities to clinch important games went begging.

In some ways Sobers had a frustrating first season in that the lack of a serious challenge for any of the domestic competitions meant that the crowds stayed away from many Notts games. Yet, despite having this important stimulus removed, the Windies captain still managed a number of near super-human feats.

The first of these imperious displays of talent came in early August against eventual championship runners-up Kent at Dover. Kent batted first and Sobers opening the bowling with his fast left-arm deliveries soon had Luckhurst trapped lbw for seven, before bowling Nicholls for six. Knott came in to partner Denness and in their contrasting styles they added 113 for the third wicket. However, after passing the 150-mark Notts' home-grown West Indian fast bowler, Clinton Forbes, dismissed both batsmen. A small stand between Leary and Shepherd added 40 more runs, but then Sobers captured 5 more wickets (Halfyard dismissing Johnson) to record a final analysis of 7-67.

The Notts first innings was a solid unremarkable affair, the county scoring 228 for 7 declared (Sobers 17, batting at number 7) and finishing 7 runs behind the home side. Once more Kent started badly as Taylor and Forbes had 4 out for 64, but again Denness, this time with Shepherd, began to guide the county out of trouble. With Kent's lead nearing 100 and time running out, Sobers brought himself on to bowl slow left-arm. Denness was the first to go, stumped by Murray. He was followed by Shepherd (raging against the dying light by scoring 57 in 78 minutes with 11 4s), Dixon and Sayer. Forbes helped mop up the tail and Sobers' match figures were 49.3-6-156-11.

Notts were now faced with the almost impossible task of scoring 186 in 2¼ hours. There was no hanging around until the fifth wicket went down for Sobers this time. He emerged from the pavilion at 38 for 1 and destroyed the Kent attack with a ferocious assault. In his first 40 minutes at the crease he scored 51 runs out of a total of 71. His next 50 came even faster as he raced to the fastest century of the season in a total of 77 minutes, hitting 2 6s and 18 4s and carrying his side to victory with 5 overs to spare.

The Kent bowlers were unable to contain Sobers from the moment he arrived at the crease, as the 80 per cent of his runs accrued in boundaries shows, and all other statistics apart it is the bowling figures that tell the true story of Sobers' majesty: Shepherd 17-3-68-0; Sayer 4-0-20-0; Dixon 6-0-32-1; and Underwood, at the height of his powers on a third-day wicket, 13.2-2-65-2.

This was the match that really whetted the appetite of Nottinghamshire's supporters and convinced the club officials that they'd made the right choice. But, despite the glory of Sobers during August on the south coast, it is another performance that barely lasted three minutes that has stayed in the minds of cricket-lovers when they dwell on 'Sir Gary's' first season in county cricket.

When Notts arrived in Swansea at the end of the 1968 season, Sobers still needed another victory to secure his bottles of bubbly from Bunty Ames. On the first day Notts batted and were 300-odd for 5,when Sobers came to the wicket looking to score quickly enough to give him the chance to declare and bowl at the Welsh side before the close of play.

The Notts captain raced to 40 and had decided that he would bat on for just 2 more overs. As Malcolm Nash came on to bowl slow–medium left-arm he began to eye the short leg side boundary. Sobers explains that his intention was 'to swing so hard at each ball that even a miss hit off the top edge would clear the boundary'.

But Sobers did not have to worry about top edges for the first four deliveries, which were all hit square in the middle of the bat and over the rope. The fifth delivery was wide of the off-stump and Sobers' flailing bat did not make such good contact. The ball soared to long-off where the fielder completed the catch, only to topple backwards over the boundary rope – another six. The sixth ball of the over was a seamer pitched short on middle and leg, and Sobers hit it so hard that when the ball was recovered by a small boy two days later he swore it was 'still rolling down the road'. In one over Nash's bowling analysis had gone from the impressive 20-3-64-4 to the more modest 21-3-100-4.

Ironically, to date the only other batsman to have hit six sixes off a six-ball over in a first-class match is Indian all-rounder (and renowned stonewaller) Ravi Shastri, who was recruited by Glamorgan during the late 1980s.

Notts declared the first innings total at 394 and bowled out Glamorgan for 254 (Sobers 2 for 63). In Notts' second innings, 4 wickets went down for 30 (a lead of just 170), but Sobers again strolled to the crease and scored 72 out of 94 in an hour and 51 minutes, allowing his side to leave Glamorgan 280 to win. However the Welsh county crumbled against Taylor and White, and were dismissed for 113. Sobers collected his champagne a few days later.

Despite the success of 1968, international commitments combined significantly to reduce Sobers' impact on Notts' performance. Without the influence and example of the West Indies captain the Notts team reverted to a very ordinary side indeed.

This was clearly demonstrated during the opening few months of the 1970 season. Sobers had missed much of the preceding English season through taking part in that summer's West Indian tour and was about to depart for the Rest of the World Series scheduled to take place as a replacement for the cancelled visit of the South African team.

If this was not enough to destroy any sense of continuity with the county, the confused situation was made worse by Sobers agreeing to take part in a double wicket competition in the then racially segregated state of Rhodesia. Sobers had made the decision to take the trip after the 1970 English season while in a position of apparent ignorance about the situation in the country. But he was a proud man and determined to stand by his commitments.

When Sobers arrived at the gates of the Oval on 20 May 1970 to take part in a county championship game with Surrey, he was astonished to find a group of protesters waiting at the Jack Hobbs gates. He was called an 'Uncle Tom' and once inside the ground was constantly booed while on the field. And if the external pressures were not enough, Sobers had to twice rescue his side as the Surrey seamers demolished the early batting order.

In the first innings, he came to the wicket at 28 for 4, and in the next 4¾ hours he straight drove 2 enormous 6s, and cut, pulled and drove 28 4s to record 160 out of 281. In reply, Surrey's batsmen all chipped in and the home side reached 278 for 4 declared with little trouble. Notts going in again soon found themselves 4 down for 60. Sobers made his way wearily to the wicket and in an atypical defensive innings scored 42 in 2 hours, fighting a tense duel with Pocock and Intikhab Alam in the process. But with support running out he stepped on the gas to crash another 61 in 47 minutes. With his score on 103 and the total 218 Sobers declared, giving Surrey 2 hours and 35 minutes to score 222. Altogether Sobers' 263 runs accounted for 52 per cent of the team's total and the next highest combined score came from Basharat Hassan, who scored just 55.

Despite the loss of Edrich, their leading batsman, Surrey went for the runs and the Notts bowlers were powerless to stop them as the target was reached for the loss of only three wickets. As the disconsolate Notts team trooped from the field many must have been too ashamed to look their captain in the eye.

In spite of a continuing series of breathtaking performances from Sobers, the initial optimism about his effect on the side began to drain away. Sobers was aware that the advances made in 1968 and maintained in 1969 were in danger of being lost, and asked to be released from the Rest of the World Series. However, he was told in no uncertain terms that if he refused to take part in the replacement test series he would not be allowed to turn out for Notts. This was a case of considerable double standards, as a few years later Geoff Boycott was able to declare himself ineligible for England, while still being allowed to play for Yorkshire.

Given his attempts to free himself from these unexpected international obligations, Sobers received some very unfair criticism from the *1971 Wisden* in which he was accused of saving his best performances for the Rest of the World games.

By the time he returned full time in 1971, the damage was done and Notts dropped back to finish twelfth in the county championship. Over the next few years the decline continued, the county finishing fourteenth in 1972 and last in 1973. Sobers was then removed from the captaincy and played one last season under former Lancashire skipper Jack Bond in 1974, the county finishing fifteenth.

Ironically it was Sobers' departure that brought the arrival of Clive Rice. Unlike Sobers he was free from the demands of test cricket and burned with an unfulfilled ambition that was finally able to craft a championship winning team for Nottinghamshire.

Despite the havoc Sobers had wreaked on his county during 1968, Glamorgan captain Tony Lewis was another who was broadly welcoming of immediate registration. In a light-hearted way he claimed that in the year 2000 his county's side would include, 'four Indians, three West Indians, an African, a Pakistani and a Chinaman'. Mind you he also foresaw another scenario, which unfortunately looks almost as unlikely now as it did in the late 1960s. 'In 2000 . . . I can imagine the Welsh team manager rushing up to Bradford . . . to sign Imtiaz Illingworth, one of the ten Yorkshire-born Pakistanis playing in the Yorkshire side.'

Lewis, of course, had plenty of reasons to approve of overseas players. In 1969 Glamorgan won the county championship for only the second time. The first had been in 1948 in only the third post-War season, a time in which English cricket had yet to recover from the effects of the conflict. In 1969, the championship was much more fiercely contested with many less fashionable sides challenging the 1968 winners Yorkshire.

The Welsh county stormed through the whole season winning 11 of its 24 games and losing none. To the fore in most games were Pakistan's Majid Khan, who topped the county's batting averages, scoring 1,386 runs in all games at 39.66, and West Indian batsman Bryan Davis who successfully adapted his cavalier approach to English conditions.

For a number of years the Glamorgan side had promised much. Lewis and Alan Jones provided the batting strength, while the county's two naturalized

Welshmen, Walker (from South Africa) and Cordle (from Barbados), formed a bowling quartet with Nash and Shepherd that had to be respected. Once the county could play two overseas stars in the place of less skilled home-grown players that promise was turned into achievement.

Outstanding individual achievements such as those performed by Sobers or Majid Khan were nothing new in county cricket. What was new was the head-to-head battle between overseas stars that Lancashire League spectators had enjoyed for decades. The most eagerly awaited game came early in the 1968 season at Trent Bridge, with Nottinghamshire against Warwickshire or, as it was billed, Sobers and Murray vs. Kanhai and Gibbs.

With the West Indies' four leading players all involved it seemed inevitable that they would dominate the game, but as cricket is anything other than an obvious game it looked initially as though they might have little influence. Warwickshire batted first, and Sobers and Forbes soon gave way to the classic English medium-pace attack of Taylor and Halfyard. Seaming the ball off a helpful pitch, Taylor took 6-42 and Halfyard 3-20, dismissing Warwick for 93. Taylor accounted for Warwick's overseas batting star, Kanhai, falling lbw to the English seamer for eight. Gibbs remained nought not out and only two catches apiece by Murray and Sobers bore testament to the presence of Notts' West Indian giants.

That presence finally began to make itself felt in the second half of Notts' innings. The home side were making a better fist of the conditions but when Sobers and Murray came together the top 4 batsmen were gone with only 76 on the board. Facing the highly effective attack (in English conditions at least) of Brown, Cartwright and Bannister, the two West Indians almost doubled their side's score. Surprisingly it was Sobers who went first, caught and bowled by occasional leg-spinner Bob Barber for 54, but Murray batted on in that irritatingly effective way peculiar to wicket-keepers to record the highest score of the game so far.

With Notts having reached 282 (Murray 92), Warwick faced a deficit 189 and were soon deep in trouble. Sobers had Barber for a duck, and Forbes dismissed Stewart and Amiss for three and one respectively. It was six for three when Kanhai and Ibadulla came together for the second time in the match. Warwickshire were still 183 runs behind and with only 7 wickets left standing, but just as Sobers and Murray had done, Kanhai, the grey-haired batting magician, and Ibadulla, an imposing mixture of West Indian physique and Pakistani grandeur, began to pull the game around.

The West Indian of Indian descent and the Pakistani with a West Indian father had their escapes earlier on but gradually began to assume control. Sobers this time shouldered his fair share of the bowling burden, but although he bowled 32 overs in all three of his styles he was unable to add to his solitary wicket. Kanhai dominated the Notts attack which had run riot during the first innings, and with Ibadulla rock-like in support, he wiped Warwick's deficit and pushed on to higher ground. When Kanhai was finally dismissed for 253, including a 6 and 36 4s, the pair had added 402 for the fourth wicket. Warwickshire declared a few overs later, leaving Ibadulla undefeated at the end of the innings with 147, having hit 16 4s.

The first season following the introduction of immediate registration was just over a month old and already two foreign players, one admittedly who had played in England since the early 1950s, had forced themselves into the county record books. The score of 402 was the highest stand in Warwickshire's history, and the exotic names of Kanhai and Ibadulla joined the common Anglo-Saxon names of Smith and Foster in the county's roll of honour.

After Warwickshire declared at 435 for 4, Notts were left to score 247 in under 2 hours, and that was beyond even Sobers' capabilities.

A month later it was Gibbs' turn to show his mettle and to overcome an opposing overseas star. Warwickshire arrived at Leyton in the days following Sobers' thrashing of Kent and both West Indians were keen to make sure that their captain did not gain all the glory that season.

However Essex's young left-arm spinner Ray East raced through the visitors' batting order, dismissing Kanhai for a duck and taking 7 for 52. Essex, as they might have feared, fared even worse. Gibbs and Brown combined to bowl them out for 47, 51 runs behind. As the game entered its third innings, the surface was growing even more unreliable and East was becoming almost unplayable. Bowling throughout the innings with John Lever, East captured Kanhai for 10 and went one better than his first innings performance by taking 8 wickets for 63.

Now came the crunch. Essex had been set 150 to win, 3 times more than they had made in the first innings. Gibbs made the first breakthrough having Edmeades lbw. for 7 and then the medium pacer Blenkiron took over to reduce Essex to 31 for 5. Gibbs then dismissed Keith Boyce for a duck and Essex were 52 for 6. South African recruit Lee Irvine, though, was still there. Fated to live in the shadow of Richards, Procter and Barlow, Irvine was slowly developing into one of the most reliably aggressive batsmen in world cricket. His greatest achievements were still ahead of him, but the size of his ambition was already clear.

Irvine climbed into Gibbs and Blenkiron, smashing 2 6s and 6 4s as the county's score began to race upwards. But, with the score on 92, Essex captain Brian Taylor was dismissed, and with one end open, Gibbs stepped in to dismiss Hobbs for a duck and leave Irvine with no option but to go down with all guns blazing. His 41, all but 5 from boundaries, was the highest score of the match and represented more runs than any other Essex player made in both innings combined. It was also symptomatic of the new spirit that overseas players had brought with them into English county cricket.

The early theory that one overseas player would not be enough if a county wanted to make a serious attempt at the championship was beginning to be proved correct. At least two were required to provide support for each other, share the burden of expectations and rise above the conditions when lesser players began to struggle. In the Warwickshire side Kanhai always threatened rival bowling attacks, while Gibbs worried their batsmen. For Notts, Sobers' one-man playing machine was kept viable by Murray's assistance in the field, boosting morale and talking tactics.

Yet still in 1969, there were those counties who, either out of inclination or poverty, chose to stick with just one. The danger of this approach was exposed in a number of games during the season. One of the best examples came when Northants, boasting Mushtaq Mohammad and Hylton Ackerman, travelled to play Hampshire and Barry Richards.

Northants batted first and the respected pace duo of Cottam and White soon had the visitors struggling. Goldstein was lbw to White for seven and Lightfoot was caught by Stevenson off Cottam for nine. At 33 for 2 Ackerman and Mushtaq Mohammad came together and transformed the struggle into a rout. Ackerman was out at 111 after scoring 54, but Mushtaq, with the help of Prideaux and Willey, carried on to score an undefeated 154 out of 325 for 5 declared.

Hampshire had lost their captain, Roy Marshall, when he trod on the ball and damaged his ankle, and faced a difficult task repelling Mushtaq and Breakwell on a spinners' wicket. Only Barry Richards, recording his fifth century of the season could cope with conditions. Yet he had no support and in any case Hants had already surrendered the initiative to their opponents by letting them score over 300 on a poor wicket.

Richards responded magnificently as Northants quickie Peter Lee dismissed Turner and Gilliat by the time the score reached 19. Richards, playing with 'soft hands' to avoid the danger of edging to the encircling close fielders, added 78 with Livingstone, but the spinners were on now and his partner went for 12, quickly followed by Wheatley for a duck. The young Trevor Jesty was frozen into inactivity by the conditions and remained scoreless while Richards added 30. Breakwell dismissed Jesty, Lee returned to have wicket-keeper Stephenson lbw. and then Mushtaq took over. What Richards must have thought as he saw the number nine White stumped with Hants still 19 runs from preventing the follow-on is best left unexplored. The master batsman was then joined by McIlwaine, playing his first county match. The young bowler carved his way to 17 before also being stumped and Richards left the field having carried his bat for 127, as well as almost single-handedly saving the follow-on.

Unfortunately, after Northants had scored 149-8 declared (Ackerman 34), Richards could not repeat the heroics and Hampshire lost by 140 runs, Mushtaq taking 3 for 55.

The mix of overseas players began to become vital to the make-up of county sides. To have one of your overseas stars unavailable seriously upset the game plan and, particularly in pressure situations, left teams vulnerable to rivals boasting a full complement of foreign hired hands. The all-conquering Glamorgan suffered their first defeat for nearly two years when they met Warwickshire at Edgbaston during May 1970. For Glamorgan Majid Khan was missing, while Warwickshire had Gibbs and Kanhai both present and correct.

After the first 2 innings, honours were even with Warwickshire enjoying a lead of just 22 runs. But the wicket was beginning to wear and Glamorgan's spin partnership of Walker and Shepherd (who had taken 5 for 41 in the first innings) looked like match winners. For Warwickshire Abberley and Jameson battled hard but wickets began to fall at regular intervals. Only Kanhai was able to counter the threat and even then the dashing strokemaker was slowed to 20 runs an hour. Kanhai finally fell to Walker for 91 and Shepherd then dismissed the last 4 Warwickshire batsmen for 9 runs to finish with 7 for 48.

However, the damage had already been done. A target of 210 on a third-day wicket without their leading batsman was always going to stretch Glamorgan, especially if their opponents had somebody like Gibbs to exploit the conditions. Blenkiron dismissed the first two Glamorgan batsmen for seven runs and from then on it was all Gibbs. In his first five overs he accounted for Williams, Jones, Davis, Walker and Lewis for just nine runs. Nash and Cordle came together to take the score from 81 for 8 to 132, but then 3 wickets in 8 balls swept Warwickshire to victory by 75 runs. Gibbs' 8 for 37 were career best figures.

What the presence of Gibbs and Kanhai gave Warwickshire was the ability to exploit helpful conditions, whether batting or bowling, and to withstand difficult situations in which other sides without that sort of talent at its disposal would crumble.

Later in the 1970 season, Kanhai was to give an almost textbook example of that second type of advantage. Warwickshire met Derbyshire at Coventry in early August. The home side batted first and as Jameson and Abberley added 63 for the first wicket, the home side looked set fair for a good first innings total. Then veteran off-spinner Edwin Smith dismissed both openers within the space of 13 runs, bringing Kanhai to the wicket. He and M.J.K. Smith took the score to 96 before fast bowler Alan Ward suddenly hit a purple patch.

Warwickshire slumped from 96 for 2 to 103 for 5 as Ward dismissed Mike Smith and Amiss for a single and Alan Smith for a duck. The Derbyshire and England paceman was one of the most feared bowlers on the circuit when on song and those batsmen whom he failed legitimately to dismiss often found themselves 'retiring' in a more painful way. Kanhai was joined by young all-rounder Eddie Hemmings who helped him add 66 runs.

At 169 Hemmings was dismissed for 30 and David Brown came to the wicket just in time to see Kanhai reach his century in a little under 2 hours. By the time Ward had dismissed Brown for a single, the pair had added 29 and taken the score to 197. Blenkiron was dismissed three runs later and Gibbs came in to join his test colleague. As Ward threw himself furiously into the attack, Kanhai responded by counterattacking with a series of breathtaking strokes. The battle continued until, with the score at 253, Gibbs was bowled by Russell for a duck. In came the number 11 Warwick Tidy, and again Kanhai and Ward went head to head.

Another 42 runs were added before Tidy was caught by Swarbrook off Ward for a single and Kanhai walked off to a standing ovation with 187 out of 295 to his name. It was the fiftieth century of his career and in all had taken him just three hours and eight minutes. He had hooked, pulled, cut and drove 7 6s and 26 4s (a total of 146 out of 187), scoring all but 6 of Warwickshire's final 126 runs. Without Kanhai's presence, Warwickshire would have been totally unable to cope with the conditions they found at Coventry or with Ward's ability to exploit them.

As the English waited to see how the introduction of immediate registration would affect the county game, there was considerable nervousness among some overseas players, officials and spectators over how the change would affect their own international sides.

The first international series after the introduction of immediate registration was between Australia and the West Indies. Sobers, Kanhai and Gibbs all played throughout the entire five-match series and did not seem to show any particular ill-effects from their county labours.

The Australian's eventual 3–1 victory seemed to have more to do with the home side's burgeoning batting strength, and the ineffectiveness of the ageing Hall and Griffith.

Kanhai had a quiet series by his own high standards, averaging only 37 in the 5 tests and did not travel on to New Zealand with the rest of the tour party. It was here, after the West Indies' victory in the first test, that signs of fatigue began to show. New Zealand won the second test by six wickets and were on level terms with the West Indians when the third finished in a draw. Sobers was clearly exhausted, averaging only 14 with the bat and taking just 7 wickets at 43. Gibbs also showed signs of chafing against the non-stop cricket, taking only eight wickets in the three tests.

But there was no rest even then for the West Indian side who, three months after finishing the third test in New Zealand, were facing the resurgent England. Kanhai was still absent, and Sobers and Gibbs seemed now to be operating at half their normal strength. England won the three-match series by two matches to nil and were favourites to win the drawn second test when time ran out. Sobers had his worst series against England, scoring only 150 runs at an average of 30 and taking only 11 wickets, 5 in England's second innings during the last test. Gibbs was almost completely ineffectual, capturing just two wickets in each test.

England's first post-1968 tour, to Pakistan, was too often disrupted by riots to give any clear indication of whether the home side players had learnt anything during the county season. But all three county recruits in the Pakistan side (Asif, Majid and Mushtaq) batted and bowled consistently. However, the real benefits of a county cricket education to an overseas player did not really show until January 1970.

Over the first three months of the new decade the greatest test team in South African cricket history destroyed a strong Australian XI. The nucleus of the side, Barlow, Proctor and the two Pollocks, was already in place but the team was further strengthened by the addition of two players who, during the previous two seasons in English county cricket, had added a steely determination to their already undoubted talents. Barry Richards and Lee Irvine both made their debuts in the first test. Obviously, both were going to succeed at test level, but their county experience enabled them to hit the ground running and achieve amazing consistency for players taking part in their first series. Richards led the way, recording consecutive scores of 29, 32, 140, 65, 35, 81 and 126. Irvine did nearly as well, hitting 42, 19, 13, 79, 73, 25 and 102. In a total of 14 innings, they hit 3 centuries, 4 50s and made not one score in single figures: in total 861 runs at an average of 61.50.

As we have seen there was considerable comment before 1968 that immediate registration would drain the playing resources of other test playing countries that were not as well stocked as England. After about three years it was possible to see that while seven day a week cricket was tiring the already ageing West Indian side, it had a positively enlivening effect on the precocious test sides of South Africa and Pakistan. It soon became obvious that whereas Sobers, Gibbs and Kanhai were the teachers, it was the pupils of the county circuit such as Richards and Asif Iqbal who had the most to gain.

As for the belief that immediate registration would weaken the England side, by acquainting foreign test stars with the weaknesses of Boycott and Edrich et al., the improvement in playing standards in fact seemed to have an improving effect on the rather workaday England side of the late 1960s. This effect was seen at its height when England defeated Australia on the 1970/1 tour and, particularly, when it provided stiff opposition to the Rest of the World team during the English summer of 1970. Although England were defeated by four tests to one, the losing margin in the last three matches was five, two and four wickets. This result, facing a side which in batting order read Richards, Barlow, Kanhai, Pollock, Lloyd, Sobers, Engineer (or Murray), Intikhab Alam, Proctor, McKenzie (or Mushtaq Mohammad) and Gibbs, was an impressive achievement.

Looking back, the introduction of immediate registration and the increasing numbers of overseas players in county sides did not abruptly change the nature of the competition. In the late 1960s, England had a strong if uninspiring line-up of established test and senior county players who managed to compete on more or less level terms with the overseas stars.

In 1968 Barry Richards took third place in the batting averages, with Rohan Kanhai fourth and Sobers eighth, but no other overseas players appeared among the top 25 batsmen or bowlers. In 1969 there were 6 overseas batsmen in the top 25 and 2, Procter and Majid Khan (who only took 15 wickets) in the bowling averages. In 1970 the trend, although a burgeoning one, was still not getting out of hand. Sobers topped the batting averages and Glenn Turner scored the most runs. They were joined by Kanhai, Richards, Lloyd and Majid in the top 25. In the upper reaches of the bowling averages, in the late 1970s and 1980s, the sole province of overseas stars, only four imports were present – Majid, McKenzie, Holder and Procter.

As far as the championship went, Yorkshire completed their last victory in 1968 and then fell sharply to thirteenth the following year. But in 1970 the White Rose county appeared to be on the way back, climbing to fourth place. The other leading side in the championship, Kent, had a similar experience, finishing in second place to Yorkshire during 1968, dropping to tenth in 1969 before coming back to win the competition in 1970. As we have already seen, the only county to have had its fortunes completely and consistently transformed by the arrival of overseas stars was Glamorgan, who, after finishing fourteenth in 1967, came third in 1968, first the year after and second to Kent in 1970.

Nothing much changed in the players' terms and conditions either. Apart from the odd 'star' contract, such as that awarded to Sobers, the wages earnt by most overseas players were little different from those commanded by leading English professionals.

At the other end of the salary scale from Sobers was Somerset's overseas recruit. Greg Chappell was signed up when the county's original choice, West Australian batsman John Inverarity, was picked for the 1968 tour to England. At the suggestion of his brother Ian, also in the touring party, the 19-year-old batsman wrote to Somerset on the off-chance and was offered a deal which included air fare, accommodation and £1,000.

Chappell had played just two seasons for South Australia, a total of 18 games, and is almost the perfect example of how early exposure to the English county game can add steel to a talented young player's repertoire.

The first shock was etiquette, for his South Australian captain L.E. Favell had been an easy-going guy who even the side's most junior players had called Les. But in Somerset, a place not exactly renowned for its authoritarian atmosphere, members had heard Chappell use the same approach to captain Roy Kerslake, as well as secretary Richard Robinson and had complained. Then in his first match he came in on a hat-trick to face two of Yorkshire's fiercest competitors, Freddie Trueman and Brian Close. Experiencing a torrid time against the two test bowlers on a damp wicket, he appealed against the light for the first time in his career, only to be told by the umpire that this wasn't 'bloody Australia' and to get on with the game. Luckily Chappell had a fellow Australian, the old campaigner Bill Alley, to show him the ropes. Chappell was forced to repay his kindness by being a captive audience for Alley's lengthy stories during numerous car trips throughout the length and breadth of England.

By his second game Chappell had stored up enough experience of English wickets, and no doubt a mild dislike of English unfriendliness, to hit 61 out of 134 as Derek Underwood ran amok through the Somerset side. His bowling too was transformed, after he abandoned his leg-spinners for medium pace in a single wicket competition and so impressed his colleagues that they insisted he try out his new bowling style in a championship game. In the next match against arch rivals Gloucestershire he bowled medium pace for the first time in a first-class match and took 4-37.

Though he did not know it then, the decision to switch to seam up would allow Australia to fill an important gap in its national attack, especially during limited overs matches.

Chappell next scored a fiercely struck century against Middlesex and his skill at hooking began to be known around the circuit. Of course the news came as a red rag to a bull when it reached the ears of Sussex and England fast bowler, John Snow, whom Somerset were due to meet in their next match. Chappell was young and arrogant enough not to adjust his game for Snow's extra pace, and received eight stitches above and below his right eye, as well as a night in hospital. This was another unpleasant experience, but another lesson learned. And, as if to make sure that he would not forget it in a hurry, the very first ball he received when returning to the county circuit was a beamer from West Indian fast bowler Keith Boyce.

He had always been a glorious leg-side timer of the ball and his on-drive was to become second only to Peter May's in power and finish. But Chappell only became a properly rounded test batsman when he developed off-side strength as well. This he managed to do because English bowlers spent two solid summers plugging way outside the off-stump trying to restrict his scoring opportunities.

After two seasons with Somerset, Chappell decided that being a year-round cricketer was reducing his employment opportunities should his sporting ambitions not live up to his expectations. He felt that six day a week cricket was dulling his enthusiasm for the game, but more importantly he had come to know English county players in their late 30s and early 40s who had no skills to support them when they finally quit the game. Their plight served as a warning to Chappell, who quit county cricket at the end of the 1969 season and began to investigate other ways of making a living. Thanks to English cricket, Chappell had matured both as a man and a cricketer.

It was a transformation that Australia had reason to welcome, and England to rue, just 18 months later. England arrived in Australia during the 1970/1 season and, after the first test had been drawn, Chappell found himself joining his brother Ian in the test side for the second test, the first to be played at Perth's WACA ground.

Driven forward by an opening stand of 171 between Geoff Boycott and Brian Luckhurst, England scored 397. This soon looked like a match-winning total as Snow and Peter Lever combined to reduce Australia to 107 for 5. Then Chappell, batting at number seven, drawing on all his experience with South Australia as well as his two seasons with Somerset, joined Ian Redpath in a spirited counterattack.

Adrian McGregor's biography of Chappell sets the scene: 'Greg knew all about the English attack . . . He had played and made runs against them on their own county cricket dunghills. They (the English bowlers) were neither awesome in anticipation nor actuality.' But they did command respect from Chappell, especially after his run-in with Snow, and the young Aussie with a coolness that was to become his trade mark, set his mind on survival. After 40 minutes he had scored just 1 run and it was not until he had been at the wicket for 1 hour and 7 minutes that he reached double figures.

After 3 hours the 22-year-old Chappell reached 50, having successfully achieved his goal of tiring Snow. With the England attack flagging in the Western Australian heat and the bowlers beginning to stray down the leg side, Chappell suddenly accelerated, racing from 48 to 92 in the hour after the tea interval. He nearly mishooked Snow to fine leg, steeled himself and brought up his first test century. The ground was invaded by more than 100 Australian supporters who beat a tattoo on Chappell's back. A few moments later he was out for 108 with 10 gloriously struck leg-side 4s, having added 219 with Redpath. McGregor sees Chappell retreating to the dressing room, contemplating that 'if he had not gone to Somerset, had not known these England bowlers, he would never have made his century'.

Chappell may have led the way for the modern generation of overseas cricketers who arrived in England as relative unknowns and emerged a season or two later as test greats, but there were a whole cavalcade of overseas players that had come to the UK to make their name during the preceding 100 years. However their experience of county cricket was often acutely different from that of modern overseas players and often meant risking much more than a cracked head courtesy of John Snow or a sore ear from one of Bill Alley's stories.

2 A touch of the exotic

For cricketers from overseas to take up the domestic game in England before the mid-1960s the decision was more than a career option; it required a wholesale uprooting of their previous life.

To become an overseas county player before the rule changes of 1968 meant serving a long, continuous residential qualification period, effectively cutting yourself off from the game at home. And once this residential period had been served and the player was again 'free' to do what he wanted with his winters, he often found himself shunned and in some cases banned from playing when he attempted to return to his home country's domestic competition.

Travel also posed a problem. The main cricket-playing countries of the world are all at least 4,000 miles away from the UK, and in the first half of the twentieth century that meant a lengthy and expensive trip for any overseas player making his way home. For all but the most wealthy it was a trip that required a careful weighing up of the pros and cons before embarking.

It is no wonder then that many of the overseas players who graced English cricket during the first 100 years of the modern game chose to make their home in this country, becoming British in all but nationality and sometimes playing test cricket for their adopted country. In fact, before the turn of the century there were so many Australian cricketing giants playing for county sides, that English cricket must have seemed like a rather rumbustious corner of the modern Earls Court.

During the late Victorian and Edwardian periods, Billy Midwinter played for Gloucestershire between 1877 and 1882, Sammy Woods for Cambridge University and then Somerset between 1888 and 1910, 'The Demon' Spofforth for Derbyshire between 1889 and 1891, J.J. Ferris for Gloucestershire between 1892 and 1895, 'Alberto' Trott for Middlesex between 1898 and 1910, Billy Murdoch for Sussex and then London County between 1893 and 1904, and Francis Tarrant for Middlesex from 1904 to 1914. Midwinter, Woods, Ferris and Trott all played test cricket for both England and Australia, while Tarrant, despite being one of the game's leading all-rounders played for neither country. Only Midwinter played for England against the country of his birth, all the others taking part in the early tours to South Africa.

W.G. Grace was instrumental in Gloucestershire's capture of both Midwinter and Ferris, riding roughshod as usual over the pious sensibilities of the day. Grace behaved like a modern cricketer in many ways and was the first to seek to increase his side's strength, and the gate takings, by adding a touch of the exotic to his county side.

Midwinter was discovered by Grace during his 'honeymoon' tour of Australia in 1873/4. An impressive athlete, with a skill for most games that would have impressed the uninhibited competitor in Grace, Midwinter was a bits and pieces all-rounder with the ability occasionally to raise his game to test level. During the tour Grace discovered that Midwinter had been born in Gloucestershire and persuaded him that, should he ever come to England, he should play for the county of his birth. When Midwinter did arrive, in 1878 with the Australian tourists, there was a squabble about which team he should play for, with Grace (naturally) turning out the winner.

Like Grace, Midwinter was a man not bound by the conventions of his time. Once he had arrived in England and established himself as a Gloucestershire player, he began to study ways in which to maximize his earnings. Like most cricketers of the day he played through the summer and then attempted to eke out some form of existence during the winter months. But why, reasoned Midwinter, when there was cricket being played somewhere else in the world, should he have to spend the close season in such an unpleasant way. All right, so the six-week passage to Australia was hard, but it could be endured, and five months of cricket and sunshine waited at the end. So for the six seasons between the English summer of 1880 and the Australian one of 1882/3 he played cricket the year round. He was aided in this effort to maintain full-time sporting employment by being picked as a member of the England team to Australia in 1881/2.

On returning to the UK in 1882, he had his most successful season, finishing one place higher in the batting averages than his county captain with the figures of 23 matches, 40 innings, 823 runs, average 26.54. This may not be impressive by today's standards but the atrocious playing conditions of the time put his achievement in context. For example, cricketer and missionary C.T. Studd topped the batting averages with 1,249 runs at 32.86 while the bowlers ran riot, Lancashire quick John Crossland taking 112 wickets at 10.06, and the first of Yorkshire's great slow left armers, Edmund Peate, capturing 214 at 11.84.

Ironically, given the difficulties he faced, Midwinter not only became England's first ever overseas player, but also established the blueprint for the careers followed by the foreign players who flocked to the UK 80 years later.

Midwinter decided against returning to join Gloucestershire in the spring of 1883 and, declaring himself, 'Australian to the heart's core', devoted his attentions towards playing for the state of Victoria in Australia. He was rewarded for his new-found patriotism by making one last visit to England, as a member of the 1884 Australian touring party.

Ten years after Midwinter decided to give up Gloucester for Melbourne, Grace secured another Australian star. J.J. Ferris was an outstanding success on his two tours of England in 1888 and 1890. His waspish medium-paced, left-arm spin and cut accounted for 199 wickets at 14.74 in 1888 and 186 at 14.28 in 1890. During his second tour, at the age of 23, he declared his attention to qualify by residence for Gloucestershire, but at the end of the trip left for Australia with the rest of the tour party. However, Grace's Gloucestershire were old hands at this game and simply rented a house in Ferris' name. Nobody questioned the arrangement and Ferris was actually picked as an English cricketer to tour South Africa in 1891/2. In the only test match he proved far too good for South Africa's fledgling internationals, taking 6-54 and 7-37 as England won by an innings.

Gloucestershire had every reason to have high expectations of Ferris when he finally joined the county in 1892, after 'serving' his two-year qualification period. Unfortunately for Gloucestershire, but perhaps justly, given the underhand manner in which he was registered, Ferris played only three seasons for Gloucestershire, never consistently showing his test form and leaving the county at the age of 28. He died in 1900 of enteric fever while fighting for the British army in the Boer War in South Africa.

English county cricket never again experienced such an invasion of Australian cricketing talent until the deregulated days after the 1968 watershed. The nearest parallel was the period following World War 2, when an explosion of talent Down Under meant that a near second XI of Australian might-have-beens had to seek employment in English league and county cricket.

During the late 1940s and early 1950s, there were four Australian cricketers of test standard in their mid-20s or early 30s playing for English county sides, having effectively abandoned their international careers. Colin McCool, born in 1915, Bill Alley (1919), George Tribe (1920) and Bruce Dooland (1923) would have walked into most Australian test sides. And when their number was added to by two post-war exiles, Jack Walsh and Vic Jackson, who both played for Leicestershire, the nucleus of a very useful test side began to form.

Walsh and Jackson both arrived in England through the auspices of Sir Julian Cahn, a man whose inherited millions were mainly used to create a truly impressive private cricket team. Sir Julian's 'agents' in Australian, including former test player Alan Fairfax, specialized in identifying young cricketers who showed promise and who, for some reason or other, did not think they could make an immediate mark on the international scene. Once identified, the players would be approached and offered what seemed to them huge sums of money to come to England and play for Sir Julian's side. Ginty Lush, for example, after missing selection for the 1938 tour party, was offered £600 by Fairfax on Sir Julian's behalf compared to the £5 a week he was currently earning as a cub reporter in Sydney. After the furniture magnate had tired of a player and wanted new talents to excite his cricketing palate, the unwanted retainers would be either sent to play for his pet county Leicestershire, retired to the leagues or returned home.

Jack Walsh was perhaps Sir Julian's most astute capture. Walsh, a slow left-arm off-break bowler, was making a name for himself in his native New South

Wales when Sir Julian's roving talent spotters drew a bead on him. He was whisked away to England at the age of 24 before he had even made his first-class debut. Walsh went on to become what many authorities of the day reckoned was the greatest left-arm googly bowler of the day, many ranking him above fellow Australian, and established test cricketer, Chuck Fleetwood-Smith.

After the war Walsh joined Leicestershire as a professional, as did Vic Jackson. Both had played as amateurs for the county before the war, but now became regular members of the team. In the mid-1930s, Jackson had been a promising all-rounder, who had like Lush narrowly missed selection for the 1938 touring party, and again Sir Julian's men had swooped.

Jackson and Walsh, like many of the Australians playing in county cricket during the late 1940s, were effectively filling the gaps left by those pre-war cricketers who had either been killed during the recently concluded conflict or were now too old to compete at first-class level. Such was the paucity of Leicestershire's pace attack in the late 1940s, for example, that Jackson's military medium was often called on to open the bowling.

While Jackson's post-war county career was relatively low-key for someone of his talents, Walsh soon became regarded as the leading spin bowler in the country. In 1946 he took 146 wickets at 20.36 and a further 174 at 19.56 the following year. He was picked to play for the Players against the Gentlemen three times between 1947 and 1951.

George Tribe and Bruce Dooland also represented the Players during the 1950s. Tribe, who played for Northamptonshire, was yet another spin bowling all-rounder, while Bruce Dooland's leg-breaks carried a weak Nottinghamshire attack for most of the 1950s. Tribe, who like Walsh varied his slow, left-arm style with the use of a chinaman, completed the double of 100 wickets and 1,000 runs 7 times, a feat matched by Dooland in 1954 and 1957. In fact, such was the all-round skill of Australia's test match rejects that five out of the six players were able to record doubles, the other three instances being Walsh in 1952, Jackson in 1955 and Bill Alley in 1962.

Colin McCool was the only one of the six ex-pats not to record the double, but a career record of 602 wickets at 27.47 showed that he was no mug with the ball. McCool had just begun to establish himself in the New South Wales side before the war broke out. The end of the hostilities found him playing for Queensland and, at the age of 30, successfully breaking into the all-conquering Australian test side of the late 1940s. A hard-hitting, middle order batsman as well as a thoughtful bowler, McCool played in all five games during the 1946/7 test series against England. He took two 5-wicket hauls, scored 95 in the first test and an undefeated century during the third game. Despite this level of success, although being part of Bradman's unsurpassed 1948 touring side, he never again played against England.

McCool had bad luck with injuries throughout Bradman's triumphal farewell tour. Only really considered for the fifth test, he lost out to Doug Ring and then in England's tour of 1950/1 he was displaced by 'mystery bowler' Jack Iverson.

McCool obviously did not have a very high regard for Iverson, who bowled off-breaks by flicking the ball out of his hand using his middle finger, and greatly enjoyed belting him out of the attack whenever they met during Sheffield Shield matches. But his replacement by a 'flash in the pan' cricketer seems to have soured McCool against test cricket.

He begins Chapter 8 of his originally titled autobiography, *Cricket is a Game*, by saying: 'I suppose I could have come to England with Hassett's 1953 Australian side. But I wasn't interested.' McCool had a two-year contract with the East Lancashire league side and told the selectors he wanted 'no further part of test cricket'. In his book he explains: 'Test cricket is a heart-burning business, and as all-rounder I'd been forced to shoulder a double load of worry'.

At the relatively advanced age of 40, McCool joined Somerset with a reputation as a has-been. When he finished the 1956 season with 1,976 runs at 37.82 and 49 wickets he felt, with some reason, that he had answered that particular criticism. Somerset, a weak side, were always on the look-out for talent beyond the south-west and a year after his county debut, McCool was joined by another Australian might-have-been.

Bill Alley was 38 and another of the highly talented Australian cricketers who had had to compete with his country's outstanding post-war stock of players. In line for a tour place in 1948 the combative opening batsman and medium-pace bowler was ruled out by having his jaw broken while practising in the nets. The freak accident, when a ball hit by another batsman found a hole in the nets, effectively ended his career in Australia and he moved to England, spending nine consecutive seasons in the Lancashire leagues.

When they met in one league game during the 1950s, McCool was shocked to see how much Alley's bowling had improved, 'here he was swinging the ball about and seaming it, things he probably never thought about in Australia'. Alley explained: 'It was the leagues. You know how it is up there, all the professionals have to bowl. Why even Everton Weekes gets wickets with those flighty off-spinners of his. So I had a go and this was the result.'

Alley played for Somerset for 12 seasons, until he was 49, and became one of the English game's leading all-rounders. In 1961 he scored 3,019 runs at 56.19 and a year later did the 'double' by capturing 112 wickets at 20.74. The injection of OAP Aussie talent obviously worked, as after four consecutive summers finishing at the bottom of championship table, Somerset climbed to third place in 1958.

Apart from Cahn's two captures, the post-war Aussie invasion began in the Lancashire Leagues and it was in the fierce club cricket of the north-west that the modern idea of the hired overseas professional really took hold.

The league clubs were able to draw huge crowds for what was effectively a contest between 20 weekend cricketers and 2 professionals. They were often supported by wealthy industrialists and had considerable sums of money to spend on hiring their overseas stars. Although foreign professionals had played in the league before World War 1, the idea of attaching glamour to a side by signing up an established overseas test player only really began in the 1920s. After World War 2 the presence of overseas players of quality became the norm and it was in the leagues rather than county cricket where most foreign crick-eters looked to make their living during the English summers. Unlike opting for a county career, playing for a Lancashire league did not necessarily have to interfere with the players' domestic or international career back home. The fact that test tours were rarer also made the problem of whether to play for country or club a reasonably rare quandary.

By far the most lucrative cricketing employment available between April and September, the leagues proved such a draw that it would be shorter to list the great overseas post-war players who did not join league clubs than those that did. Between the wars, though, the league played host to three cricketing immortals, the Australian fast bowler Ted McDonald, and the West Indians George Headley and Learie Constantine.

McDonald had first come to England with the Australian touring party of 1921. A fast bowler of feline grace, he was to improve vastly on his mediocre performances of the previous Australian summer and establish himself as one of his country's greatest cricketing assets. He left England to play a series against South Africa on the return trip home to Australia. Then, after playing 11 test matches in just under 2 years and taking 43 wickets, he retired for ever from the international stage. Despite the protestations of *Wisden*, he had signed a con-tract with league club Nelson while touring England. McDonald's motives are unclear, but perhaps his taciturn character rejected the unreliability of test cricket and opted instead for the steadier work of the league.

Age may also have played its part. When, in 1923, he had his most successful season in the leagues, McDonald was already 34, old for a fast bowler. He had lost his youth to the war years and many thought that his 112 wickets at the ridiculously low average of 6.67 would be his final fling. They could not have been more mistaken, since the next year he took 99 wickets and after that joined Lancashire to propel them to three consecutive championship titles in 1926, 1927 and 1928. In those three seasons he took 175, 150 and 178 wickets respectively.

The phrase 'silent but deadly' might have been invented for McDonald. He ran on slipper feet to the wicket, according to some leaving no mark upon even the dampest turf. To secure MacDonald Lancashire had to pay Nelson the then enormous sum of £500 (roughly equivalent to half the club's annual gate money) and promise to hold two first-class games at Nelson's home ground, but there was little doubt that they got their money's worth from the Australian fast bowler.

In fact, in an echo of the debate which was to take place 40 years later, Lan-cashire had tried to have the residential qualification for players born outside the county reduced from 24 to 12 months. They were defeated by the votes of other counties, but had they been successful the history of overseas players in English cricket might have been considerably different.

McDonald may have been the first truly great overseas cricketer to play in the Lancashire Leagues, but incredibly Nelson were able, just five years later, to sign a player who made an even greater impact on the English game.

Learie Constantine has become the archetype for West Indian cricket. A resourceful and fearsome fast bowler, a batsman who had an attacking stroke (some quite outrageous) for every ball and the world's most accomplished fielder, Constantine was also the first black person many English cricket watchers had ever seen. During his nine years as Nelson's professional, he added thousands to the gate takings, redefined attacking cricket, rewrote league records and, by dint of his ready intellect and easy humour, put an end to centuries of prejudice in the minds of many English men and women.

C.L.R. James, in *Beyond a Boundary*, claimed that: 'Constantine by his cricket, by the demeanour of himself and his wife in what all could realise was no easy situation . . . had created an enormous interest in the West Indies and the West Indians'. And, in a peculiar way, the league paid back the entire of the West Indies for Constantine's brilliance. With money made from the league, Constantine was able to finance the publication of James' *The Case for West Indian Self-Government*, raising the issue for the first time outside the Islands.

Constantine's performances in the leagues beggar description and his tussles with the greatest of all bowlers, Sydney Barnes, are legendary. But one bowling performance particularly stands out and demonstrates his mastery. Playing against Accrington in an early season match during 1934, Constantine contributed just 4 runs to Nelson's score of 116. Accrington's professional, former Lancashire stalwart Dick Tyldesley, took 5 wickets, but in reply the West Indian dismissed the powerful Accrington side almost single-handedly for just 12 runs. Nine batsmen were either bowled or trapped lbw by Constantine, six of them making ducks. Only the catching of Tyldesley by Winslow for another duck stood in the way of Nelson's professional recording the perfect bowling return. Constantine helped Nelson win the Lancashire League in all but two of the nine seasons in which he was the side's professional. After Nelson's triumph during Constantine's last season of 1937, the side has won the competition just five more times to 1993.

Constantine was followed to Lancashire by two other West Indians. Manny Martindale was Constantine's opening partner for the West Indies and his success on the international circuit persuaded Burnley to sign him in 1936. Martindale thereafter played for Lowerhouse and Bacup, settling with his family in Lancashire, and he was still playing as a professional in the Ribblesdale League in 1963.

The other recruit was George Headley, still considered by many to be the greatest ever West Indian batsman. In England and Australia, Headley was the 'black Bradman', but in the Windies it was Bradman who was the 'white Headley'. The West Indian joined Haslingden in 1934 and still holds the club's record for the number of runs by a professional, scoring 1,360 in 1937.

While Nelson were dominating the league during the 1930s, their great rivals

Accrington were plotting a move even more audacious than the signing of Constantine. And ironically it was Constantine himself who suggested that Accrington approach Don Bradman.

The world's greatest batsman was struggling to find employment in the recession-hit Australia of the early 1930s. Bradman did not want to become a 'professional' cricketer, preferring to learn another way of making ends meet should his comet-like career fade as quickly as it had grown in stature. He knew that taking up the post of Accrington's professional would mean an end to his test career, at least for the duration of the contract, but even so times were hard and he seriously considered the move.

Bradman's mind was finally made up for him when the Associated Newspapers Group linked up with a local radio station to offer Bradman employment with them. He gladly took up the offer, though his agreement to write articles for Associated later got him into trouble with the Australian cricketing authorities and again nearly saw a premature end to his international career.

Writing in his 1950 book *Farewell to Cricket*, Bradman actually remarks on the Lancashire Leagues of the late 1940s, which had secured the talents of Tribe, McCool et al. He expressed 'anxiety' that the leagues were proving a drain on his country's cricketing resources. He is moved to write: 'There are sufficient Australians in the League to create an eleven of international standards. The number of front-line players in Australia at any time is limited and any defection from the ranks in this country has the same effect as retirement.' He argues that 'Australia is not able at this juncture able to support professionalism in cricket', comments on the large sums available to league cricketers which are 'hard to resist' and concludes that the problem of test team players leaving for the Lancashire Leagues 'threatens to become worse, and must seriously exercise the minds of legislators and players in the future'.

Bradman's words serve as a timely reminder that, before the days of immediate qualification and modern air travel, the presence of overseas players in county and league cricket was seen as a threat to the domestic and international cricket of other test-playing nations. It could also be argued that once this 'weakening' factor was added to the benefits of playing against test-class overseas players in domestic cricket, the presence of these foreign stars was a significant contributor to England's success against Australia during the 1950s. The migration of Australian talent in the 1940s and 1950s was created by the commercial strength of English domestic cricket, and it is ironic that it was the financial weakness of the county competition which led directly to the scrapping of the existing qualification rules in 1967.

There were a number of other countries, apart from Australia, that might have echoed Bradman's concern during the 1950s and 1960s. The rapidly increasing availability of air travel meant that the rising cricketing powers of India and later Pakistan began to add to the cavalcade of cricketing talent that the league presented.

But, increasingly, the situation, as far as the supporters of other test-playing countries were concerned, was improving. Clubs became more willing to let overseas professionals return home in the English winter and foreign cricketing authorities began to take a less prejudiced view against those who wanted to play cricket all year round. By the early 1960s it was accepted practice that overseas players could seek employment as league professionals during the English summer, and return home to domestic and sometimes international cricket in the close season. County cricket was to take another ten years to come to terms with this idea, but already international sides (particularly the West Indies) were beginning to benefit from the experience their leading players had gained in the English leagues.

In the 1950s and 1960s, the league was overrun with test stars. Apart from those already mentioned, Australians playing league cricket included Ken Archer, Bobby Simpson, Sidney Barnes, Bob Cowper, Ray Lindwall, Neil Hawke, Ian Chappell and Keith Stackpole. From the sub-continent and South Africa came Eddie Barlow, Hugh Tayfield, Fazal Mahmood, Vijay Hazare and S.P. Gupte. But it was the West Indians that provided the majority of Lancashire League professionals during this period. Especially in the 1960s, league players had to accustom themselves to facing international class fast bowlers in most matches. Again, it is worth pointing out that if English county cricket is now used to giving young West Indian test players a thorough cricketing education, it was the leagues that provided the finishing school for the brilliant West Indian sides of the 1950s and 1960s.

Almost without exception, all the leading West Indian players of the day played for Lancashire League sides. Week in, week out, league players could pit their talents against the likes of Wes Hall, Roy Gilchrist, Lance Gibbs, Charlie Griffith, Chester Watson and Clyde Walcott.

A representative side chosen from the West Indian players employed as league professionals during the 1950s and 1960s would possess all the cricketing talents, particularly fearsome fast bowling, and appear almost unbeatable. For openers the selectors could choose Roy Marshall and Conrad Hunte. The middle-order powerhouse would be led by the most awesome of all West Indian strokemakers, Everton Weekes, supported by Basil Butcher, Seymour Nurse and spin bowling all-rounder Ollie Smith, and further strengthened by wicketkeeper Clyde Walcott. Smith could form a more than effective spin bowling partnership with Lance Gibbs, while the pace bowling attack of Wes Hall, Charlie Griffith and Roy Gilchrist would have most batsmen praying for rain. All but Marshall played regularly for the Windies, and he was perhaps the last to sacrifice what would have been an undoubtedly brilliant test career to play county cricket, in his case for Hampshire.

The Lancashire League is still full of overseas professionals and every now and then, as for example when Rishton captured Viv Richards after his sudden departure from Somerset, a truly world-class player will grace the competition. But now most of the professionals are perhaps slightly below test status, often young players on the way up or old ones winding down. The overseas pros playing for league clubs in 1992, for example, included those whose test careers had never quite taken off (Dipak Patel, Roger Harper and Alan Dodemade) or those who were just establishing an international reputation such as Mark Priest, Phil Simmons and Keith Athurton.

Over the last 25 years the international stars have been tempted away by the cash and kudos of the county circuit. But it will be interesting to see how this picture changes now that the regulations restricting each county to one overseas player applies to all 18 first-class sides. The number of places open to overseas players in county cricket are now less than half of what they were in the mid-to-late 1970s and, providing the money is there, a return to the leagues of the world's leading players may not be too much of a pipe dream for the cricket lovers of northern England.

As well as the Australians, there have been dozens of players, from South Africa, the West Indies, India, New Zealand and Pakistan, who joined the county circuit and made England their home in the years before the introduction of immediate registration. This book is not about them, since their experience was very different to that of the overseas players who have taken part in county cricket since 1968. But it is worth recalling the finest hours of two of the most unusual overseas players to play county cricket before the late 1960s if only to drive home this point.

For social and economic reasons the majority of pre-1968 overseas players had come from Australia and South Africa. Those from the Indian sub-continent played county cricket as amateurs, were usually from royal and/or moneyed families, and considered the game a diversion from more pressing and unpleasant duties back home. The glorious uncle and nephew pair of Ranjitsinhji and Duleepsinhji always considered themselves 'English' as far as cricket was concerned.

West Indian county players were much rarer but, in the early 1900s, two in particular were skilful enough to make an impact during English cricket's most dazzling decade.

In 1906 white West Indian Sydney Smith was made one of *Wisden*'s 'cricketers of the year'. He made his name on the second West Indian tour of 1906 and stayed behind to qualify by residence for Northamptonshire, finally being made captain for the side. He was an attacking, middle-order batsman and slow left-arm bowler of 'immaculate length' who played for the Gentlemen against the Players three times, playing match-winning innings of 52 and 50 in the 1914 Lords match.

But Smith, novelty though he was to the English cricket lovers of the Edwardian age, was still white skinned. Elsewhere in the country, 70 years before Gordon Greenidge first brought his particular brand of batting savagery to county cricket, a batsman with a striking resemblance to the Bajan was treating Derbyshire's opponents with exactly the same sort of disdain.

Charles Augustus Ollivierre was the star batsman of the first West Indian tour of England in 1900. He headed the batting averages, scoring 883 runs at

32.70, and as his team went down to defeat at the hands of county sides time and again, he alone resisted the county pros, many of whom were openly contemptuous of a black man's ability to play first-class cricket.

Twice he was involved in double century opening stands. Against Leicestershire, opening the batting with the West Indian born Plum Warner, he put on 238 for the first wicket: Warner 113; Ollivierre 159. Against Surrey he scored 94 in an opening stand of 208, which was accumulated at such a rate that the West Indians, after being dismissed for just another 120 runs, had the time to reduce the county to 86-7.

After the tour Ollivierre, like Smith, stayed behind to qualify for an English county, making his debut for Derbyshire in 1901. The decision, as seen from this end of the century, seems a curious one. This was 30 years before Constantine had helped break down northern prejudice against those without a white skin. But it is pleasing to note that Ollivierre's colour was no bar to him being accorded amateur status, his name appearing as Mr C.A. Ollivierre on the score card.

Ollivierre formed an exciting opening partnership with another amateur, Levi Wright. They were a brilliant but unreliable pair whose greatest hour came when Derbyshire most needed it.

The county did not possess strength in depth and were regularly steamrollered by stronger sides. The Essex side which faced Derbyshire in May 1904 was not Yorkshire or Kent, but when they had rattled up 597 (Percy Perrin 343 not out), an hour before lunch on the second day, the gulf between the sides seemed just as great.

Ollivierre and Wright, however, seemed blissfully unaware of the hole Derbyshire were in. During the remaining 55 minutes before the break they put on 144 and, going into lunch, the West Indian opener was already on 91. After the break the onslaught continued until, with Derbyshire's total on 191, Wright was out for 68. Ollivierre plundered on, however, reaching 100 in 95 minutes and 200 in just over 3 hours. He mingled Edwardian elegance, cutting late to the boundary, with what then must have seemed the most vulgar exuberance, pulling deliveries pitching outside the off stump over square leg. Finally, after hitting 37 4s and with his score standing at 229 out of 378, he was bowled by Reeves.

The other Derbyshire batsmen carried on the fight-back and the northern county was finally dismissed for 548, just 49 behind. A draw seemed to be the only possible result and, buoyed up by his performance, Ollivierre celebrated well but not too wisely. Taking the field on the third day he was nursing a raging hangover and almost immediately dropped a catch. He took advantage of the amateur's prerogative and, summoning a substitute, retired to the pavilion and a soothing ice pack.

But he was not to be left in peace for very long, because the Essex side which had also rather overdone the celebrations, both for Perrin and then Ollivierre, crashed to 91 all-out. Middle-order batsman, The Revd F.H. Gillingham, was, as you would expect from a man of the cloth, the only Essex player to escape censure – he was in bed with lumbago.

To win the match Derbyshire had to score 147 in just over 2 hours and the Chesterfield ground soon filled with 2,000 spectators eager to see a historic win. Ollivierre, roused from his sick bed, was in no mood to hang around. He started where he had left off in the first innings and after 65 minutes was on 74. This time though Wright was out early and the game took its final turn.

Ollivierre was joined by Bill Storer, a hard-bitten north-country professional who had played for England both as a batsman and wicket-keeper. Storer, to put no finer point on it, had racist tendencies and did not like the idea of his county providing employment for a black man, especially one who adopted the airs and carefree playing style of an amateur. Storer was also a pragmatic cricketer and quickly worked out that he still had time to score 50 runs, and therefore collect the bonus money on offer to encourage professionals towards achieving batting and bowling milestones. As Hampshire's Philip Mead used to say, as he tickled the ball round the corner to bring up yet another century, 'That's another bag of coal for the winter'.

So as the game entered its final hour, Storer began manipulating the strike. Ollivierre, who was just as keen to achieve the extremely rare record of a double century and century in a match, and who was perfectly aware of Storer's views about his playing ability, began to fight back. On the two went, fighting the Essex attack, the clock and each other. As the close of play approached and the total neared the target of 149, the original two opponents of Derbyshire and Essex were almost forgotten as the race for talent, money and a place in the record books intensified. Eventually, after an hour and 20 minutes, the winning runs were made, but neither Storer (48) nor Ollivierre (92) had quite achieved their goal.

3 Overseas players 1968–1992; a county-by-county guide

Ninety years after the Ollivierre match of 1904, English cricket-lovers have grown used to witnessing players from overseas taking the leading role in games between counties. Twenty-six seasons have now passed since the introduction of immediate registration for overseas players, and each county can look back on a lengthy and illustrious list of foreign recruits. In 1992, even Yorkshire succumbed to the spirit of the age and signed Sachin Tendulkar, the latest in a line of boy geniuses from the Indian sub-continent with, as far as we know, not a drop of tyke blood flowing in his veins.

The rule changes pushed through in the late 1970s eventually resulted in every county being able to register only one player not qualified to represent England, but for the great majority of the period between 1968 and 1993 counties have usually had at least two overseas cricketers on their books.

Initial enthusiasm for the idea saw most counties exercising their prerogative to sign up an overseas player under the immediate registration rule. Other overseas recruits qualified to play for a county under the old residential qualification rule, usually by playing league cricket nearby and, by the mid-1970s all but a couple of counties had two overseas players, while many had three or four.

From then on the pattern of employment began to change. The rule changes of the late 1970s left counties such as Hampshire, Sussex and Somerset able to field two overseas players. Other counties not in this fortunate position attempted to reduce their disadvantage by signing two overseas players and only playing one at a time. In terms of team strength this was not as good as being able to field both, but had the advantage of reducing the workload of overseas players, therefore keeping them fresh and free of injury. It also enabled counties to pick two players of differing types to make the most of changing conditions, and the different demands of the first-class programme and the three one-day competitions.

For example, it was a common practice in the mid-1980s for counties to employ two West Indian fast bowlers, therefore always having a fit and hungry strike bowler to throw at the opposition. Other teams opted for a fast bowler to take part in first-class games, while a batsman or a seam bowling all-rounder was selected for the three one-day competitions.

The use of this loophole in the new registration rules – adopted by almost every county as they lost their right to field two overseas players – was obviously against the spirit of the late 1970s rule change if not the letter. During the mid-1980s steps were taken to close the loophole and the relevant law now prevents counties from registering more than one overseas player. No cover is allowed and if your resident overseas player is injured during the course of the season, as happened with Derbyshire's West Indian player Ian Bishop in 1993, then bad luck.

So, a quarter of a century later, the employment of overseas cricketers is now at a level which most of those backing the introduction of immediate registration would have expected and desired. But in the intervening period there has been a massive importation of foreign talent into English cricket, the like of which nobody in the late 1960s would ever have envisaged. In this chapter the story of this mass migration is told by examining each county's record in employing overseas cricketers.

From Mike Procter to Corrie Van Zyl, from the sublime to the ridiculous, from signing an unknown Antiguan who turned out to be a world beater to asking an Indian spinner to perform on green tops in Chesterfield, many of the triumphs and disasters of English domestic cricket during the last three decades have centred on the much maligned/heralded overseas player.

Key to county tables

The information included in the list of overseas players for each county is as follows.

1 Number of first-class matches played for the county
2 Name of player
3 Type of player – opening batsman, pace bowler, all-rounder etc.
4 Period of county career
5 Nationality: A = Australia; SA = South Africa; WI = West Indies; P = Pakistan; I = India; NZ = New Zealand; Z = Zimbabwe/Rhodesia; EA = East Africa

Therefore, the entry, 151 G.D. McKenzie (pace bowler) 1969–75 A, means that Garth McKenzie was an Australian pace bowler who played 151 first-class games for Leicestershire between 1969 and 1975.

For the sake of practicality, only those players who played at least ten first-class matches for a county are included in each list or, in most cases, in the analysis that follows. At the end of each list of players the total number of appearances made by overseas players is included to enable comparison between the counties.

Derbyshire

71	C.P. Wilkins (batsman, medium-pace bowler) 1970–2	SA
46	S. Venkataraghavan (off-spin bowler) 1973–5	I
17	L.G. Rowe (batsman) 1974	WI
60	E.J. Barlow (batsman) 1976–8	SA
156	J.G. Wright (opening batsman) 1977–88	NZ
106	P.N. Kirsten (batsman) 1978–82	SA
66	M.A. Holding (fast bowler) 1983–9	WI

43	I.R. Bishop (fast bowler) 1989–92	WI
10	A.P. Kuiper (batsman) 1990	SA
20	M. Azharuddin (batsman) 1991	I

595

Apart from Yorkshire, who until 1992 excluded overseas players altogether, Derbyshire's recent history has been the least influenced by overseas players. Although Derbyshire has had 10 overseas cricketers play more than 10 games for the county since 1968, their combined total of 595 games is the lowest of all the first-class counties. Derbyshire did not even employ an overseas cricketer in the first two seasons following the introduction of immediate registration and for six out of the next seven seasons they only had one foreign recruit on the books. New Zealand opening batsman John Wright joined South African all-rounder Eddie Barlow at Derby in 1977 and, for the next 12 seasons the two players shared the duties of the overseas professional. But only once, in 1978, have Derby had three overseas players to pick from.

There was some resistance in the county to signing an overseas player following the 1968 watershed and this view held sway until the end of the 1969 season. Derbyshire had won through to the Gillette Cup final after a famous semi-final victory over Sussex. Against Yorkshire though, things went against Derbyshire from the start and they were defeated by 69 runs with 5 overs still left to bowl. An overseas player might have made all the difference it was felt, and one was duly sought out and signed up. But, even then, Derbyshire did not sign some world-famous recruit. The 25-year-old South African batsman Chris Wilkins was a trier in the true Derbyshire mould, but he was hardly a name to conjure with. Over his three years with the county he acquitted himself well, becoming particularly renowned for his fierce driving and outstanding fielding, especially at slip.

By 1973 Derbyshire felt comfortable enough with the idea of overseas players to sign someone who might not have come from Chesterfield or South Normanton. It was pretty obvious that Srinivasaraghavan Venkataraghavan had not freshly arrived from a Derbyshire pit village and any bonds with past prejudices were sharply snapped. Venkat turned in some good performances for the county but Derbyshire already had a strong spin bowling attack and the Indian's presence did not add much to the county's all-round strength. Added to this was the fact that the Indian spinner found playing conditions as unfamiliar from those of his own country as could be possible. Not for the first time a player from the Indian sub-continent arrived to play for an English county to find, what seemed to him, bitterly cold weather, green pitches and people, who if not actively unfriendly, seemed strange and distant.

Likewise, Lawrence Rowe's arrival in 1974 to fill in for Venkat while he was touring England with his national side proved to be another case of a square peg to fill a round hole. It was not until Eddie Barlow arrived from South Africa that the county really found an overseas player to meet the needs of the side. Two long-established batsmen, Mike Page and Brian Bolus, had left the county in 1975, and the need was for a batsman. Barlow, with his massive experience and indomitable fighting spirit fitted the bill perfectly. But at 35 he was only ever going to be a short-term bet and the more significant signing was that of John Wright in 1977. Barlow took over as Derbyshire captain when Bob Taylor resigned his position in June 1976. This move allowed the South African to influence the attitude as well as the performances of the team, vastly improving the fitness and fielding ability of the side, and when Barlow left in 1978, Derbyshire were a much more positive team.

Barlow's replacement was another South African – Peter Kirsten. Kirsten had in fact arrived at Derbyshire a year before in the company of Allan Lamb and Garth Le Roux. All three had been brought over by Barlow to play in the county's second XI and to gain a taste of English county cricket.

The Wright and Kirsten partnership continued for four years, but their greatest moment came towards the end of the third year. After losing two Lords finals, in 1969 and 1978, Derbyshire had fought their way to a showdown with Northamptonshire in the 1981 Benson & Hedges competition. Northants started well, and Cook and Larkins put on 99 for the first wicket, but after that 3 run-outs and some tight bowling from Wood and Newman saw the Midland's county restricted to 235 off 60 overs. In Derbyshire's reply Wright immediately attacked the bowling of Sarfraz Nawaz and when Alan Hill was lbw to Mallender with the score at 41, the New Zealander was joined by Kirsten. The two then put on 123 runs in 33 overs, a bit slow for some of the nervous Derbyshire supporters, but enough to give the middle order a licence to slog their county to victory. The fact that the match was won by Derbyshire off the last ball, did little to disguise the fact that 12 years after the county had gone down at the hands of Yorkshire, an overseas player (or more correctly two) had helped the county add to its silverware collection for the first time in 45 years.

But, in the view of Bob Taylor, the policy of employing two overseas batsmen unbalanced the side and he was much happier when Michael Holding replaced Kirsten, who had never really taken to county cricket, in 1983. Unfortunately for the county and the two players concerned, Holding's registration coincided with the Test and County Cricket Board's (TCCB) decision to restrict most counties to one overseas player. During the 6 years that they played together, Holding took the field for first-class games on 56 occasions and Wright for just 49. Holding's 14 games in 1986 were the most that either player managed in one season.

History once again repeated itself when, in 1989, Holding brought Ian Bishop to Derbyshire in the place of the retiring Wright. Bishop, a born-again Christian whose quoted hobbies include reading 'theological books', was a Holding disciple and, together with Devon Malcolm, offered the promise of the county's fastest ever opening attack. Bishop was an immediate success, outbowling his mentor by taking ten more wickets in just one more game at a considerably lower cost. Holding, in fact, had brought Bishop along at just the right time because it was obvious that Holding was finally beginning to lose some of his pace and effectiveness.

With Holding gone, Derbyshire once again reverted to the policy of having one fast bowler and one batsman as their two overseas players. Adrian Kuiper was brought over from South Africa mainly to play in one-day games but Bishop's injury problems, which were just beginning to come through, meant that he ended up playing in ten championship matches.

Kuiper had arrived in England with a glowing reputation as a hard-hitting all-rounder. One innings played against Mike Gatting's rebel team was described by the English players present as the most fiercely struck they had seen since Ian Botham's 118 at Edgbaston in 1981. But, unfortunately, Kuiper's technique was not up to coping with the seaming English wickets and he finished the season having scored only 288 runs at 19.20, his performance seeming even worse in the light of the fact that Bishop, previously regarded as a tail ender with no batting pretensions, managed 326 at 29.63 and a highest score of 103. By 1991 Bishop was experiencing severe back problems which eventually resulted in him having to undergo a series of operations and remodel his bowling action. Indian captain Azharuddin stepped into the breach and, after an uncertain start, played some innings of rare brilliance.

In 1992 the remodelled Bishop returned and was fit enough to play 20 championship matches. He captured 64 wickets at an average of 17.46, by far the best performance of any Derbyshire bowler in that season, and the county breathed a sigh of relief. Unfortunately their peace of mind was short-lived as Bishop again broke down, leaving Derbyshire without an overseas player for the great majority of the 1993 season.

Durham

14 D.M. Jones (batsman) 1992   A

Dean Jones, 'the legend' had a sticky start to his county cricket career and it was particularly unfortunate for Durham's inaugural season that he should be called away on international duty once he had started to get the swing of things. In hindsight it is possible to see that with only one Durham bowler taking more than 50 wickets, an overseas bowler would have suited the make-up of the county's fledgling team that much better.

An overseas bowler is what Durham got in 1993 when they signed West Indian quickie Anderson Cummins. But Cummins was only recruited because Durham assumed that Jones would be touring with Australia during the summer of 1993. When, in fact, Jones was not picked he turned the clock back to the late 1950s and said he was considering emigrating to England to establish a career in county cricket. He did in fact apply for a work permit to join Durham as a youth coach for the 1993 season, but was turned down. Jones then simply jumped on a plane and turned up at Durham claiming that he would work for free, an offer that was quickly and gratefully accepted.

Essex

211	K.D. Boyce (all-rounder, pace bowler) 1966–77	WI
54	B.L. Irvine (batsman) 1968–9	SA
47	B.C. Francis (batsman) 1971–3	A
282	K.S. McEwan (batsman) 1974–85	SA
144	N. Phillip (all-rounder, pace bowler) 1978–85	WI
39	A.R. Border (batsman) 1986–8	A
12	H.A. Page (pace bowler) 1987	SA
59	M.E. Waugh (batsman) 1989–92	A
22	Salim Malik (batsman) 1991	P

870

Poor Hugh Page has been the only failure in 25 years of solid and often spectacular performances from Essex's overseas players. In hindsight the selection of the county's overseas players seems to have been inspired and the policy driving it amazingly simple. Discounting Page, Essex have only ever picked two kinds of overseas players: West Indian pace bowling all-rounders (one replaced the other, giving a continuity of service lasting 20 years) and hard-hitting, middle-order batsmen. This policy has worked remarkably well and the county has seen no need to change it. Essex have never had more than two overseas players on their books at any one time. Indeed, they have never needed to, as their original choices have nearly always done the job required of them.

Essex's selection policy to begin with was forced on the county by economic necessity. Never the richest county, while other clubs had their pick of the high-profile 1960s West Indian and South African test teams, Essex had to make do with an unknown all-rounder spotted playing for Barbados by Les Ames and later recommended to Trevor Bailey. But Keith Boyce, for it was he, never forgot that he had been signed up by Essex before making any mark in West Indian cricket and remained fiercely loyal to the county even after winning international honours.

Boyce, who came close to performing the double in his first full season for the county, was joined by South African Lee Irvine in 1968. Irvine was another obscure (and cheap) overseas player who, after playing for Essex, graduated to his national side. After making his name with the county as one of the cleanest strikers of the ball in world cricket, the left-handed batsman was picked as a member of the great South African side of 1969/70. He made a slow start, but in the third test he hit 79 and 73, and in the fourth and last game of the series made his maiden (and of course only) test century. Essex expected Irvine to be selected for South Africa's cancelled 1970 tour of England and replaced him with yet another unknown, Australian batsman Bruce Francis. The Australian arrived as a middle-order batsman, but was promoted by the county to the opening spot. One year later he was accompanying Keith Stackpole out of the Old Trafford pavilion as his country's number two. But despite the success of

Boyce, Irvine and Francis, Essex's greatest discovery was still to come.

Ken McEwan had only played 10 first-class matches when he joined Essex in 1974 and his 439 runs for Eastern Province had included just two 50s. The South African stylist had been recommended to Sussex by Tony Greig, but that county, as well as Northamptonshire, had declined the chance to sign him up. In 1973 out-going Essex captain Brian Taylor had his chance to study McEwan's form and with remarkable speed offered a three-year contract to this supposed no-hoper. Taylor's decision was to secure the biggest bargain in English county cricket history as McEwan, joining in the year that Fletcher became captain, and Gooch, Hardie and Neil Smith all won regular places, was to score over 18,000 runs for the county and to play a major part in the team's dominance of the domestic cricket scene.

In 1976, after ten years with Essex, the strain of carrying the county's bowling attack, as well as setting games alight with displays of brilliant batsmanship and boundary fielding, began to tell on Boyce. The county attempted to sign Richard Hadlee as a replacement, but the TCCB, which has often resisted the signing of one-season stopgaps in the event of injury to a county's existing overseas player, would only agree to the move if the New Zealand all-rounder signed up for three years. He refused and the deal was off, which was just as well for the other 16 counties who would have had trouble winning anything if Hadlee had linked up with Gooch, Fletcher, Lever and McEwan.

Instead of Hadlee the county found themselves being approached by and signing another unknown West Indian all-rounder, Norbert Philip. Here was a player who, while lacking Boyce's grace, seemed able to fill his predecessor's shoes and, over a slightly shorter county career, his batting and bowling figures bear comparison with his more illustrious fellow West Indian. Indeed, it was the opinion of Mike Denness, the former Kent and England captain who played in Essex's 1979 championship winning side, that it was the selection of Philip which enabled the county to win their first trophy. He argued that Boyce had lost much of his zip over his last few years with the county and that it was only after Philip joined that Lever finally had a pace bowling partner who could be relied upon to maintain the pressure on opposing batsmen.

Essex won the county championship twice more, in 1983 and 1984, but after the 1985 season both Phillip and McEwan finally called it a day. The West Indian was growing too old to be a consistently successful fast bowler and the South African was fed up with plugging along British motorways without the lure of test cricket to keep him going. So one, highly successful era ended and another, even more productive, began.

Whereas in the past, Essex had selected unknowns through lack of cash, now they used their new-found wealth to take their pick of the world's best. But in doing so they avoided the mistake made by so many other counties of selecting a player, however talented, who was not going to perform to his potential through a lack of temperament. Every overseas player picked by Essex since the mid-1980s, no matter how big a name, has been selected first and foremost because the club believed he would not upset the constructive harmony of the Essex dressing room.

Allan Border was the first of this new breed and served as a role model for those who came after. Not only did he score thousands of runs in his two seasons, he also attended most of the sponsor's events at which his presence was required, and took time out to coach up-and-coming Essex players like Paul Prichard.

The enormous demands that international cricket placed on Border meant that he could only spend two summers with Essex. In 1987 the county experimented with a young South African pace bowler Hugh Page. However, his below par performance and a drop to twelfth place in the table soon had Essex hurrying back to pick a batsman, first Australian Mark Waugh and then Pakistani strokemaker Salim Malik. Chopping and changing overseas players in this manner is usually highly dangerous to a county's team spirit and therefore its performance on the field. However, Essex's careful consideration of character as well as talent has stopped this problem arising and has produced astonishingly consistent performances from its overseas players.

Over the six seasons Border, Waugh and Malik played for Essex, their combined career figures for the county read 120 matches, 9,248 runs at an average of 61.24, and 32 centuries. In terms of sheer weight of runs at a consistently high average it is an unparalleled rate of return from a group of overseas players over an extended period.

In 1992, with Pakistan touring England, Essex again chose Mark Waugh as their overseas player. But a year later it was the Australian's turn to tour 'the old country' and Malik returned to Chelmsford. It will be interesting to see in 1994, with both players theoretically available, who gets the nod.

Glamorgan

312	A.E. Cordle (pace bowler) 1963–80	WI
60	B.A. Davis (batsman) 1968–70	WI
154	Majid Khan (batsman) 1968–76	P
45	R.C. Fredericks (opening batsman) 1971–3	WI
82	J.W. Solanky (all-rounder, off-spin bowler) 1972–6	EA
30	G.D. Armstrong (pace bowler) 1974–6	WI
76	R.C. Ontong (all-rounder, off-spin bowler) 1975–80	SA
16	C.L. King (batsman, medium-pace bowler) 1977	WI
44	P.D. Swart (all-rounder, pace bowler) 1978–9	Z
83	Javed Miandad (batsman) 1980–5	P
35	E.A. Moseley (pace bowler) 1980–6	WI
45	W.W. Davis (fast bowler) 1982–4	WI
58	Younis Ahmed (batsman) 1984–6	P
13	D.J. Hickey (pace bowler) 1986	A
12	C.J.P.G. Van Zyl (pace bowler) 1987–8	SA

| 62 | R.J.Shastri (all-rounder left-arm spin bowler)1987–91 | I |
| 32 | I.V.A. Richards (batsman) 1990 and 1992 | WI |

1,159   (950 without Solanky and Cordle before 1968)

Glamorgan have employed more overseas professionals than any other county side. This is not surprising given that the county has always looked outside its own borders, and limited resources, to build a successful team. But what that glib reason hides is the fact that, with one or two noticeable exceptions, Glamorgan's choice of overseas players has proved at best doubtful and at worst a complete disaster.

Glamorgan's supporters have had particularly bad value from their county's overseas players. On average each turned out just 68 times for their adopted county. Remove Solanky, who as an East African was unlikely to play test cricket, Ontong, who as a Cape coloured was never likely to play for his country and who became English qualified in 1981 anyway, and Cordle, who although born in the West Indies only ever played there once, and the average appearances falls to just 63. The total appearances of the 14 remaining players equal 689, just 24 more than Sussex who employed only 8 overseas players in the same period. Glamorgan is not the richest of counties and sometimes it has to satisfy itself with overseas players who were either unproven or past their prime, but time and again they have selected players who, either through temperament, suspect fitness or sheer lack of talent, were never going to make the grade.

Like Kent, Glamorgan did enjoy a stable and successful period immediately after the introduction of immediate registration. From 1968 to 1970, Bryan Davis and Majid Khan were part of a championship-winning side. When Davis left at the end of the 1970 season he was replaced by an even more exciting player, West Indian opener Roy Fredericks.

It was in 1974 that Glamorgan's selectors' judgement began to go slightly haywire. The club wanted a fast bowler and decided not to re-engage Fredericks who they thought was restricting playing opportunities for promising home-grown players. After considering Sarfraz Nawaz, who opted to return to Northants, Dennis Lillee and Jeff Thomson, Glamorgan contacted the West Indian selectors to see if they had useful young fast bowlers. Yes, they replied, they had three – Uton Dowe, Greg Armstrong and Michael Holding. Glamorgan chose Armstrong. The West Indian was fast, but very erratic and left the club after three seasons.

Majid Khan also finally left the club in 1976, after his less than successful term as county captain had severely affected his playing ability and brought a sad end to his otherwise successful career with the county. Glamorgan were determined to make sure they picked a stone-cold cert for their next overseas player. Peter Kirsten, Garth Le Roux and Allan Lamb were all debated, but the final decision was to hunt out an all-rounder. West Indian Collis King was the club's choice, but although he helped the county through to a Gillette Cup runners-up place, his free-swinging batting and straightforward medium-paced bowling proved ineffective in English conditions.

The selection of an all-rounder was still considered the right policy when the club came to choose King's replacement, though many supporters raised an eyebrow when the club announced that it had signed a 31-year-old Rhodesian called Peter Swart. Swart had been successful in the Lancashire League and was to put in some solid performances for Glamorgan. But his gentle medium-pace put the county in no position to trade blows with teams boasting a Roberts or a Daniel, and it was Swart himself who recognized the inevitable and quit at the end of the 1979 season.

Looking back on Glamorgan's approach to employing overseas players during the 1970s, former captain Tony Lewis claimed that the county's attempt to compete without a world-class fast bowler was a 'form of suicide.'

In 1980 the club appeared to get it right, but then only by chance. The signing of a world-class batsman Javed Miandad, as well as a fast and consistent West Indian fast bowler Ezra Moseley, saw the county climb off the bottom of the championship table and rise to thirteenth place. But these two only came together after the club had talked to Kapil Dev, Vincent Van der Bijl, Australian quickie Alan Hurst and Pakistani batsman Parvez Mir. During the 1980 and 1981 season Moseley played 29 times for the county in first-class matches and took 103 wickets. Unfortunately for Glamorgan, just when they appeared to have found a fast bowler who was the genuine article, Moseley broke down and only played briefly for the county again five years later.

Glamorgan looked around for a replacement and, after attempting to sign Franklyn Stephenson, Terry Alderman and Steve Jefferies, settled on Winston Davis. This created a problem for the county as a change in the TCCB's regulations meant that Glamorgan could only play one overseas player in its first team. The club were forced to choose between Miandad, who had already proved himself the best batsman ever to play for the county, and Davis, who as an effective West Indian fast bowler was considered by most as the key to any championship success.

During 1983 the decision was made to play Davis during the majority of three-day matches and Miandad, once he had returned from World Cup duty with Pakistan, in the limited over matches. Neither policy proved a great success, though Davis (despite being hampered by the slow Welsh pitches) did top the county's bowling averages with 52 wickets at 26.71.

In 1984 Younis Ahmed joined the county. The 36-year-old Pakistani batsman had already enjoyed a successful 19-year career in county cricket, playing for Surrey and Worcestershire. His test career had lasted just two matches and he had not played first-class cricket in his home country for over ten years. In terms of qualification he was no longer considered an overseas player by the TCCB, allowing Glamorgan to play him alongside Davis and/or Miandad.

But, at the end of the 1984 season, Davis was released to create more opportunities for up-and-coming Welsh fast bowlers such as Greg Thomas. Although the two Pakistani batsmen played well, the county had a poor season and captain Rodney Ontong disappeared back to his native South Africa, claiming that he was not prepared to lead a side without an overseas fast bowler. Approaches were made to Bruce Reid and Craig McDermott, but eventually the club settled for re-signing Moseley, and Ontong agreed to return. However, this move upset Miandad, whose fiery temperament was not best suited to the club's constant changes of strategy when it came to employing overseas players. Following Pakistan's success in the Sharjah trophy, when Miandad had hit the last delivery of the final for six to win the tournament, he simply stayed at home to soak up the adulation.

Later in the season he did try and return, asking for a two or three-year contract, but was turned away. After all this the 1986 season was always going to be problematic and so it proved. Moseley, who because of his Lancashire League commitments could only play mid-week matches, took just 11 wickets at 40.63, and Dennis Hickey, the young Australian fast bowler who stood in for Miandad, 17 at 58.58.

Starting afresh in 1987 the club again switched strategies and this time decided to look for a spinner, who would be able to exploit the 'slow and low' Welsh pitches, as well as a fast bowler. The quickie they chose was an obscure South African called Corrie Van Zyl, who took just 17 wickets in 2 seasons, while the spinner was Ravi Shastri. Unfortunately, bowling had always been the weakest part of the Indian all-rounder's game and in $3\frac{1}{2}$ seasons he only took 95 first-class wickets. To replace Shastri while he was touring England with his country in 1990, Glamorgan signed West Indian captain Viv Richards who enjoyed a highly successful season, scoring 1,425 runs at 61.95. However even the great West Indian seemed affected by the Welsh air, and his second season at the club was marred by injury and was much less successful.

Gloucestershire

259	M.J. Procter (all-rounder, fast bowler) 1965–81	SA
16	R.W. Phillips (batsman) 1968–70	WI
193	Sadiq Mohammad (batsman) 1972–82	P
206	Zaheer Abbas (batsman) 1972–85	P
71	J.N. Shepherd (all-rounder, pace bowler) 1982–7	WI
122	C.A. Walsh (fast bowler) 1984–92	WI
24	B.F. Davison (batsman) 1985	Z
138	K.M. Curran (all-rounder, pace bowler) 1985–90	Z
16	V.S. Greene (pace bowler) 1987–9	WI
20	T.M. Alderman (pace bowler) 1988	A
20	D.R. Gilbert (pace bowler) 1991	A

1,085

It is not unreasonable to suggest that for much of the 1970s, Procter, Sadiq and Zaheer *were* Gloucestershire County Cricket Club. They scored the runs, took most of the wickets and held a good few catches. Indeed, the majority of great or even very good cricketers who have played for Gloucestershire since the late 1960s were born outside the UK. The feats performed by these players in Gloucestershire's name engendered the strongest feelings of affection for imported players on the county circuit. To this day, Gloucestershire supporters yearn for a return to the heady days of Procter, Zaheer and Sadiq. Gloucestershire have bred very few high-class players of their own during the last 30 years, for if they had the county would surely have added significantly to the two trophies they won during the heady 1970s.

The story of those two cup final wins (the Gillette in 1973 and the Benson & Hedges in 1977) shows how much the side owed to their overseas players. In the 1973 game Procter made easily the highest score of the game after coming to the wicket with the score at 22 for 2 (Sadiq and Zaheer both out for 9). When Sussex batted, Procter bowled nearly 11 overs for 27 runs and 2 wickets. At Lord's in 1977 Sadiq and Procter managed just 25 each, but Zaheer took the attack to Underwood and just failed to make the highest score of the match by 1 run. During Kent's reply Procter bowled 7 overs and took 1 wicket for 15 runs. The story was the same in most of the games Gloucestershire played during the 1970s; one of the county's overseas players could always be counted on to come good. Sometimes it did not prevent defeat (or lead to victory), but at least the county went down fighting.

Procter, in particular, seems to have dominated the county side during his time at Gloucestershire, a feeling reinforced by the fact that 2 of the 13 chapters in David Green's recent history of the county refer to Procter by name (Chapter 9: The arrival of Procter and Chapter 11: Mike Procter's captaincy). His arrival in the county was like that of Waqar Younis and Ian Botham combined. He bowled sharp in-swingers and had a particularly nasty bouncer, while his batting was classical but almost unbelievably powerful, especially in the V between mid-on and mid-off. Like Botham, no cause was lost while he still had a bat or ball in his hands.

For four seasons, Procter joined Brown, Mortimore and Allen in one of the country's leading bowling attacks, but Gloucestershire's batting was too inconsistent for the county to pose a realistic challenge for the county championship. In 1969 they finished second behind Glamorgan but otherwise their positions were sixteenth, seventeenth and eighth. Roy Phillips, a West Indian who had qualified by residence, had one good season but faded after that.

The situation changed in 1972 when Sadiq Mohammad qualified by residence and Zaheer Abbas was registered. Over the ten seasons during which the two Pakistanis and the South African played together, Gloucestershire were to average eighth place in the county table and to finish third three times running. In 1977 in particular Gloucestershire only trailed eventual joint winners Middlesex and Kent by five points after having two games rained off without a ball being bowled. During that season Gloucestershire won 9 of their 20 finished games. Zaheer hit 1,584 runs at 52.80, while Procter took 109 wickets at 18.04 in 1977, which was also the first of Procter's five years as Gloucestershire captain.

Sadiq, a compact, left-handed batsman whose ability to improvise bore much resemblance to Javed Miandad, would open the batting usually with the aggressive Knight or Stovold. Zaheer batted at three and Procter at four. As Alastair Hignell, who usually batted five or six, remembered later, batsmen commonly arrived at the wicket to find the score 150 for 4 – before lunch on the first day. Their dominance reached a peak in 1976 when Zaheer scored 2,431 championship runs and twice made a double century and a century in a match (without being dismissed in each of the four innings), Sadiq hit 1,600 runs at an average of 47, and Procter scored over 1,000 runs and took 65 wickets.

Not surprisingly, Procter's retirement from the English game at the end of the 1981 season took the wind out of Gloucestershire's sails, especially as it was followed by Sadiq's departure a year later. Zaheer was still there, but it was the ebullient characters of Procter and Sadiq, as much as their talent that had driven Gloucestershire for the last ten years. An attempt was made to plug the gap with West Indian all-rounder Franklyn Stephenson, but his appearances were restricted by the fact that the TCCB regulations prevented him playing alongside Sadiq and Zaheer. Gloucestershire had to make do with the 38-year-old John Shepherd, who was no longer classed as an overseas player after leaving Kent.

A more durable replacement for Procter (if there could ever be such a thing) arrived in 1984 in the shape of Courtney Walsh. Unfortunately, his first-class appearances for the county were cut back to only six after he was picked as part of the West Indian touring party and Gloucestershire finished at the bottom of the championship table. In 1985 the story was different as Walsh played 20 games and took 82 wickets at 19.95. This, combined with David Lawrence's promise and the arrival of the 'English-qualified' Zimbabweans Kevin Curran and Brian Davison, shot the county into third place.

Walsh has proved one of the most reliable of overseas players and in partnership with Lawrence he has made rival batsmen almost as nervous about visiting Gloucester as they were in Procter's heyday. But Walsh's effectiveness, like Garner's, was dampened in later seasons through his continuous selection by the West Indian test team, in which he fulfilled the role of stock bowler. Vibert Greene, a fast–medium bowler from Barbados, was hired to provide support and did a solid enough job in his 16 appearances for the county.

Gloucestershire have had mixed success in finding a replacement for Walsh during his summers touring England with the West Indies. In 1988 they struck gold and pulled off something of a coup by persuading Terry Alderman to return to English county cricket. Alderman, after his two highly successful seasons with Kent in 1984 and 1986, had claimed that the daily grind of English domestic cricket was not for him. Gloucestershire changed his mind and he returned to take 75 wickets at 22.81, and form an effective and contrasting bowling attack with Lawrence and Curran.

In 1991, Gloucestershire chose Australian fast bowler David Gilbert to replace Walsh. Unfortunately he had few of Alderman's wiles and at the age of

31 was considerably less pacy than Walsh. Gilbert took only 55 wickets at 30.81 and although he proved himself a great trier, most Gloucestershire supporters were glad to see Walsh return in 1992. The warm welcome was well justified as Walsh captured 92 first-class wickets at an average of 15.96, a sharp contrast to the general paucity of Gloucestershire's home-grown bowling which was led by slow left armer Mark Davies's 55 wickets at 27.94.

Hampshire

204	B.A. Richards (opening batsman) 1968–78	SA
275	C.G. Greenidge (opening batsman) 1970–87	WI
26	D.R. O'Sullivan (left-arm spin bowler) 1971–3	NZ
58	A.M.E. Roberts (fast bowler) 1973–8	WI
197	M.D. Marshall (fast bowler) 1979–92	WI
29	C.L. Smith (batsman) 1980–2	SA
15	R.A. Smith (batsman) 1982–4	SA
20	E.L. Reifer (left-arm pace bowler) 1988–9	WI
22	S.T. Jefferies (all-rounder, left-arm pace bowler) 1988–9	SA
18	Aquib Javed (pace bowler) 1991	P

864

The sometimes arbitrary nature of who is and who is not an overseas cricketer, and the way in which that affects a player's county career, has been thrown into sharp relief more than once at Southampton. Gordon Greenidge arrived in Berkshire from Barbados in 1965 at the age of 14 and by the time he made his debut for the West Indies in the 1974/5 series against India he had played the great majority of his first-class cricket in England. In fact he had already played for the English Schools team and had been sounded out in 1972 by Hampshire's cricket committee chairman over whether he wished to play test cricket for England. Greenidge, although disappointed about missing out on the 1973 West Indian tour of England, said no and before he could change his mind the Windies snapped him up.

The Smith brothers, on the other hand, arrived as ready-made cricketers from South Africa, spent two seasons qualifying as English and then went on to enjoy test careers with their adopted country. Barry Richards of course never seriously contemplated playing for another country, but because his nation was banned from test cricket he was able to give most of his efforts to Hampshire. Therefore Hampshire had uninterrupted service from South Africa's leading bat while losing their West Indian-qualified Englishman every four seasons and having to do without their two English-qualified South Africans on a regular basis.

It was this rather confused and cosmopolitan approach that gave Hampshire the 'league of nations' tag during the 1970s and 1980s, and marked their employment policy out as one of the most flexible, wide-ranging and ambitious.

During the 1986 and 1987 seasons, Hampshire's playing staff included three West Indians, three South Africans, a Kenyan and a Dutchman. Counting Paul Terry as German (he was born in Osnabrück) is misleading both in terms of his allegiance and his nationality.

This uninhibited approach to team building began during the captaincy of West Indian ex-pat Roy Marshall, the last of the great white West Indian players. It was carried on by enterprising skippers such as Nick Pocock and Mark Nicholas. Hampshire have always looked to possess depth in resources. From 1970 onwards Hampshire have only twice (during the summers of 1976 and 1988) had to depend on one overseas player and once, when the Smith brothers were qualifying for England, Hampshire had four 'foreign' players to call on. The ability to play two (sometimes three) overseas players in most games has aided this approach, as has the county's policy of having an overseas bowler as well as one or two (or three) batsmen. The question as to why, given all this careful planning Hampshire have only managed to win the county championship once since 1968 is for another chapter.

But it is clear that the championship victory of 1973 would never have been possible without Hampshire's three overseas players. Richards led the way with 1,452 runs at 51.85, while Greenidge actually beat that run tally, knocking up 1,656 runs at 48.70. But often the forgotten man in the trio was New Zealand left-arm spinner David O'Sullivan. Never a success during his 11 tests, the first of which had come in the previous winter, O'Sullivan formed an effective partnership with Hampshire vice-captain and veteran slow left-armer Peter Sainsbury. Sainsbury did not spin the ball much (if at all) and O'Sullivan was never such a force again, but such was the mesmerism they managed to weave over opposing batsman that they became the county's leading bowlers, taking 100 wickets at under 20 apiece between them.

O'Sullivan lost his place in 1974 to Andy Roberts, who at 23 tore into English county cricket and terrified almost every batsman he bowled against. In 1974, Roberts was a sheer terror. He played in 21 first-class matches and took 119 wickets at 13.62. But, as Barry Richards has been at pains to point out, Roberts's success was based on thought as well as frightening pace. His two-speed bouncer fooled many experienced batsmen, who hooked the first medium-pace delivery easily and then found themselves fearing for their lives as the second lightning-fast bouncer reared up at their face. In one famous, and photographed, incident, Colin Cowdrey was sent crashing back through his stumps by Roberts's two-card trick for the most spectacular hit wicket dismissal ever. There was to be no relief for Hampshire's opponents after Roberts left the county in 1978, for he was replaced by Malcolm Marshall, the Antiguan's rightful heir as both hit man and strategist in the West Indian pace quartet.

Hampshire were actually a stronger side in 1974 than they were in their championship-winning year and, if it had not been for a game against Yorkshire being abandoned without a ball bowled, Hampshire would have almost certainly picked up their second consecutive trophy. As well as Roberts's wickets,

Richards scored 1,406 runs at 61.13 and Greenidge 1,093 at 35.25, including 259 against Sussex with 13 6s!

Similar attempts were made by Marshall and Greenidge in the mid-1980s to drive Hampshire to the top of the table, but without the support O'Sullivan and Roberts provided in the 1970s, the county's 'English' resources were not enough.

In the early 1970s the Richards and Greenidge partnership was fit to rank alongside that most exciting of county cricket opening partnerships, that of Lancashire's MacLaren and Spooner. But after the success of the mid-1970s, Richards began to become bored with the county circuit. His captain Richard Gilliat admitted that in 1973, 'for once our success gave Barry Richards the motivation to keep trying throughout the season'. When Richards finally left Hampshire he had some harsh words to say about county cricket, but the move apparently caused the South African a lot of heartache and in later life he has begun to regret that he appeared so dissatisfied with his life in the game. He is admired particularly by overseas players for being one of the first to secure terms and conditions from his employers which reflected the size and nature of his contribution to the county's competitiveness and financial success.

Roberts soon followed Richards, his move encouraged by his belief that he was being over bowled by Hampshire captain Richard Gilliat and ill-founded rumours that he was a 'disruptive' influence in the dressing room.

Hampshire chose a relatively unknown West Indian fast bowler as Roberts's replacement. Malcolm Marshall's commitment to county cricket could not have been more different from that of Richards, even though both had a talent which marked them out from even the very best of their Hampshire colleagues. In the winter before the 1982 season in which he took a record 134 wickets for the county, Marshall had been touring Australia. Playing in a one-day international he was facing Dennis Lillee who bowled him a perfect leg–cutter, pitching leg and missing off. Marshall learnt how Lillee accomplished this delivery and perfected it himself. In the following county season he used it to such devastating effect that he estimates that he captured a third of his wickets for the county with it. Many other overseas fast bowlers would have saved this delivery and only used it, along with the surprise factor, in international matches.

Not so Marshall, who backed his own talent to defeat any batsman, however familiar he might be with the West Indian's skills. Those skills would be on show during a Sunday League game against Glamorgan, as much as they would against England at Lord's, and for that approach Marshall became one of the most valuable overseas players during the 1980s. This fact was recognized by Hampshire supporters, who made sure that the £61,006 raised during his 1987 benefit year was a record for a West Indian cricketer.

However, during this same period cash was becoming a sore point with Hampshire's other West Indian. Greenidge, who would have been 38 at the start of the 1989 season, asked for a contract worth £29,000. The club refused and Greenidge left the county displaying a considerable amount of bad feeling.

Hampshire has shown a willingness to experiment during the seasons when its West Indians have been touring. Twice they went for left-arm pace bowlers, but not to any great success. In 1991, with Marshall touring again, Hampshire signed up Aquib Javed, who had already done sterling service as Waqar and Wasim's henchman. His 53 wickets at 31.24 were a disappointing return and the rumour on the county circuit was that he had been instructed by the senior Pakistani test players not to let on about any of the Pakistanis' 'aids' to swing bowling that might come in useful during the 1992 tour of England.

Hampshire's disappointment with Javed was particularly strong as Robin Smith had brought back tales of how much late swing the Pakistani pace bowler had achieved during that winter's World Cup final. Graham Gooch also described Javed's bowling in that match as 'a revelation'.

Marshall returned in 1992, but was a shadow of his former fearsome self. However, the 49 wickets at 27.51 he took in championship matches were less important than the part he played in Hampshire's capture of the Benson & Hedges trophy. During the final with Kent, the West Indian fast bowler smashed 29 off 22 balls and then turned in a match-winning spell of 3 for 33 as Hampshire won through by 41 runs.

Kent

303	J.N. Shepherd (all-rounder, pace bowler) 1966–81	WI
243	Asif Iqbal (batsman, medium-pace bowler) 1968–82	P
80	B.D. Julien (all-rounder, pace bowler) 1970–7	WI
82	E.A.E. Baptiste (all-rounder, left-arm pace bowling) 1981–7	WI
40	T.M. Alderman (pace bowler) 1984 and 1986	A
45	R.F. Pienaar (batsman, medium-pace bowler) 1987–9	SA
12	F. De Villiers (pace bowler) 1990	SA
26	T.A. Merrick (pace bowler) 1990–1	WI
21	C.L. Hooper (batsman) 1992	WI
852		

The self-deprecating humour that Kent fans developed during the 1980s after their team failed to match its achievements of the previous decade had more than a little to do with the county's quixotic selection of overseas players. As county after rival county took their pick from the world-class fast bowlers being mass-produced in the Caribbean, Kent recruited a series of pale imitations and a couple of South Africans that few had ever heard of.

As usual with fans' humour it is generalized and in some cases grossly unfair. Eldine Baptiste turned in a number of solid performances, while Roy Pienaar helped Kent get within one point of the county championship in 1988. Kent's one unquestioned recruiting coup in the 1980s came with Terry Alderman's two seasons for the county. Here was a bowler who had proved his worth in English conditions and, given even merely competent support, could have won the championship for almost any county. Kent succeeded in overcoming his fears about the wear and tear a full English season would wreak on his injury-prone body, but failed to persuade him to make a long-term commitment.

Lack of continuity in the overseas playing staff, as displayed by Alderman's on–off stay with Kent, marks out two distinct periods in the county's recent history. Kent employed just 9 overseas players in the 27 seasons between 1966 and 1992, but recruitment accelerated sharply towards the end of the period. In the glory years of the 1970s and late 1960s Kent fielded just three overseas players, who between them racked up 626 first-class games for the county. In the care-worn 1980s and early 1990s, 6 overseas cricketers played for the county, appearing just 214 times in all. Such was the continuity offered by Asif, Shepherd and Julien that between 1971 and 1981 Kent signed no new overseas player. That ten-year gap between signings is without parallel in English county cricket since the late 1960s.

All but two of Kent's overseas players (Alderman and Merrick) have had some claim to being all-rounders. The county's continuing attraction to players who can perform with both bat and ball stems from the success of the county's original trio of overseas players.

Kent in the 1970s and late 1960s had a side packed full of highly talented home-grown specialists. In batting it boasted Colin Cowdrey, Luckhurst, Denness, Knott, Tavare and Woolmer, while the bowling was spearheaded for the entire period by the masterful Underwood, ably supported by John Graham and later by Graham Dilley. What the county required to transform this promise into championship-winning potential was to stiffen the batting in the middle and lower order, therefore protecting the tail end specialists, as well as providing bowling support. Asif, Shepherd and Julien managed to do all this and much more, and Kent appeared to be one of the first counties to learn one of the golden rules governing the employment of overseas players – 'Don't waste your money duplicating resources'. Kent lacked home-grown all-rounders, so it went out on to the newly open market and bought them. A typical early 1970s Kent line-up of Luckhurst, Nicholls, Cowdrey, Denness, Asif, Knott, Shepherd, Woolmer, Julien, Underwood and Graham was a carefully constructed team boasting everything but a high-class wrist-spinner.

Given the huge success the employment of all-rounders brought, it was not surprising that the county has stuck to the policy. Eldine Baptiste's recruitment in 1981 was an obvious attempt to perform a like-for-like replacement with the ageing Shepherd. On paper the switch appears to have been a success. The two West Indians' playing records are remarkably similar, both averaging between 25 and 30 with bat and ball, as well as fielding to the high standard expected of Kentish cricketers. But by the early 1980s the Kent team had changed in nature: in players such as Chris Cowdrey, Ellison, Penn and Potter, it had its own domestically produced all-rounders, admittedly of a more prosaic kind. What the county lacked was penetration in its bowling attack, with only the rock steady Underwood providing any sort of consistent threat. This might have been provided in 1982 when Kent attempted to register leg-break bowler Abdul

Qadir for the first half of the season, Pakistan being due to tour England in the second half. Unfortunately for Kent the request was turned down by the TCCB's registration committee.

In 1984 Baptiste toured as part of the all-conquering West Indian side and Terry Alderman, a specialist swing bowler and batting rabbit, took his place in the Kent side. The difference was immediately noticeable and Kent started bowling sides out, winning two more matches than in 1983 and rising two places to fifth in the championship table. Only a wholesale collapse in batting form (in 1983 6 players had averaged more than 40, in 1984 not 1 reached that mark) prevented the county from making a concerted attempt on the championship title.

Baptiste returned in 1985 to have his most successful season with the county, playing 21 games, scoring 897 runs at 30.93 and capturing 52 wickets. But the effect on the county's bowling performance was noticeable. Underwood and Ellison repeated their heroics of a year earlier but the county won only four games and slipped to ninth place in the championship. Kent recognized that something had to be done, and produced a workable and highly effective compromise. Baptiste was to play in the one-day games (one of the advantages of all-rounders was that they apparently offered the most value for money in limited-overs matches) and Alderman would feature in the county championship side. The county was rewarded for such a flexible approach with a better performance in the county championship and a runners-up medal in the Nat West trophy. During 1986, age finally caught up with Underwood, who was to announce his retirement a year later, otherwise even greater feats might have been within the county's grasp.

The next year, 1987, was Baptiste's last season with Kent and Alderman's absence was painfully obvious. The West Indian took his usual 50 wickets, but with no Dilley and with Underwood winding down, it was obvious that this was a season too far for Kent's continued employment of Baptiste. The county slipped to fourteenth place and the dangers of not attempting to match the choice of overseas player to the needs of the side finally came home to roost.

After choosing another all-rounder in South African Roy Pienaar and enjoying a freak season in 1988, when Chris Penn for one year became the strike bowler Kent had been looking for since Dilley's departure, Kent recognized their weakness and picked West Indian fast bowler Tony Merrick, who had previously played for Warwickshire. The move paid off to an extent in 1991, with Merrick taking 58 wickets and Kent rising to sixth place in the championship table.

Carl Hooper, another all-rounder, was chosen to play for the county in 1992 and, with Igglesden, Ealham and McCague all growing in effectiveness, his selection has proved a luxury Kent were finally able to afford. The West Indian played every county championship match, scoring 1,329 runs at 47.46 and taking 35 wickets at 37.34. Like Asif before him, Hooper proved the perfect linchpin between the county's aggressive specialist batsmen, and a varied and constantly threatening bowling attack.

Lancashire

219	C.H. Lloyd (batsman) 1968–86	WI
175	F.M. Engineer (wicket-keeper, batsman) 1968–76	I
49	C.E.H. Croft (fast bowler) 1977–82	WI
19	M.F. Malone (pace bowler) 1979–80	A
32	S.T. Jefferies (all-rounder, left-arm pace bowler) 1983–5	SA
70	B.P. Patterson (fast bowler) 1984–90	WI
44	Wasim Akram (all-rounder, left-arm pace bowler) 1988–91	P
14	D.K. Morrison (pace bowler) 1992	NZ

622

When Clive Lloyd played his last game for Lancashire in 1986 he had become so closely associated with the county that he was used in a national TV advertising campaign for the (Manchester) *Guardian*. The former West Indies captain turned down an initial approach from Hampshire and became registered as one of Lancashire's overseas players for 19 seasons, easily a record for a player who was also enjoying a lengthy and highly successful test career. That he felt at home in Lancashire is evident in the fact that he settled there after retiring from county and test cricket. Like Learie Constantine before him, Lloyd played Lancashire League cricket (for Haslingden) and – as he became connected in the minds of the county's supporters to the glorious and highly successful cricket played in their name – they welcomed him as one of their own.

Between 1968 and 1986 Lloyd was as important to Lancashire as he was to the West Indies. He exuded an aura of success developed with Lancashire's one-day wonders during the 1970s and with the Windies team during the 1980s. He had played alongside the Indian wicket-keeper Farokh Engineer for the first nine seasons and together they provided the impetus behind the county's capture of the Gillette Cup (four times) and the Sunday League (twice).

The choice of Engineer as an overseas player was considered an odd one at the time. Top-class wicket-keepers are usually not that difficult to find among the ranks of English county players. Lancashire, however, were able to claim that as well as signing a high-quality keeper they had also secured a test-class batsman. Engineer's performance for the county proved that Lancashire's judgement was sound, but ironically this owed more to his enthusiastic role as keeper and the centre of Lancashire's vibrant fielding side of the early 1970s than to his batting. Engineer never once passed 1,000 first-class runs in an English season, and his batting average for Lancashire of 26.64 with only 4 centuries compares poorly to his test average of 31.08. Like Lloyd, Engineer also settled in Lancashire after his career in top-class cricket was over.

After Engineer left and was replaced with the fearsome but unreliable Colin Croft, Lancashire found success more difficult to come by. Lloyd's star, however, was still in the ascendant as his West Indies team began to emerge as the strongest in test history. When Lloyd was made captain of Lancashire in 1981 there were many who thought it was a good decision taken rather too late. Yet, without his four-man pace attack, Lloyd found winning cricket matches rather more difficult and in his three years of captaincy the county under-performed to finish sixteenth, twelfth and thirteenth respectively. However, such was the loyalty felt towards Lloyd that he was given a second chance in 1986. Again it appears to have been the wrong move, as the county slipped one place down the county table to finish fifteenth. In fairness to Lloyd it should be pointed out that he was able to play in only six county championship games. He also led Lancashire to the 1986 final of the Nat West Trophy against Sussex. Unfortunately for the West Indies captain, Lancashire lost and Lloyd himself was dismissed for a duck by eventual man of the match Dermot Reeve.

Lloyd was also granted a second benefit during the 1986 season, a clear sign of the esteem in which the club held him. But in the eyes of many supporters giving a player the chance to make £100,000 tax free when they had only played three championship games in the last two seasons was deemed a bit rich. Here, many thought, was a clear example of a player, admittedly a great one, getting bigger than the game.

While Lloyd continued to be considered as Lancashire's number one overseas player, three fast bowlers actually shared the bulk of the burden between 1977 and 1985. Of the three Colin Croft was the fastest and the finest, but unfortunately his temperament was as unreadable as his sharply slanting deliveries and, despite the presence of the Windies' captain in the Lancashire side, he was rarely able to live up to the fearsome reputation he earned in test cricket.

Mick Malone was a fast bowler from Perth, who had a promising test career ended by his involvement in the Packer Circus. Of Lloyd's three supporting acts he was perhaps the most consistently successful, taking 64 wickets at 24.20. The South African left-arm pace man Stephen Jefferies appeared to lack the necessary penetration on English wickets although he did play a part in Lancashire's 1984 Benson & Hedges Cup final victory by taking 3 for 28 off his 11 overs, as Warwickshire crashed from 102 for 2 to 139 all-out.

Patrick Patterson emerged from under Lloyd's shadow in 1987, when he was employed as Lancashire's sole overseas player. But it soon became apparent that Lancashire had another Colin Croft on their hands. Patterson was fast, sometimes frighteningly so, but unlike his colleagues in the West Indies' pace attack he lacked a keen tactical sense as well as the ability to consistently move the ball. In 1987 Lancashire came second to Nottinghamshire in the county championship, losing out on the title by only five points. The county could have rightfully expected more than 52 wickets at 26.13 from their West Indian fast bowler and, had Patterson delivered then, Lancashire would have surely walked away with their first county championship for 37 years.

With Patterson touring with the West Indian side in 1988, Lancashire signed Wasim Akram, the Pakistani left-arm pace man who had impressed so much when playing for his country in England the previous year. Wasim was only able to play 10 first-class games for the county in 1988, but he took 31 wickets at

21.48 and his arrival signalled the start of a mini golden age for the county. In fact, so keen had Lancashire been to sign the Pakistani all-rounder before any other county, they had met Wasim as he stepped off the plane at the start of Pakistan's 1987 tour of England and offered him a six-year contract.

From 1989, Patterson and Wasim have proved the most effective pairing of overseas players for the county since Lloyd and Engineer. Patterson has been used mainly for first-class games and Wasim for one-day competitions, where his all-round abilities offer greater scope for influencing the game. Splitting the workload kept both fresh and fit. In the bowler-friendly summer of 1989, both bowlers finished the season with first-class bowling averages under 20, and the county came fourth in the county championship as well as winning the Sunday League title. In the run-soaked year of 1990, Wasim and Patterson's skills were not so effective in first-class cricket, but the county still finished a respectable sixth. However in one-day cricket Lancashire were almost unstoppable. They finished runners up in the Sunday League, just two points behind Derbyshire, and achieved the unparalleled feat of capturing both one-day knock-out cups.

Wasim's influence was most keenly felt during July's Benson & Hedges Cup final. Coming in at number six, he smashed 28 runs off 21 balls, hitting 2 6s and a 4 to set a decent target for Worcestershire to chase. Then coming on to bowl as first change he wrapped up the game for Lancashire by having both Curtis and Hick caught behind. In September's Nat West final all Wasim had to do was bowl a tight 12 overs after Phillip DeFreitas had taken 5 wickets to reduce Northamptonshire to 5 for 39. However, he did also run out Northants' top scorer, Curtly Ambrose, two short of his half-century.

In 1991, Patterson was touring again and Wasim had to shoulder the burden alone. The strain began to tell and, despite the Pakistani pace star topping the bowling averages with 56 wickets at 22.33, the county slipped to eighth place. Once again the county also missed out by three points on picking up the Sunday League title and made the final of the Benson & Hedges Cup. Once again their opponents were Worcestershire, but this time Graeme Hick proved to be Wasim's master, making 88 before he was caught and bowled by Allott. Worcestershire won by 65 runs and it was the critics' consensus that Lancashire had lost the game by allowing Hick to get settled in before introducing Wasim.

During 1991 Wasim was becoming steadily disillusioned with county cricket. His heavy international workload had given him a fitness record which was the cause of some some concern (and complaint) at Old Trafford. This sort of reaction seemed ungrateful at best to Akram and he soon had further reason to feel hard done by. Playing in a championship match he was warned by the umpire, and ex-policeman, Nigel Plews for over-using the bouncer. Once again the Pakistani's fiery temper got the better of him and he showed dissent. In his heart of hearts Akram must have expected some reprimand, but when Lancashire chairman Bob Bennett imposed a £1,000 fine (around 5 per cent of his season's wages) and the rumour was spread that Bennett was acting in a zealous fashion so as to cement his position as England tour manager, it seemed to be the last straw.

Akram was missing from the Lancashire side in 1992, but only because he was touring with the successful Pakistani team. New Zealand fast bowler Danny Morrison filled in none too successfully, but the big question was whether the Pakistani fast bowler would return in 1993. The chances seemed against it, but after what Lancashire captain Neil Fairbrother described as 'a struggle' Akram said yes. Fairbrother said he felt as if a 'monstrous weight' had been lifted from his mind.

Leicestershire

151	G.D. McKenzie (pace bowler) 1969–75	A
303	B.F. Davison (batsman) 1970–83	Z
219	P.B. Clift (all-rounder, medium-pace bowler) 1975–87	Z
36	A.M.E. Roberts (fast bowler) 1981–4	WI
71	G.J.F. Ferris (fast bowler) 1983–90	WI
75	W.K.M. Benjamin (all-rounder, pace bowler) 1986–92	WI
24	J.N. Maguire (pace bowler) 1991	A

879

As with Kent, Leicester's experience with overseas players has seen the county enjoy a period of remarkable consistency during the 1970s, only to struggle during the 1980s to find the foreign recruits who would match the needs of the side. 'Garth' McKenzie and Brian Davison joined within a season of each other and began to power their adopted county towards its first ever county championship title in 1975. Their selection demonstrated secretary Mike Turner's determination to catch up with other counties which had secured their overseas players in time for the 1968 season. But, as early as May 1969, Turner had his doubts about the new system, writing to the other counties and warning against the possible effects of allowing too many overseas players on to the county circuit.

Turner's reservations have not stopped him picking players who would have the maximum possible impact on the county's performance. Amazingly, Leicestershire have only ever lost their overseas player to a tour of England once since 1969. Winston Benjamin toured with the West Indies in 1988, but Leicestershire already had George Ferris waiting in the wings and about to enjoy his most successful season for the county. Altogether, Leicestershire's overseas players have played only 28 test matches during their time with the county. The Rhodesians, Davison and Clift, as well as the West Indian quickie George Ferris, never played for their countries, while Maguire's test career finished seven years before coming to Leicestershire.

In 1975 Turner and Leicester received their first and greatest reward both for choosing its overseas players so well and trawling other counties for available English-qualified stars like Illingworth and Higgs. Although by 1975 McKenzie was feeling his age, gracefully accepting his exclusion from the side as the championship race hotted up, Davison was going from strength to strength.

The rugged southern African batsman blasted 1,498 runs in 21 championship games at an average of 53.50 to achieve the highest position in the English batting averages for a Leicestershire player since another southern African, Clive Inman, in 1963. The combination of two overseas players, carefully selected recruits from other counties and promising young home-grown players such as David Gower, allowed Illingworth's side to pip Yorkshire for the championship, much to the captain's delight, and capture the Benson & Hedges Cup – the first county to win the championship and a one-day title in a single season.

Brian Davison played for Leicester during 14 seasons. His total of 303 first-class and 273 one-day games during his county career puts him among the most hardworking of overseas pros. But most impressive of all is that he managed to average nearly 22 first-class games every season for Leicester, a level of consistency unmatched by other overseas players over such a long period. Davison became such a fixture on the English county circuit that moves were made to get him qualified to play for England. The campaign worked, with the Test and County Cricket Board ruling that in September 1980 that he and South African all-rounder Mike Procter were English as far as international cricket was concerned. But the English selectors were never really interested and, despite performances such as scoring 1,800 runs at 54.54 in the 1982 season, Davison simply played out the last three years of his career as English qualified.

Davison's fellow overseas player and Rhodesian, Paddy Clift, played for eight seasons with Leicester as a medium-pace bowler and middle-order batsman. Rarely able to perform the sort of match-winning feats that gave Procter and Clive Rice prominence, despite their absence from the international stage, Clift was nevertheless extremely valuable to the Leicester side. The flexibility offered to the side by his solid batting and accurate bowling allowed Leicester to employ a series of West Indian fast bowlers, giving the already useful pace attack a keen edge.

That edge has been provided by three players over a ten-year period, unfortunately none of them has proved consistent enough to maintain its sharpness. Andy Roberts arrived at Leicester with his reputation as a great fast bowler already established. Unfortunately injury problems got in the way and his 4 seasons with the county (between 1981 and 1984) saw him play 11, 13, 4 and 8 first-class games respectively. In 1983 Roberts introduced one of his protégés to the county, George Ferris, who stayed with the county for eight seasons. But, although Ferris took 224 first-class wickets for the county he was only a regular fixture in the side during the 1988 season while he was Leicester's only overseas player.

Ferris played two seasons with Roberts and Clift, as well as one with the Rhodesian alone, before he was joined at Leicester by Winston Benjamin. Like Ferris, Benjamin was from Antigua and bowled, on occasions, very quickly. Both were also the same age, born in 1964, and only Benjamin's superior batting skills marked the two apart. Yet it was Benjamin the late-comer who became the first choice between 1986 and 1990. Excluding the 1988 season when Benjamin was touring, the all-rounder played 50 games for the county, while Ferris played only 28.

This swapping back and forth of two fast bowlers, as Lancashire have done with Wasim Akram and Patrick Patterson, and Surrey attempted to do with Sylvester Clarke and Tony Gray, allowed the county to keep their strike bowlers fresh. The policy worked in that Ferris and Benjamin played a total of 23 games in 1986, 20 in 1987, 19 in 1989 and 16 in 1990. However their combined bowling performance only once approached the level which a county would expect from a competent overseas professional. In 1989, the two captured 79 wickets at 19.03, but in the following year it appeared that without the benefit of the previous season's thick-seamed balls the pair were not a force to be reckoned with. In 1990, the year of modern batting's high summer, they took only 36 wickets at 32.58. Benjamin, whose performances for the West Indies proved that his bowling could contain real hostility, decided to quit county cricket claiming that it was adversely affecting his game (only to return to the county in 1992), while Ferris was reluctantly released.

Into the breach stepped not one man, but two; both Australian but only one planning to take any active part on the field. Western Australian guru Daryl Foster was already working his magic on Kent, but Leicester's signing of Australian coach Bobby Simpson was still treated as big news. Many of the county's supporters expected him to bring along one of his country's established test stars to fill Leicester's vacant overseas player's post. Would it be Dean Jones or Steve Waugh they asked themselves, and when it was announced that the county had signed the 34-year-old John Maguire they were more than a little puzzled.

But the appointment of the pace bowler, who had been banned from international selection for touring South Africa, did have some logic. With no Benjamin, Ferris or Agnew, the side needed a bowler of experience to shore up the promising talent of Millns and Mullulay. The Australian provided that by playing in every first-class and one-day game during the season. His bowling may have lacked the penetration of the West Indians, but after ten years of nursing the injury-prone frames of Ferris and Benjamin, Leicester welcomed the return of a player who, like Davison, McKenzie or Clift, would turn out regardless.

In 1992 Maguire and Simpson departed, the coaching magic having failed to work at Grace Road, and Benjamin returned. It was a low-key comeback with the West Indian scoring just 453 runs and taking only 47 wickets.

Middlesex

170	A.H. Latchman (leg-break bowler) 1965–73	WI
216	N.G. Featherstone (all-rounder, off-spin bowler) 1968–79	Z
44	A.N. Connolly (pace bowler) 1969–70	A
42	H.A. Gomes (batsman) 1973–6	WI
214	W.W. Daniel (fast bowler) 1977–88	WI

21   V.A.P. Van der Bijl (pace bowler) 1980–1   SA
63   D.L. Haynes (opening batsman) 1989–92   WI

770

Since signing Wayne Daniel in 1976, Middlesex have usually exercised the same clear-minded approach to recruiting overseas players as they have to anything connected with winning cricket matches over the last decade and a half. They have decided on the job that the overseas player has to perform and then selected someone to fit the bill. In this way Middlesex made their own luck when they chose Wayne Daniel.

Here was a West Indian fast bowler of the highest rank, who for most of his career was out of favour with the talent-soaked West Indian selectors and (freed from the demands of the international circuit) therefore able to remain almost injury free. Vincent Van der Bijl was chosen in 1980 as much for his take-no-prisoners approach as for his ability to partner Daniel. Here was no one-season piece of opportunism, but a man who would fling himself body and soul into playing for the county as if he had been born in St John's Wood. Mike Gatting was sure of the South African's contribution: 'He not only bowled well himself but helped and inspired and kidded the other bowlers in the side. He was a team man and a lovable character. In his own field, he was the finest I've ever seen.' Unsurprisingly, with an opening attack of Daniel and Van der Bijl operating in harmony, Middlesex won the county championship title in 1980 by a clear margin.

When Daniel's fitness, effectiveness and temperament all went to pot during the 1987 season, it took Middlesex a couple of seasons to respond to the problem. Many at the club felt that since the county had enjoyed great success during the late 1970s and early 1980s it could afford a couple of fallow seasons. This, they argued, would allow the club to take their time and not risk botching the recruitment of Daniel's replacement. However, many of the club's senior players, including captain Gatting and vice-captain Emburey, believed that the team needed the presence of an overseas player to challenge for trophies. As it happened, the 1988 season, in which Daniel played only two first-class games, was a relatively successful one for Middlesex. They improved their position in the county championship from sixteenth to seventh and won the Nat West trophy, defeating Worcestershire complete with a run-gorged Hick in the final.

With the arrival of Angus Fraser, the county had an embarrassment of bowling riches, but lacked stability at the top of the order. When they picked Desmond Haynes to fill the gap left by Graham Barlow it seemed, like most good decisions, a painfully obvious choice. Here was a hugely experienced batsman who had lost none of his enthusiasm for the game, would fit sweetly into the Middlesex dressing room, and had considerable experience of English conditions through league cricket and numerous International tours. Everybody was left asking, 'Why has no one ever picked him before?'

It had not always been so simple for Middlesex. The high cost of living in London, coupled with Middlesex's relative lack of success (and therefore money) in the 1960s and early 1970s made it difficult to attract players of the highest calibre. Mushtaq Mohammad, for example, who had become disenchanted with Northants, turned down an offer from Middlesex in 1971. Middlesex's first post-1968 overseas professional, Australian fast bowler Alan Connolly, spent two unhappy seasons at the club, after the other players discovered that he was being paid more than established English test players such as Titmus and Murray.

Connolly was a cocky player whose attitude set him at loggerheads with the hard-bitten county pros who dominated the Middlesex dressing room at that time. The Australian was also prone to over-experiment when bowling and this reduced his effectiveness in county cricket, as well as increasing the tension between Middlesex's English-qualified players whose playing style was dominated by a 'give nothing away' attitude.

Solid but unspectacular performers, such as Latchman, Featherstone and Gomes, did not expect large pay packets and therefore were within Middlesex's price range. But then they could not be expected to perform like test regulars either and Larry Gomes found himself in the unusual position for an overseas player of being dropped to make way for a young English batsman. Again the county made the right choice, for the home-grown player was Mike Gatting.

Once Middlesex were able to pick up a bargain in Wayne Daniel, who at the time was relatively unproven and therefore did not command the sort of salary which years of consistent success in the county games rightfully brought him, they made sure they looked after him. Daniel was spotted playing for the West Indian under-19 side against their English counterparts by the Middlesex pair of Gatting and Emburey, who were playing in the series. His most widely used nickname was 'Black Diamond', but fellow fast bowler Mike Selvey also christened him 'Rent and Rates', stressing how vital the West Indian was to the county's continued success. In 1982, when Middlesex won the county championship in Mike Brearley's last year as captain, Daniel bowled an average of 25 overs a game and captured 71 wickets at an average 17.50. Surrey fast bowler Sylvester Clarke, on the other hand, averaged 30 overs a game over 22 matches and his 85 wickets cost 20. Not much of a difference there, but it is symptomatic of the relative freshness of the two fast bowlers and therefore their continuing value to their English employers.

Daniel had to be watched though. One season he almost gave up his very effective bouncer altogether and resorted to bowling overs full of yorkers. It was eventually revealed that he was trying to win a prize offered by the *Sun* to the bowler who hit the stumps most often in that season. Daniel, much to his disgust, finally failed to be crowned by the newspaper as that season's 'demon bowler', when his arch rival Clarke secured the prize.

Daniel's physique did not make it easy for him to maintain pace throughout an English county season, since he was muscle-bound and therefore prone to injury. Middlesex had tried to extend his playing career as long as possible, but in 1987, at the age of 32, this problem began to catch up with him. He managed to bowl 333 overs, but only took 29 wickets at an average of 42.96 and he left the county a year later with Mike Gatting claiming that Daniel had been 'the best overseas player in the land'.

Replacing Daniel was always going to be difficult, and wisely Middlesex chose not to try and replace like with like. In any case they did not need a bowler. An attack that included Fraser, Ellcock, Cowans and Williams to bowl pace, and Emburey and Tufnell to provide spin was not going to need much support, not in English county cricket anyway. An opening batsman was what they needed and, when they signed Dessie Haynes, Middlesex actually got two.

At the age of 33, Haynes was never going to have a long career with Middlesex so it was important, if the county were to get their money's worth, to make as much of the West Indian's experience as possible. At the end of the 1988 season, Mike Roseberry had scored 830 runs in 29 first-class matches at an average of 23.05 and had suffered from never having had an experienced or regular opening partner. With Roseberry benefiting from Haynes's positive attitude at the wicket and his constant on-field encouragement, the young English opener blossomed. In 1989 he scored 703 runs at 29.29 and in 1990 finally came into his own with 1,497 at 40.45.

Roseberry is in no doubt himself about Haynes's influence:

The one thing that helped my batting in 1990 was that Desmond was back in the side. The year before I played much more negatively. But he is such a huge influence. Not just on me, he helps everyone. Mark Ramprakash will confirm that. He keeps talking a lot during the innings as well as off the field. A great asset – maybe with Desmond at the other end I simply relax and play better.

Roseberry's cricketing education was complete and Middlesex, having shelled out for an established overseas opening batsman, made good on the deal by gaining an established and effective opening partnership.

Despite the lessons of the late 1980s, Middlesex went into the 1991 season without an overseas player, Haynes touring England with the West Indian team. Despite Mike Gatting's 2,000 plus first-class runs, and a good performance from the spin partnership of Tufnell and Emburey, Middlesex slipped to fifteenth place in the championship with, significantly, Roseberry only contributing 1,222 runs at 33.02. In 1992 Haynes was back and everything was looking better. Roseberry actually out-performed his mentor, scoring 1,724 first-class runs at 49.25 compared to Haynes's 1,513 at 45.84, and Middlesex won the Sunday League.

Northamptonshire

262	Mushtaq Mohammad (all-rounder, leg-break bowler) 1964–78	P
97	H.M. Ackerman (batsman) 1967–71	SA
10	F.S. Goldstein (opening batsman) 1969	Z
151	Sarfraz Nawaz (pace bowler) 1969–82	P

110	B.S. Bedi (left-arm spin bowler) 1972–7	I
92	A.J. Lamb (batsman) 1978–81	SA
16	Kapil Dev (all-rounder, pace bowler) 1981–3	I
11	J.A. Carse (pace bowler) 1983	Z
17	R.A. Hanley (pace bowler) 1984	SA
54	R.A. Harper (all-rounder, off-spin bowler) 1985–7	WI
57	W.W. Davis (fast bowler) 1987–90	WI
42	C.E.L. Ambrose (fast bowler) 1989–92	WI
18	E.A.E. Baptiste (all-rounder, pace bowler) 1991	WI
21	K.M. Curran (all-rounder, pace bowler) 1992	Z

958   (901 discounting Mushtaq's appearances before 1968)

Thirty years before Sachin Tendulkar helped end one particular English taboo, another teenager from the Indian sub-continent was in the vanguard of another significant sea change for English cricket. Mushtaq Mohammad had made his test debut at the age 15 of during the March 1959 test match against the West Indies. Five years later he was signed up by Northamptonshire to begin his residential qualification period and became arguably the first overseas player of the modern era. Like his younger brother Sadiq, who played for Gloucestershire, Mushtaq seemed to have little trouble adjusting to English county cricket or to an English way of life and captained Northants to their first ever trophy in the 1976 Gillette Cup final. In that year the county also finished second in the county championship table behind Middlesex, and Mushtaq topped the batting averages with 1,620 runs at 50.62. Unusually for a modern overseas player, Mushtaq played for Northants when Pakistan toured England in 1967 and 1971, taking part only in the test matches.

Mushtaq was joined by Hylton Ackerman in 1968. The county was forced to grant the South African batsman immediate registration after he had broken the residential qualification rules by over-staying during a holiday trip to his home country. Pakistani seam bowler Sarfraz Nawaz also joined the county in 1969, playing his first game in 1970. But he was considered to have shown a lack of commitment when he resisted joining Northants after the 1971 split tour of England and was not re-engaged until 1974.

Bishan Bedi was a more immediate success, although there were some rumblings that Northants were forced to sack some promising young players to be able to afford the famous left-arm spinner. However, most people soon forgot about this unhappy by-product of Bedi's employment when the Indian spinner began to get to work. He has by far the best record of any overseas spin bowler in English county cricket and his capturing of 434 wickets at 20.89 puts him on a par with the most feared fast bowlers of his time.

Bedi was dismissed by Northants in 1977 following his involvement with the Packer Circus. He fought the decision through the courts, but lost, and left county cricket a very bitter man.

The 24-year-old South African batsman Allan Lamb joined the county in

1978 following Bedi's departure. Over the next five seasons there was growing speculation over the prospect of Lamb becoming English qualified and playing test cricket. As with Hick, there was much to excite the pundits in Lamb's performances in county cricket. Arriving relatively unheralded he finished his first season for Northants occupying eleventh place in the national batting averages. The following year he was third and in 1980 first, and although he slipped back to third place in 1981, it was obvious that Lamb was an international-class performer.

The temptation was too much for the English selectors surveying their choice of prospective batsmen recently denuded by the defection of the South African rebels. Under the rule which allowed those 'foreign' players with a British-born parent and a four-year residency to be treated as 'English' as far as international cricket was concerned, Lamb was selected for the first one-day international against India. At the same time Keith Fletcher was deposed from the English captaincy and the position given to Bob Willis. The official reason was Fletcher's negative tactics and poor results during the recent tour of India, but most commentators believed that his sacking had more to with the creation of a space in the English team for Lamb.

Whether the move was a good one for the English test team remains debatable, but Northants certainly suffered from Lamb becoming an Englishman. In the four seasons between joining the county and playing for England, Lamb averaged 23 appearances for the county each year and scored 6,679 runs at 60.17. In the 11 seasons following his England debut he averaged only 13 matches a year for the county and has scored 10,078 runs at 51.68.

Lamb's conversion to an English qualified player, as well as Sarfraz's advanced age, began a disastrous period for Northants as they attempted the selection of a replacement overseas player. Their first choice seemed a banker, as Kapil Dev appeared made for English county cricket, but as Worcester were to find out later his talents duplicated those already found in most English sides. Kapil also had an understandable desire to take it a bit easy while playing county cricket. He was prepared to act as both stock and strike bowler for his country, but doing the same for an English county six or seven days a week was just not on.

In 1983, with Kapil Dev taking part in the World Cup, Zimbabwean fast–medium bowler James Carse was recruited as a replacement. Something of a sporting renaissance man, he had represented Zimbabwe at rugby, football and athletics, but he could do nothing on Northants' soggy pitches and finished the season with just 22 wickets at 32.82. Worse was to come in 1984, when the county threw all their eggs into one basket by selecting another South African pace man, the 32-year-old Rupert Hanley. Unfortunately, 'Spook' Hanley fared no better than Carse and, despite playing in 17 games, was only able to capture 37 wickets at 31.94.

A change of tack was called for and was provided by the selection of West Indian off-spin bowler and all-rounder Roger Harper. His arrival was greeted as an inspirational choice, bringing one of the most exciting all-round players in the world to the full-time attention of the English cricket-watching public. It was a moot point whether or not Richard Williams, Northants' home-grown off-spinning all-rounder and test prospect, agreed with this move, leading as it did to the sharp restriction in his playing opportunities for the county and (it is alleged) to the ending of his first-class career. But then, in hindsight, Harper himself probably now questions the wisdom of the move. When he joined Northants Harper was considered the best fielder in the world, one of its most promising all-rounders and a future West Indies captain. His first season with the county was a triumph, Harper scoring 734 runs at 38.63 and taking 56 wickets at 35.64, and the next year was even better, with 921 runs at 36.84 and 62 wickets at 26.93. But in 1987 the strain of carrying the weak Northants attack (Harper had bowled 1,604 overs in two seasons) was beginning to tell and injury reduced the all-rounder to just five appearances for the county. It was a setback from which Harper has still to recover, his bowling action disintegrating to such a degree that he was sometimes unable to pitch the ball on the wicket.

The following year, 1988, Northants attempted one of the boldest experiments in the history of county cricket. At the age of 38, Australian fast-bowling legend Dennis Lillee was signed up to make his début in English domestic cricket. To begin with it seemed that the audacious move might just work, especially when Lillee destroyed the Gloucestershire batting with 6 for 68. But the onset of a recurring injury ended Lillee's county career after just seven matches and Winston Davis, who had served as Harper's understudy since 1987, filled the breach for the rest of the season.

Davis and new arrival Curtly Ambrose shared the onerous burden of bowling fast on Northants' lifeless pitches during the 1989 season. However Ambrose's blossoming into one of the world's most dangerous bowlers in 1990 coincided with a dramatic loss of form on Davis's part and the unlucky pace man was released. In 1991 former Kent all-rounder Eldine Baptiste filled in for the touring Ambrose with reasonable success and a year later the wandering Kevin Curran made Northants his third county.

Ambrose returned in 1992 to capture 50 wickets at 26.14, a reasonably impressive performance but not up to the standard he is currently maintaining in test cricket, in which he vies with Waqar Younis as the most persistently destructive fast bowler. Even more than his West Indian predecessor Joel Garner, Ambrose is a private (sometimes almost mysterious) man who appears to find it hard to motivate himself during the daily grind of county cricket. It is also widely believed that Ambrose, unlike his test colleagues Walsh and Marshall, has not sufficiently adapted his normal bowling style to take account of the demands of county cricket and therefore consistently pitches the ball too short, restricting wicket-taking chances as well as run-scoring opportunities.

After Sobers' departure from the county game at the end of the 1974 season, Nottinghamshire had to wait another three seasons before they finally discovered the match-winning combination of overseas players that the county had hoped would be provided by Murray and his West Indian captain. And even then it was another three years until Richard Hadlee was able to play a full sea-

Nottinghamshire

329	B.S. Hassan (batsman) 1966–83	Kenya/ East Africa
97	D.L. Murray (wicket-keeper) 1966–71	WI
107	G. St A. Sobers (all-rounder, pace and left-arm spin bowler) 1968–74	WI
32	N. Nanan (all-rounder, leg-spin bowler) 1971–80	WI
44	D.R. Doshi (left-arm spin bowler) 1973–8	I
40	H.C. Latchman (leg-spin bowler) 1974–6	WI
283	C.E.B. Rice (all-rounder, pace bowler) 1975–87	SA
22	W.K. Watson (pace bowler) 1976–80	SA
148	R.J. Hadlee (all-rounder, pace bowler) 1978–87	NZ
82	F.D. Stephenson (all-rounder, pace bowler) 1988–91	WI
31	C.L. Cairns (all-rounder, pace bowler) 1988–92	NZ

1,215   (without Hassan 886)

son at Trent Bridge. Hadlee and Rice were the greatest pair of overseas match winners ever possessed by an English county. The fact that individually they were both highly talented fast bowlers, as well as being international class batsmen, gave them a head start, but it was their partnership in the middle of the batting order and with the new ball which added a new dimension to their threat.

In 1981 Nottinghamshire beat Sussex by two points to claim their first county championship for 52 years. Throughout the season the chase for the championship became a battle for supremacy between four of the world's leading all-rounders. For Sussex, Garth Le Roux took 81 wickets at 19.53 and Imran Khan 66 at 22.18, but Rice cancelled out Imran's contribution by taking 65 at 19.20 (as well as scoring 1,462 runs at 56.23) and Hadlee overshadowed every performance by capturing 105 victims at 14.89.

That summer, glorious though it was for England's test team, must have been one long nightmare for domestic county batsmen. Among the top 20 leading bowlers in the end of season averages, in addition to Hadlee, Rice, Imran and Le Roux, were six West Indian fast bowlers, namely Clarke, Garner, Holding, Moseley, Marshall and Daniel. During the Ashes Series Ian Botham may have been the undoubted king of cricket, but back on the county circuit it was the overseas quicks who held all in their sway. Indeed, E.W. Swanton, opining from on high at the end of the season, claimed that it was Rice and not Botham who was the leading all-rounder of the age.

But Nottinghamshire's glory in this year of living dangerously might have been just a pipe dream if Hadlee had stuck to his original plan of retiring from county cricket at the end of the 1980 season. In the three seasons since he had joined the county, injuries and international calls meant that he had only played

27 times for Nottingham. Hadlee had tried to combat the wear and tear county cricket was wreaking on his body by sometimes bowling from a shortened run up. Though still managing to take 113 wickets in those 27 games Hadlee decided that 'this wasn't the way I wanted to play the game'.

But the Trent Bridge officials were not going to let him go without a fight and enlisted his father, New Zealand cricketer Walter Hadlee, to help change his mind. Hadlee jun. was told that he was wanted back at Nottingham even if he only bowled off two paces. The New Zealand strike bowler then made the leap of logic that was to make him a force in county cricket and greatly extend his effectiveness as a test cricketer. Using a shortened run for the first time as a staple rather than an emergency measure, he played through the 1981 season and only missed one county championship match. The shortened run up became a fixed feature in Hadlee's game and it is doubtful if New Zealand would have achieved the success it enjoyed during the 1980s if playing for Nottingham had not exerted such a strong pull on Hadlee.

In 1987, the year of Hadlee's eventual retirement from Nottingham, the county won the championship for the second time during the 1980s. At the age of 36 he took 97 wickets for the county and topped the batting averages as well, with 1,075 runs at 53.75. Three years later, now 39 and freshly knighted in the new year's honours list, he played his last test series and took 16 wickets in the three-match series to finish with a world record tally of 431. Hadlee's experience is a clear example of how the sheer weight of English domestic cricket can sometimes push overseas players to discover new depths and talents.

Rice's contribution to Nottingham was perhaps every bit as valuable as Hadlee's. He joined Notts at the age of 26 and perhaps felt South Africa's exclusion from test cricket more keenly than any other potential international. When South Africa finally did return to the international circuit, Rice was judged as being too old and perhaps too closely connected to the rebel tours of the early and mid-1980s, and so his only 'legitimate' appearance on the world stage at test level was during the MCC's bicentenary game in 1987. But, before his back went, Rice was a bowler to be feared, faster than Hadlee though not as skilful. He was also a hugely determined batsman, but perhaps his most impressive ability was his skill as a captain and, following Notts' capture of the 1981 county championship, he was described by *Wisden* as 'the most complete player in world cricket'.

After Rice left Notts, the divisions and personal tensions that had always been present, but not allowed to surface, broke free and badly damaged a still strong side. This had not happened before because Rice's will to win had imposed a steely determination on a Notts side that contained characters as diverse as Robinson, Broad, Randall, Hassan, French and Hemmings. On the field he did not have to say much because the atmosphere in the dressing room told the players, more clearly than any sergeant majorish barking, what was expected from them in terms of effort and concentration.

Replacing not only Rice but Hadlee as well was always going to be impossible, especially following a championship-winning year. When Notts manager Ken Taylor revealed that he planned to sign Franklyn Stephenson he was told 'He's useless, you'd be an idiot to sign him'. Six months later at the end of the 1988 season, Stephenson smashed a Yorkshire attack for 111 and 117, and then ripped their batting apart to take 4 for 105 and 7 for 117. In doing so he became only the second player to perform the double of 100 wickets and 1,000 runs since the number of county championship games was reduced. The other player was, of course, Richard Hadlee who performed the feat in 1984, but his ghost had now been well and truly laid to rest. Stephenson had come from nowhere to be made one of *Wisden*'s five cricketers of the year.

Stephenson's route to Notts was not an easy one and many say that his is one of the great wasted talents of modern cricket. After two injury-hit and unhappy seasons with Gloucestershire, he signed up for two of the rebel tours of South Africa at the age of 24. A West Indian touring the land of apartheid was always going to be beyond the pale for most of his compatriots and a promising international career was effectively cancelled out. When he joined Notts he came charged with an impossible task and entered a dressing room that was in the process of turning in on itself and then disintegrating. That he remained aloof from all the back-biting and turned in such an impressive performance was perhaps the greatest of his achievements. But, at the end of the 1991 season, it finally did all become too much for the easygoing but thoughtful Bajan and he decamped to the somewhat sunnier atmosphere at Hove.

Rice and Hadlee gave Notts two county championships as well as considerable one-day success, but their legacy of superhuman achievement may cast an unhealthy shadow over the county's overseas' recruits for some time to come. However, Chris Cairns, son of former New Zealand test star Lance, at least appears to be making a good fist of the challenge, and has formed an exciting bowling and batting partnership with England all-rounder Chris Lewis.

Somerset

52	G.S. Chappell (batsman) 1968–9	A
46	K.J. O'Keeffe (all-rounder, leg-spin bowler) 1971–2	A
205	H.R. Moseley (pace bowler) 1971–82	WI
191	I.V.A. Richards (batsman) 1974–86	WI
94	J. Garner (fast bowler) 1977–86	WI
15	S.M. Gavaskar (opening batsman) 1980	I
11	H.E.I. Gore (left-arm pace bowler) 1980	WI
48	M.D. Crowe (batsman) 1984–8	NZ
19	S.R. Waugh (batsman) 1987–8	A
71	S.J. Cook (opening batsman) 1989–91	SA
16	R.P. Snell (pace bowler) 1992	SA

Somerset's employment of overseas cricketers has been dominated by the drama and crisis which accompanied the county careers of Garner and Richards. That period in Somerset's history, as well as the county's first overseas signing Greg Chappell, is dealt with at length elsewhere in this book (in Chapter 6). But there have been other overseas players to pull on Somerset colours and it is those who we will deal with here.

After a year without an overseas player Australian leg-spinner Kerry O'Keeffe arrived to join the south-west county in 1971. He was an immediate success in a summer which produced pitches to encourage bowlers and spinners in particular. Hampshire's Sainsbury took 107 wickets at 17.51, Gibbs 131 at 18.89 and Underwood 102 at 19.47. O'Keeffe only took 77 wickets at 23.57, but that was no bad return for a 21-year-old Australian leg-spinner who had never played cricket outside his home country before. But, like Greg Chappell, his rough-edged approach to the game (and to life in general) did not endear him to the more stuffy players and club officials. When, in his second season, the batsmen began to get after him, there was very little help forthcoming from team mates or ex-players and he left at the end of the 1972 season, having added only 16 wickets to his 1971 tally.

Ask even the most dedicated cricket historian which overseas cricketer played most times for Somerset and they will have to think hard before coming up with the name of Hallam Moseley. In fact the West Indian pace bowler played for the county between 1971 and 1982, and appeared in 205 first-class games, 14 more than his nearest rival Viv Richards. It was he who filled in for Richards and Garner, when injury, international calls or some other distraction got in the way of them appearing for the county. This he did more than adequately and his final return of 547 wickets at 24.10 would be a set of figures that many counties would consider acceptable in a first-string overseas player.

Moseley, in fact, was one of those highly competent cricketers for whom the new arrangements for overseas players actually prevented them from developing their county career to its full potential. Moseley recognized that, given the depth of fast-bowling talent in the West Indies, he was never likely to get a test call up. Once he had seen England on Barbados' 1969 tour and Gary Sobers, no less, had recommended him to Somerset, Moseley decided to try and make a career out of county cricket, and effectively emigrated to Somerset, playing only two more seasons in the West Indies. He tried many times to become registered as English qualified, not because he wanted to play for England but because he wanted to maximize his playing opportunities for Somerset. However, the TCCB now saw matters in black and white, and an overseas player with even the slimmest chance of representing his native country would find it very hard to be treated as anything other than a foreign interloper. Constantly changing the qualification rules did not help either.

Moseley made his only appearance at a Lord's final in the 1982 Benson & Hedges clash with Nottinghamshire. Like all the Somerset bowlers he made good use of a helpful pitch and took 1 for 26 from his 11 overs as Somerset won by 9 wickets. Two months later, after 11 years with the county, Moseley was released without warning; another victim of Somerset's less than diplomatic approach to team management.

In Somerset's records Moseley stands as the county's seventeenth highest first-class wicket taker. Only Vic Marks among modern Somerset cricketers has taken more, and yet Peter Roebuck and David Foot in their respective histories of the county mention Moseley just eight times in total. Both men are sympathetic to the way in which the county treated the West Indian quick, but the lack of space they give his achievements reflects just how insignificant his place in Somerset's cricket history seems to have become.

The two other forgotten men of Somerset's overseas staff were an oddly matched pair. Needing one-season replacements for the touring Richards and Garner, the club opted for the world's leading opening batsman Sunil Gavaskar and an unknown left-arm seamer, Hugh Gore, who had been recommended to the club by fellow Antiguan Richards. Gore was, to put it mildly, not a great success. When he arrived in England his fitness was nowhere near the level required to get a fast bowler through an English summer. In the end he played only 11 games and took just 14 first-class wickets at 47.74. Gavaskar, of course, made much more of an impact without ever setting Taunton alight as Richards had done. There were a number of brilliant set pieces, but a wet summer and the lack-lustre cricket never really engaged Gavaskar's mind. Therefore, at the end of the season he left with a disappointing record of just 686 runs at 34.30.

In 1987 the storm over the departure of Garner and Richards was beginning to blow itself out. What the county needed to lift it out of its self-inflicted gloom were deeds of derring-do and unsullied nobility. And if there were ever two batsmen well equipped to perform such feats they were Martin Crowe and Steve Waugh. Not since the time of Palairet can the county have enjoyed such a feat of classical batsmanship. Crowe led the way, as he had to, considering what Somerset had just given up for him, by scoring 1,627 runs at 67.79. But Waugh, sneaking into the side late in the season, was not to be outdone. In four championship matches the Australian hit 2 centuries and finished the season with 340 runs at 113.33.

In 1988 the glory continued with Waugh taking over the lead role from the injured Crowe. Both players left the county to concentrate on their international careers at the end of the season, but they left behind them countless memories of perfectly executed cover drives and late cuts, as well as a statistical record to envy: Crowe, 22 matches, 2,100 runs, 8 centuries, average 70; Waugh, 18 matches, 1,626 runs, 8 centuries, average 86. Somerset supporters had suffered over recent years as their team pulled itself apart, but in the performances of these two Antipodean batsmen they were well rewarded for their loyalty.

And still, incredibly, the best was yet to come. South African Jimmy Cook arrived in 1989, a ready-made master batsman about to rewrite the county's batting records. With Somerset's home-grown players failing to perform and the team sliding down every possible table, the supporters had to have something to cling on to and Cook was a rock. He was 36 when he joined Somerset and had never played first-class cricket overseas before, yet he scored over 2,000 first-class runs in every one of his three seasons for the county and was one of *Wisden*'s five cricketers of the year in 1990. His unassuming mastery and quiet courtesy instantly made him one of the county circuit's best loved players, although what he made of being nicknamed 'Mutley' because of an alleged facial resemblance to Dick Dastardly's canine side-kick is unrecorded.

Cook was a challenge that county bowlers had not even begun to meet by the time he slipped out of the English game at the end of the 1991 season.

With hindsight it is clear that Somerset's faith in their English-qualified bowlers was misguided and that the employment of an overseas fast bowler would have improved the county's performances. But then again it could be argued that, Tavare apart, there was no English player to hold the batting together either. Indeed, the signing of South African paceman Snell in 1992 turned out to be almost a complete disaster. The arrival of Pakistani leg-breaker Mushtaq Ahmed in 1993 looks a much more promising choice.

Surrey

262	Younis Ahmed (batsman) 1965–78	P
232	Intikhab Alam (all-rounder, leg-spin bowler) 1969–81	P
186	G.P. Howarth (batsman) 1971–85	NZ
160	S.T. Clarke (fast bowler) 1979–88	WI
39	A.H. Gray (fast bowler) 1985–8	WI
31	Waqar Younis (fast bowler) 1990–1	P
11	R.J. Bryson (pace bowler) 1992	SA

921

On the surface, in terms of consistency and number of games played, it may appear that Surrey was the county that benefited most from the introduction of immediate registration and the resulting flood of overseas players into the county scene. Surrey were lucky (and wise) enough to employ six overseas players who, though perhaps not all reaching the heights touched by other overseas professionals, provided good service for the county over an extended period of time. Howarth stayed for 14 seasons, Younis Ahmed and Intikhab for 13, and Clarke for 10. The injury-troubled Tony Gray perhaps did not possess the staying powers of his predecessors, but only Rudi Bryson and Dirk Tazelaar (the Australian left-arm fast bowler signed to replace Clarke and Gray) proved a complete failure, and Surrey soon made up for that slip of judgement by employing a little-known Pakistani fast bowler called Waqar Younis a year later.

The truth behind Surrey's seeming good fortune is a little less palatable for the London-based side. Of its seven overseas players only Clarke and Waqar were consistent match winners and the majority of the foreign recruits were dogged by controversy of one kind or another while at the Oval.

Younis Ahmed joined Surrey in 1965, but did not qualify by residence to play for the county until 1967. After playing two tests in the early 1960s, the Pakistani batsman had effectively given up his international career to concentrate on building a life in England and English cricket. Although he did play again for his country in the late 1980s, Younis was really a throwback to those pre-1960s overseas cricketers who, realizing that they could not make a living from the game at home, had moved to England in search of steady employment.

Like a number of talented Pakistani cricketers Younis Ahmed was highly strung, and although he played with great style and increasing technical sureness, his arrogance would sometimes get the better of him, both on the field and off. His record for Surrey is a consistent one, and he played an important part in the county's 1971 championship victory, as well as top scoring in the side's 1974 Benson & Hedges Cup final win, but many players and supporters were surprised that he stayed for as long as he did.

Surrey's first 'proper' overseas player was the Pakistani all-rounder Intikhab Alam and the reputation that he left behind could not have been more different than that which remained after Younis Ahmed left the county. After joining the county in 1969 he played for Surrey right throughout the 1970s and was another vital cog in the side's 1971 triumph. Although in the mid-1970s his leg-spin was ill suited to the Oval pitches, Intikhab never gave anything less than his all for his adopted county. The debt that Surrey felt they owed Intikhab after 12 years of service was due in equal measure to his solid performances with bat and ball, and to the feeling of fun which he injected into what could often be a dour and troubled dressing room.

The last of Surrey's trio of 1970s overseas players was a young New Zealand batsman called Geoff Howarth, who made his debut in 1971. The extent of his talents only really became obvious after he was capped by his country in the 1974/5 New Zealand summer. A year later he had his best season in English county cricket and in 1978 scored 296 runs, average 74, in the three test series against England. But just as he was moving into his best form, changes to the rules governing overseas players severely restricted his playing opportunities for the county.

In 1984 Howarth, now captain of New Zealand and considered by some to be the best team leader on the international circuit, was appointed to captain Surrey. In an unspectacular year for the county Howarth did nothing to throw his captaincy ability into doubt, but like many before him his form following the appointment nose-dived. In 1985 Howarth's career with the county came to a premature end. Clarke was injured and the need to appoint another overseas bowler prevented Howarth from playing a single championship game. Given his talent, especially as a captain, and his dedication to the county, it was a sad way for Howarth to leave the Oval.

Sylvester Clarke is considered by many leading English players to be the most fearsome of all the West Indian fast bowlers who have played county cricket since the late 1960s. As late as 1987, when Clarke was 32, Gatting and Gooch both said the Bajan fast bowler should have played in the MCC Bicentenary match which attempted to assemble the world's finest 22 players. The former Leicestershire paceman John Agnew agrees, describing Clarke as 'the most feared man in county cricket' with a particular liking for 'having a go at tail enders'. On learning that Clarke would not be playing in one championship match, Agnew said the news was 'almost like a stay of execution'.

The description 'mean and moody' could have been invented for Clarke and, unlike most of his countrymen, this applied on the field as well as off. All this said, Clarke's value to Surrey was immeasurable. He captured around one-quarter of Surrey's wickets in the 160 county games in which he played and effectively took countless more for bowlers at the other end as the batsmen tried to escape from his ferocious assault. It is extremely doubtful whether Robin Jackman would have taken the hat-full of wickets that he did in the late 1970s and early 1980s had Clarke not usually been bowling at the other end. Against Warwickshire in the 1982 Nat West final, Clarke bowled his 11 overs and 2 balls for 17 runs and 2 wickets, and Surrey won by 9 wickets.

Clarke made the decision to go on a rebel tour of South Africa and the resulting ban by the West Indies meant that he was able to concentrate his considerable energies on winning matches for Surrey. However, as we have already seen, a back injury which had affected the West Indian on and off throughout his career with the county prevented him playing during the 1985 season. Clarke's fitness problem was accentuated by his failure to curb his liking for good food and drink.

The county signed Tony Gray from Trinidad to replace Clarke for that season alone, but the young 6 ft 8 in West Indian did so well in capturing 79 wickets that he was kept on at the expense of Howarth. In the next two seasons Gray and Clarke, playing separately because of the overseas players regulations, captured 209 wickets between them.

In 1988 Clarke's uneasy relationship with Surrey came to a head and the West Indian fast bowler made moves to sign for Lancashire League club Rishton as the replacement for Viv Richards. The county had to 'buy' him back, but at least were well rewarded when he captured 63 wickets at 14.49.

The period between the loss of Gray and Clarke and the signing of Waqar Younis was a scrappy one. It was characterized by the selection of the woefully inadequate Australian Dirk Tazelaar and an aborted attempt to re-sign Gray. In the final event Waqar Younis was unearthed and, after a few searing in-dipping yorkers were bowled, a five-year contract was signed.

Waqar's recruitment had an element of luck about it, Pakistan captain Imran Khan offering the young fast bowler to Sussex first. Imran admits that it was the fact that his former colleague Ian Greig was captaining Surrey which led him to approach the London county once Sussex had turned Waqar down. Imran praises Greig for his foresight in deciding to replace the injury-prone Gray with the Pakistani fire-brand. Greig's perception was rewarded when Waqar (signed for just £7,000) took 57 wickets at 23.80 in his first season.

But even after Waqar's success during 1990, Surrey nearly let the fast bowler slip through their fingers. They originally refused to deal with Waqar's agent, Jonathan Barnett, and the young Pakistani star was on the brink of leaving the county. The crisis was settled at the eleventh hour by the intervention of Surrey cricket chairman Jimmy Fulford, but the whole episode shows how the signing of overseas players in the 1990s (even those with relatively little test experience) has become a much more complicated process than that which led to the informal deals struck during the 1960s and 1970s. Fulford had been recruited for Waqar (as well as Wasim Akram) by their mentor Imran Khan as soon as the young fast bowler secured a place with Surrey.

Unfortunately, Surrey have yet to master Essex's skill in selecting replacement overseas players when contracted players are on tour and come the next Pakistan summer in England the county will be looking for somebody considerably more effective than Rudi Bryson. The South African was marketed to Surrey as the next Alan Donald, but he played in just ten championship games and took only 17 wickets at the embarrassing average of 68.52.

Bryson did, however, manage to pick up the 'Corrie Van der Zyl award for the worst overseas player' given by cricket fanzine *Johnny Miller 96 not out*. The runners-up in 1992, a year full of under-performing overseas players were Somerset's Richard Snell and Lancashire's Danny Morrison. Indeed, *JM96*'s 'Worst ever Surrey XI' includes no less than five overseas players: Rudi Bryson and Dirk Tazelaar, as well as (rather unfairly) Geoff Howarth, Intikhab Alam and Tony Gray.

Sussex

152	G.A. Greenidge (batsman) 1968–75	WI
76	U.C. Joshi (off-spin bowler) 1970–4	I
40	Javed Miandad (batsman) 1976–9	P
53	K.C. Wessels (opening batsman) 1976–80	SA & A
129	Imran Khan (all-rounder, fast bowler) 1977–88	P
136	G. Le Roux (all-rounder, pace bowler) 1978–87	SA
61	A.I.C. Dodemaide (all-rounder, pace bowler) 1989–91	A
18	F.D. Stephenson (all-rounder, pace bowler) 1992	WI

665

Sussex, along with Derbyshire, Lancashire and of course Yorkshire, showed the greatest resistance to the surging tide of overseas players which swept over the country in the late 1960s and early 1970s. True they had the South African born 'Englishman' Tony Greig on their books, but the county's only real bona fide overseas players before the mid-1970s were the largely unsuccessful Geoff Greenidge and Udaykumar Joshi. Throughout its history, despite the great names that have graced the side, Sussex have never appeared particularly concerned about winning championships and, although this is no longer true, a certain *laissez-faire* attitude does seem to have informed the selection of some of their overseas players.

Greenidge was unrelated to his namesake, Gordon, at Hampshire, and unfortunately for Sussex he was nowhere near as good a player. An all-rounder of some promise, he had only played a handful of first-class games when the county took him on, his one performance of note being a score of 205 for Barbados against Jamaica in 1966/7. His first two seasons brought nothing special, but in 1970 at the age of 22 he scored five first-class centuries, the youngest Sussex player to achieve this feat. After that, although Greenidge turned in some solid performances, a batting average of under 30 was a sign of a player out of his depth, and at the end of the 1975 season the West Indian retired and returned home. Joshi, a little known and not hugely successful off-spin bowler, took 74 wickets in 1971 (his first full season with Sussex), but after that declined in effectiveness and drifted out of the county game a year earlier than Greenidge.

After these two failures of selection, Sussex then disastrously rejected a young South African batsman called Ken McEwan, who had played for their second XI at the invitation of Tony Greig. McEwan was told that the county was looking to sign an Indian player and accepted Doug Insole's invitation to join Essex.

Sussex finally fully grasped the nettle of the need for an overseas player of high quality during the 1976 season by signing two contrasting young batsmen. Kepler Wessels was 19 years old and as rugged an opening batsman as his Afrikaner background could make him. Javed Miandad was also 19, a street-fighting middle-order strokemaker who was to make his test debut at the end of the year against New Zealand, scoring 166. In fact, Sussex were so eager to blood their young Pakistani star that they played him in a game against Leicestershire before his registration was complete and so lost the points they gained from taking part in the match. However, Miandad initially more than repaid the county's faith in him, scoring 500 runs in his first five games for Sussex.

Both Javed and Wessels had their successes for the county, particularly the South African, who scored well over 3,000 runs in his last two seasons with the county at an average of around 60, but neither was destined to remain with the county. As Glamorgan were to discover later on, Miandad's talent and temperament did not always happily co-exist, and he parted company with the county when it became clear that the club thought more highly of the skills of Imran Khan. The Pakistani all-rounder had joined the county from Worcestershire in 1977, but was then forced to miss most of the season after the TCCB banned him for violating his contract with Worcestershire. Wessels, on the other hand, could have stayed but chose to emigrate to Australia at the end of the 1980 season. Luckily Sussex had a ready-made replacement in South African all-rounder Garth Le Roux who had been signed up during the 1978 season.

For the next seven seasons, saving the Pakistanis' test duties, Imran and Le Roux formed one of the most exciting batting and bowling partnerships in county cricket, giving Sussex another Pakistani–South African duo which was considerably more cohesive and effective than the one that had preceded it. It very nearly brought the county its first ever county championship in 1981.

Imran took 66 wickets at 22.18, Le Roux 81 at 19.53 and Ian Greig 76 at 19.32, as Sussex finished just two points behind Rice and Hadlee's Nottinghamshire.

But the Imran–Le Roux partnership was only put together after some difficulty and a hint of a possible crisis for English cricket. His decision to leave Worcestershire and join the more cosmopolitan atmosphere at Sussex's Hove base was not widely welcomed by the more conservative cricket followers. The *Daily Telegraph* said that Imran's move 'cheapened club-loyalty, diluted county identity and created a money market with all the attendant unpleasantness'. Unsurprisingly, the TCCB rejected Imran's initial application in May 1977, but Sussex, who were desperate for a fast bowler, having already unsuccessfully approached both Jeff Thomson and Gary Gilmour, took the case to the Cricket Council and successfully had the decision overturned. The fears that Imran's defection from Worcester was the start of a football-style transfer system have proved largely unfounded.

A second threat to the partnership emerged in 1983, when the club forgot to apply for a work permit for Le Roux. The South African was facing a wait until late May while the Department of Employment processed the application, but the day was saved when Conservative MP Tim Sainsbury used his influence to speed things along.

Unfortunately for Sussex the success of 1981 was not to be continued. By 1983 Le Roux had a serious groin strain and Imran was suffering from the stress fracture from which he was later to make a dramatic recovery. Imran's relationship with the county he joined to escape the small-town boredom of Worcester also began to sour. In his autobiography he makes but two passing mentions of the county where he played a significant part of his cricket. Around the county circuit it was well known that there were days when the enigmatic Imran would be 'trying' and that those were the days to avoid. However, as the successful team of the early 1980s began to disintegrate, those days became fewer and fewer. The 1986 Nat West final was won not by Imran's swing and speed or Le Roux's seam-bowling skills, but Dermot Reeve's 'wobbly' medium pace, although it is fair to note that Paul Parker must have been reassured to see Imran coming to the wicket to help him put the finishing touches to the cup final victory.

Sussex were in a sorry state at the start of the 1989 season, their first without either Imran or Le Roux since 1977. Waiting to take on the workload of these two giants was Tony Dodemaide, an important part of Australia's one-day side but only gaining access to international honours through the defection of bowlers like Terry Alderman to Kim Hughes's South African rebels.

Sussex might have had a considerably more famous overseas player if their negotiations with Viv Richards had been successful. The West Indian captain, who had just played a season of league cricket for Rishton after his dismissal by Somerset at the end of the 1986 season, apparently asked for a salary of £35,000. Sussex said that 'it had to be careful with our wage structure' and ended the negotiations. A few months later Yorkshire also rejected an offer by Richards to play for the county. This time the asking price was said to have risen by £1,000.

Dodemaide was a solid performer, and certainly more reliable than Le Roux with the bat, but at the end of the season a return of 65 wickets at 30.52 was a poor contrast compared to Sussex's embarrassment of riches in the early 1980s. Dodemaide did come second to Alan Wells in the Sussex bowling averages that year, but it was still somewhat of a surprise that the county persisted with him. The following year his batting was solid and he once against finished second in the county's bowling averages, this time taking 56 wickets at 39.39 in a batsman's summer. Sussex finished last in the championship table, winning just three matches. In 1991 Sussex climbed up to eleventh place, thanks to consistent contributions from most of the regular first team members. Dodemaide was among these solid performers, but even the undemanding seaside club felt they could do better and the Australian was released.

To fill their overseas players post, Sussex turned to one of the nomads of the county scene, Franklyn Stephenson. The easygoing Bajan had been unhappy in the highly strung atmosphere of the Nottinghamshire dressing room, feeling that, despite his outstanding record for the county, he was not properly appreciated. Like Imran before him, the all-rounder thought that Hove might be a more pleasant place to play cricket. Unfortunately for both the tall West Indian all-rounder and his new club, Stephenson was not to make the immediate impact that he did at Nottingham. His batting lived up to expectations, with 680 finely struck runs, including a century in his second game for the county, but his bowling, which had proved so devastating at Trent Bridge, did not seem to travel well.

The bowler, who only a few years ago had taken well over 100 wickets in a season, was only able to manage 40 (at an average 34.37) for Sussex in 1992, with 11 coming in one match against Worcestershire. His best return in the 17 other county games in which he played was 4 for 65 against Durham. Stephenson also scored 126 runs in the Worcester match, so he was obviously still capable of the big performance, though now at the age of 33 not on a consistent basis.

Warwickshire

109	L.R. Gibbs (off-spin bowler) 1967–72	WI
173	R. Kanhai (batsman) 1968–77	WI
285	A.I. Kallicharran (batsman) 1971–90	WI
58	D.L. Murray (wicket-keeper) 1972–5	WI
59	W.A. Bourne (all-rounder, pace bowler) 1973–7	WI
138	A.M. Ferreira (all-rounder, pace bowler) 1979–86	SA
43	D.R. Doshi (left-arm spin bowler) 1980–1	I
12	B.M. McMillan (all-rounder, pace bowler) 1986	SA
34	T.A. Merrick (pace bowler) 1987–9	WI
96	A.A. Donald (fast bowler) 1987–92	SA

1,007

In 1972 Warwickshire won the county championship for the third time. They won 9 of their 20 twenty matches and drew the other 11. Kent, the runners-up, trailed by 36 points and lost 4 games. But the county champions' opponents could argue with some cause that the trophy should really have been awarded to a side called, in the manner of Victorian invitation XIs, 'Warwickshire with four gentlemen of the West Indies'. During the 1972 season, Warwickshire were able to call on the Windies' leading batsman, Rohan Kanhai; its rising star, Alvin Kallicharran; its leading spin bowler, Lance Gibbs; and its wicket-keeper Deryck Murray. The club only failed to win the Gillette Cup because another West Indian, Lancashire's Clive Lloyd, hit 126. Warwickshire also made the semi-final of the first Benson & Hedges competition and only disappointed in the John Player League, in which they finished twelfth – and even this perfor-mance was a considerable improvement on the year before when they finished bottom of the table.

It was the exuberant cricket of the 1966 West Indian team, of which only Kallicharran of the Warwicks quartet was not a member, that played a large part in bringing about the introduction of immediate registration. The Midlands county was the quickest to make sure that it secured the greatest amount of reflected glory following the 1968 watershed. The club lost the main prize (Sobers) to Nottinghamshire, but decided to make up for that loss by selecting as many West Indians as possible (although they did also approach South African all-rounder Eddie Barlow). Gibbs was registered under the pre-water-shed rule in 1966, which allowed Warwickshire to take immediate advantage of the 1968 rule change by hiring Kanhai and being able to field two of the West Indies' brightest stars. And once it was clear that Kanhai and, particularly, Gibbs were reaching the end of their careers, the club moved quickly, signing Kallicharran in 1971, Murray in 1972 and William Bourne in 1973, ensuring a smooth changeover.

Warwickshire had little difficulty securing a work permit for Kallicharran as the immigration authorities judged that the length of the contract offered to the West Indian confirmed his 'eminence'. This was a significant decision as Mid-dlesex, while attempting to register Larry Gomes, were refused a permit, the Home Office interpreting the rules governing the registration for overseas cricketers as only applicable to those regarded as 'eminent'.

In terms of talent and 'glamour' there was no doubt that Warwickshire had chosen wisely in originally selecting Kanhai and Gibbs. But there was also the question of temperament and here as well the West Indian pair were well suited for making a big impact on a new stage. Kanhai had already played for Western Australia by the time he arrived at Edgbaston and Gibbs was later to enjoy a highly successful season with South Australia. Here were two cricketers whose natural exuberance and self-belief enabled them to cope with both a new set of social as well as playing conditions.

The period of West Indian dominance came to end in 1977 when Bourne and Kanhai both left the county. In the 11 seasons the 5 West Indians had played well over 500 first-class games for the county and given Birmingham's West Indian community a focus for their strong, if sometimes beleaguered, racial pride.

Kallicharran stayed on, but the player chosen to replace the West Indians could not have been more different to his illustrious predecessors. Anton Ferreira was a second-string South African all-rounder, and the loyalty shown to him by Warwickshire was encouraged by his commitment and determination rather than by his achievements on the field. A great team man he may have been but more than a few questioned the wisdom of continuing to employ an overseas player who in eight seasons scored only two first-class centuries and captured five wickets in an innings just six times. Neither was Warwickshire's next overseas signing a huge success.

Dilip Doshi had floated in and out of English county cricket for a number of years without his flighted left-arm spin proving particularly effective. He captured a sackful of wickets for Warwickshire, 146 in two seasons, but his average of 31.84 compared poorly to the other Indian spin wizard Bishan Bedi, to whom he was always being compared. His extended run in Warwickshire's first team did bring Doshi one clear benefit, however. It gave him a good chance to weigh up the weakness of England's leading batsmen. During England's 1981/2 tour of India, which immediately followed Doshi's release from Warwickshire, the left-arm spinner captured 22 test wickets, including a match-winning five for 39 in the first match at Bombay.

Kallicharran and Ferreira continued to fill the overseas post at Warwickshire alone until 1986, at which time they were joined by South African all-rounder Bruce McMillan. Picked to supplement the county's bowling resources he was a somewhat strange choice. His batting proved to be a revelation, but his medium-pace bowling was even more ineffective than Ferreira's. What was more, because he had been recruited after the 1981 rule changes, if McMillan played then Kallicharran and Ferreira could not.

Kallicharran had tried to solve that particular problem throughout the final period of his career with Warwickshire. Banned by the West Indies for taking part in a rebel tour to South Africa, and warned never to set foot again in his native Guyana, Kallicharran declared as early as 1984 that he sometimes 'felt more English than West Indian'. A few years later he was considering legal action against the TCCB in order to have himself registered as English qualified.

West Indian fast bowler Tony Merrick was chosen as McMillan's replacement and, as Ferreira had also left the county, the problem of who should play (batsman or bowler) was less complicated. Or so it should have been. As well as bringing Merrick on to the books, Warwickshire also signed up a little-known South African fast bowler called Alan Donald. That had not been their original intention. Donald was being given a season's second XI cricket by Warwickshire and, as is usual with these sort of deals, was expected to do more than his fair share of net bowling whenever the first team batsmen needed the practice. Warwickshire opener Andy Lloyd and the county's leading elder statesman Dennis Amiss both found themselves groping at thin air when facing Donald's fast, swinging deliveries and he was soon registered as Warwickshire's second new overseas signing.

Even so Donald was not expected to play a large part in the county's plans, but he proved to be such a success that he effectively took Kallicharran's place, taking 37 wickets at 26.16, compared to Merrick's 57 at 25.24. Merrick continued to hold the pole position in 1988, but it was clear that Donald was coming up fast on the inside. This time Merrick was the clear winner in terms of wickets, taking 64 at 22.12, but Donald played 9 less games and still managed to capture 26 victims at the significantly lower average of 19.50. Having given his rival a clear warning, Donald went for the kill in 1989 and blew away any question that he was the more talented bowler.

The 1989 season saw Donald play 19 matches, compared to Merrick's 2, and the South African took 86 wickets at an average of just 16.25. More importantly he was widely recognized as the great white hope, a fast bowler to rank alongside the best pace bowlers from the West Indies and Pakistan. The injury-hit Merrick knew he was beaten and the county released him after three seasons in which he had taken 134 wickets at 23.85. Unfortunately, by the time Kent took him on in 1991 he had lost much of his fire and stayed only one season.

Ironically, as soon as soon as Donald had seen off his fast-bowling rival he seemed to suffer a crisis of confidence and nearly lost his county place to a batsman. The South African played in 14 championship matches, but took only 28 wickets (just 2 per game) at 35.28. He was completely overshadowed by Warwickshire's new overseas recruit, Western Australian batsman Tom Moody, who used every inch of his 6 ft 6 in frame to blast five centuries in just seven matches. One of them, against Glamorgan's declaration bowling, was scored in just 26 minutes, at that time the fastest ever first-class ton. But to the surprise of many it was Moody and not Donald who was released at the end of the season, the batsman immediately being snapped up by Worcestershire. It was a 'brave' decision which ran the risk of being labelled foolhardy if the gamble did not come off. However, luckily for the club's administration Donald recaptured his old form, taking 157 wickets at 20.90 during the next two seasons and blasting the county to a runners-up spot in the county championship during 1991.

Worcestershire

284	G.M. Turner (opening batsman) 1967–82	NZ
181	V.A. Holder (pace bowler) 1968–80	WI
42	Imran Khan (all-rounder, fast bowler) 1971–6	P
61	J.M. Parker (opening batsman) 1971–5	NZ
30	G.G. Watson (pace bowler) 1978–9	A
85	Younis Ahmed (batsman) 1979–83	P
38	H.L. Alleyne (pace bowler) 1980–2	WI
26	R.M. Ellcock (pace bowler) 1982–7	WI
24	Kapil Dev (all-rounder, pace bowler) 1984–5	I

129   G.A. Hick (batsman) 1984–90   Z
 33   T.M. Moody (batsman) 1991–2   A
  ───
933

Captain of Worcestershire Tim Curtis describes English domestic cricket as a finishing school for overseas players and, in the 1970s at least, his county could claim to have completed the schooling of Pakistan's and New Zealand's finest modern players. However, the experience of Glenn Turner and Imran Khan shows that, far from being a free master class for young overseas professionals, the inexperienced test hopefuls had to fight for recognition just as hard as the home-grown players.

Glenn Turner arrived in England during 1967 as a 19 year old with only 15 first-class games to his credit. Originally set for Warwickshire, the Midlands side's over-abundance of established overseas test stars meant that he ended up at Worcester. The Worcestershire side of Graveney, D'Oliveira, Headley, Gifford and Flavell felt that it could hold its own in the post-immediate qualification period without an established overseas star and was happy to pick up Turner, as well as up-and-coming West Indian fast bowler Vanburn Holder, as cheap novelties. Seventeen seasons and 22,298 first-class runs later, Turner became the nineteenth man to score 100 hundreds in the process of hitting 300 in a day against Warwickshire.

The New Zealand opener began as an almost strokeless stonewaller, but after arriving in the county cricket school of hard knocks, he began to discover a depth of talent which even Turner himself had previously not suspected. Playing as an 18 year old against New Zealand's fastest bowler Dick Motz, Turner remembers: 'He became very frustrated bowling at me. I couldn't understand what was going on, he should have been able to get me out.' There is no time to hide your light under a bushel in English county cricket, especially when plenty of people are waiting to pour scorn on an unsuccessful young overseas batsman, and Turner was forced to unearth a belief in himself that surpassed even that of the other great run accumulator of the 1970s, Geoff Boycott.

Imran Khan's background could not have been more different from that of Turner's, but his experience in county cricket was similar in many ways. Imran and New Zealand opener John Parker had been signed up in 1971 as covers for Turner and Holder, who like Turner had emerged as a world-class player the year before. Imran arrived in England as a member of Pakistan's 1971 touring party. He only played in the first test and contributed just 5 (run out) to Pakistan's record-breaking 608 for 7 declared. He opened the bowling, but the inexperienced 18 year old could not control the huge swing he was able to produce, and in, as he admits, perfect conditions for swing bowling, he failed to take a wicket, costing Pakistan the victory they deserved.

This was hardly an auspicious introduction to English cricket and when, later in the season, he arrived at Worcester for the first time, his bowling ambitions were treated with contempt. Turner, perhaps forgetting his lonely apprenticeship of only a few years before, belittled Imran's ability as a bowler, an opinion backed up by Parker. In Imran's own words, the county 'stuffed' him into a 'medium-pace strait-jacket', which he was only able to shrug off in his games for Oxford University. In 1976, after he had graduated, Imran's new-found confidence brimmed over and he gave Worcester a one-season example of what they could have had, before leaving for the bright lights of Brighton, expressing the desire to be nearer London and to play under a 'dynamic' captain like Tony Greig.

In the winter season following Imran's departure from Worcester, Pakistan met New Zealand in a three-test series. Imran bowling, flat out for the first time in test cricket, took 14 wickets in the tests. Turner had four innings in the series and was dismissed by Imran on two occasions (for 1 and 49), Parker played six innings and was Imran's victim four times (for 9, 22, 7 and 24). Revenge was sweet.

Worcestershire, however, were incensed by Imran's move to Sussex, believing it a betrayal of the investment of time and money that they had made in the Pakistani all-rounder. Many on the county circuit agreed with the county, especially when it was hinted that Worcestershire, as well as going to considerable lengths to get him registered as an overseas player, had paid for Imran to undertake his high-quality English education – a claim that he has always fiercely denied. Although banned by the TCCB for much of the 1977 season, talk of other counties refusing to play against a team containing the Pakistani all-rounder came to nothing.

Ironically, in 1979 Worcestershire nearly stole South African fast bowler Garth Le Roux out from under the nose of his long-term county employer, Sussex.

The winter of 1976/7 was also a landmark for Turner. After scoring 261 runs at 43.5 in a three-match test series against India, he quit test cricket. At 29 Turner was at the peak of his powers, having scored 2,900 runs at 45 in 39 tests, but he felt that the financial rewards and the recognition that he was receiving for carrying the New Zealand test team on his back were insufficient. Reasoning that English county cricket was his main source of revenue, he decided to concentrate his efforts on playing for Worcestershire. Exactly what New Zealand was missing is evidenced by the fact that in his final five seasons for the county, between 1978 and 1982, Turner scored 8,469 runs at an average of just under 60. Effectively, English county cricket deprived New Zealand of the world's most consistent opening batsman.

Towards the end of the 1970s, Worcestershire were joined by Younis Ahmed, now considered English by the TCCB. He performed well for his second county (Surrey being his first), but once again temperament was his downfall and he was dismissed after it was discovered that he had bet against his own side during a 1983 John Player League match with Leicestershire.

Typically, after the consistency provided by Turner and Holder, Worcester spent four seasons thrashing around trying to find a long-term replacement. Hartley Alleyne and Turner had shared the burden between them in 1982, and in 1983 the whole weight fell on the very slim shoulders of 18-year-old West Indian fast bowler Ricky Ellcock, although Collis King did play two championship matches. In 1984 the cavalry arrived in the form of Kapil Dev.

The Indian all-rounder seemed to be the perfect overseas player, as his fast–medium bowling was ideally suited to English conditions, while his hard-hitting batting style meant that he could play a full part in all the one-day competitions. But test calls and injuries restricted his appearances for the county and his very suitability counted against him on the county circuit. His batting was unsuccessful during one-day cricket, in which the stolid Worcestershire side especially needed the acceleration which Kapil was expected to provide, and his bowling simply duplicated the skills of Pridgeon, Newport, Inchmore, Radford and McEwan. Worcestershire had swing and seam bowlers coming out of their ears, and what they needed from a bowler was someone who would take a couple of early wickets and then return to blast out the tail.

Worcester were not to get that until Graham Dilley arrived from Kent in 1987, but they did discover their second 18-year-old boy batting genius under their nose. It is extremely unlikely, since counties are only allowed to field one overseas player, that somebody like Turner would now be signed on a whim and a nod. Hick's arrival was greeted with greater expectation, but only Kapil's on-off appearances gave him the chance to shine so early. Again, a young batsman was able to rise to the challenge of the English county circuit, with almost no first-class experience. Unfortunately, Turner seems to have taken the part of the script which tells how to translate that success into triumphs at test level back with him to New Zealand.

At the start of the 1991 season Tom Moody, the Australian batsman released by Warwickshire, joined Hick and Botham to give Worcester one of the most fearsome batting line-ups in county cricket history. In his first season he maintained the brilliant form of the previous season, hitting 1,770 runs at 65.55. This success came just at the right time for Worcestershire as Hick, in his inaugural season as an English-qualified player, experienced his first poor season. A year later the situation was reversed and Hick finished the season with almost twice as many runs at twice the average of Moody's 624 at 36.70. Unsurprisingly Moody made way for the West Indies' latest fast-bowling discovery, Kenny Benjamin, in 1993. It appeared to be a sad and rather premature end to Moody's short but eventful county career.

Yorkshire

16 S.R. Tendulkar (batsman) 1992   l

The debate over whether Yorkshire should drop its 'Yorkshiremen-only' selection policy has raged with varying degrees of intensity ever since the introduction of immediate registration changed the pecking order. The matter came to a head in 1989 when the Yorkshire players wrote to the club's executive commit-

The vitality and enterprise of the 1966 West Indians helped popularize the idea of introducing immediate registration for overseas players. When the necessary rule changes were forced through a year later the three leading members of that team, Rohan Kanhai (above left), Lance Gibbs (above right) and Gary Sobers (below), were among the first to be snapped up by the counties.

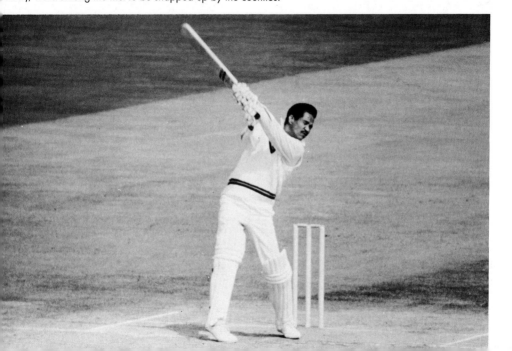

Following the introduction of immediat
registration, English county cricket
began to fill up with the world's leadin
players. Some, like Barry Richards (lef
and Majid Khan (below), had already
established themselves on the test mat
scene while others, such as Greg
Chappell (opposite above) and Alvin c
Kallicharran (opposite below), were o
the threshold of lengthy international
careers.

Though hard to imagine today, the early 1970s saw the county circuit blessed with a dozen overseas spin bowlers. Greatest of these was the Indian slow left-armer Bishan Bedi whose county career with Northamptonshire came to a controversial end among allegations of racism.

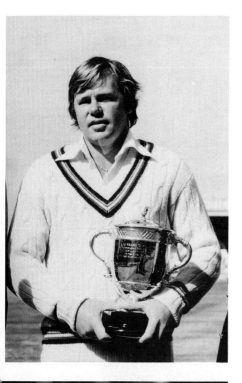

In the 1970s the county of Grace and Hammond became dominated by three overseas players. Mike Procter (left), Zaheer Abbas (below left) and Sadiq Mohammad (below right) turned their adopted county into one of the most exciting and enterprising teams on the circuit, but their dominance (reflected here as Procter collects the trophy for scoring the fastest century in the 1979 season) left little room for development among Gloucestershire's home-grown players.

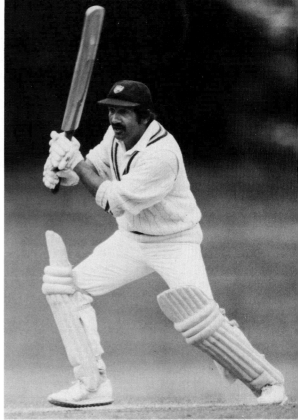

Fast bowling exiles. Wayne Daniel
(above), seen here with Middlesex
county captain Mike Gatting, and
Sylvester Clarke (below) may have
been considered surplus to
requirements by the West Indies, but
they quickly became feared and
respected opponents on the county
circuit.

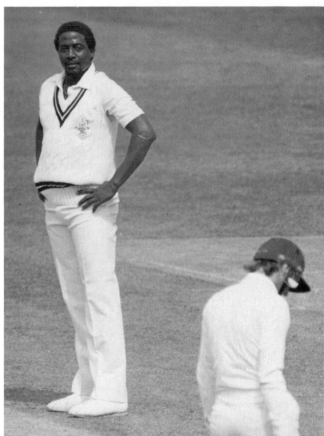

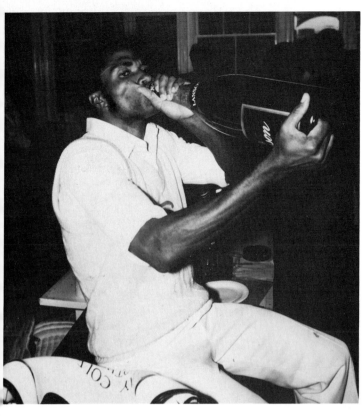

The men who made a difference. It was the arrival of Norbert Phillip (left) at Essex which led to that county's first championship triumph in 1979, while Vincent van der Bijl (below) teamed up with Wayne Daniel to secure victory for Middlesex in the following season.

Even the most promising overseas players can sometimes disappoint their English employer. The great Indian all-rounder Kapil Dev (above) did not make the expected impact at Northants or Worcester and Huge Page (below) was Essex's only failure in 25 years of employing highly successful overseas cricketers.

tee asking for the selection policy to be dropped. The final decision to allow those not born in the county to play for Yorkshire was made early in 1991.

Australian fast bowler Craig McDermott was Yorkshire's original choice to become the county's first overseas player. A three-year contract worth £100,000 was set up in conjunction with Yorkshire Television. When McDermott withdrew through injury, the county made a foolhardy/courageous (delete to taste) decision and signed up 19-year-old Indian batting sensation Sachin Tendulkar. To give one so young the responsibility of throwing off more than a century of tradition seemed incredible, though some said that as he was not old enough to know what he was getting into, Tendulkar would not be overawed by the situation. In fact Tendulkar knew perfectly well what was going on, since unlike many young test stars he is a student of cricket history, but his precocious maturity allowed him to cope with the strain.

The accepted analysis of Tendulkar's first season was that he performed adequately on the field but secured a major triumph off it. Yorkshire were always going to be glad of a batsman who could score over 1,000 runs at a decent average, but where Tendulkar really succeeded was in winning over Yorkshire's players, supporters and club officials. Yorkshire county cricket manager Steve Oldham told *The Independent*: 'You can't measure the lift he's given the dressing room. They are all better players for his presence. His confidence is infectious and they all want to bat with him.' County captain Martyn Moxon, speaking a few days before Tendulkar's debut for Yorkshire, was confident of the young Indian's positive role.

'Nasser Hussain and Mark Ramprakash grew up with great players around them', remarks Moxon. 'In the past our youngest were expected to play the leading roles from the start.'

There was just one area in which Tendulkar did not succeed, and that was in attracting Yorkshire's large Asian community to county cricket. Tendulkar was, of course, contracted by Yorkshire to play cricket and not to serve as some sort of ambassador for the club, but many Yorkshire supporters had hoped that the signing of the young Indian would scotch the rumours of racism which still clung to the county's cricket set-up. As we have already seen, Tendulkar was a hit with almost everybody connected with the club but, although being idolized by Indians living in England, very few turned up to watch him play.

There are many reasons why Tendulkar should not have attracted a new Asian audience to Yorkshire's cricket grounds (including the fact that Leeds' Asian community is primarily Pakistani in its allegiance), but it is clear that allegations of tokenism will still haunt the club until at least a couple of English-qualified Asian players establish regular places in the county side.

Outside the ground Tendulkar was regularly mobbed by the young Indian girls to whom he is the Asian equivalent of Jason Donovan (even, we must assume, to those from Pakistani families). The groups of girls following him around became so ever-present that he had to ask for his name to be removed from the side of his sponsored car. But when that car drove through the gates of

Headingley, the magic seemed to wear off and these young fans stayed away. Oldham is optimistic about the future claiming that 'Tendulkar broke the barrier', but the effects of his arrival will not be instantaneous.

As far as Tendulkar's first year in county cricket went, Yorkshire Television thought him worth the £30,000 they spent on sponsoring his employment and wanted to extend the deal, as did the club. Unfortunately for both, Tendulkar decided that, for the moment at least, county cricket was not for him and announced that he would not be returning for the 1993 season.

Tendulkar did at least believe that his year in county cricket had improved him as a player. He told *Wisden Cricket Monthly* that: 'I am a better player for the experience, more compact and tighter in my technique. I have learnt how to adapt to different conditions, and especially how to cope when the ball is moving about.' These were improvements that the England test team were soon to have plenty of evidence of.

Richie Richardson was chosen as Tendulkar's replacement, but the decision to employ another batsman as Yorkshire's second overseas player was once again a matter of heated debate within the club. Many of the ex-players on the club's cricket committee, who had originally proposed the recruitment of McDermott, still believed that Yorkshire needed a fast bowler as an overseas player. However, the club's choice was constrained by Yorkshire TV's insistence that the overseas player should be a 'big name'.

Geoff Boycott, a member of the committee at the time, remembers that although Yorkshire TV did not mind what type of player the county recruited, they did stipulate that he should be a 'world-class player'. As the TV station were paying the money, their word had to be heeded, but, as Boycott explains, cricket still being predominantly a batsman's game there were relatively few 'big name' bowlers to choose from and those wanting to play county cricket had already been signed up by other sides.

Yorkshire TV were, of course, well within their rights to demand that the player employed with their money should produce the maximum possible publicity for the sponsorship deal. However, in effect, the terms of the deal meant that the choice of an overseas player was not made on cricketing grounds alone. Despite the fact that Richardson is a great batsman and a willing team man, there are still many at Yorkshire who believe that the balance of the side might have been better served by signing a lesser known international bowler such as Danny Morrison or one of the young West Indian fast bowlers constantly hovering on the edge of international selection.

4 Overseas players and county cricket

Regardless of any conclusion history may reach about the good or ill that overseas cricketers inflicted on English cricket during the last 25 years, it is clear that the influence of 'foreign' players on the country's domestic game is declining. Compared to the mid to late 1970s, the number of overseas players gaining regular employment in English first-class cricket has halved. In both the 1991 and 1992 seasons, fewer overseas cricketers played county cricket than at any time since 1968.

An analysis of the number of overseas players registered by counties over the last 25 years shows the dramatic rise and fall of their potential influence: 1968 – 24; 1969 – 29; 1970 – 31; 1971 – 37; 1972 – 40; 1973 – 42; 1974 – 44; 1975 – 43; 1976 – 37; 1977 – 42; 1978 – 43; 1979 – 42; 1980 – 40; 1981 – 41; 1982 – 37; 1983 – 31; 1984 – 32; 1985 – 36; 1986 – 33; 1987 – 33; 1988 – 25; 1989 – 24; 1990 – 25; 1991 – 17; 1992 – 19.

The peak for the employment of overseas cricketers came between 1973 and 1981. During this time most counties had taken advantage of the existing registration rules, and commonly had one or two players signed up under the immediate registration provision and another one or two qualified by residence. But in January 1979 new regulations were introduced which stipulated that from the start of the 1982 season counties would only be allowed to play two overseas cricketers in competitive matches and only then if both were registered before 28 November 1978.

The fall off in the numbers of overseas players employed by the counties was quite pronounced over the two seasons following introduction of the new regulation, a 25 per cent decrease taking place between 1981 and 1983. But, despite this reduction in their number, overseas players still continued to dominate the first-class averages during each English season.

In 1981 10 out of the top 25 batsman were overseas recruits, and in 1983 the number had only fallen to 8. In bowling the reduction was greater, but only just, going from 10 to 7. It was not to be for another five seasons, by which time most of the overseas players registered before 1978 had left the game, that the new regulations really began to make a difference. Helped by the fact that there was a West Indies tour taking place that summer, the number of overseas players fell to 25, with the overseas batsmen in the top 25 averages dropping to just 4 and the bowlers to just 5.

The changing level in the number of overseas players taking part in English domestic cricket has two obvious corollaries.

1 How was the performance of the counties that employed the overseas players effected by the changes in the number of overseas stars available to them?

2 How was the ability of the English test team to beat its international rivals affected by the presence of overseas players?

The first question, which has been unfairly down-played in the debate surrounding overseas players, will be tackled in this chapter, and the second question will be looked at in Chapter 5.

The best starting point towards determining how the balance of power within county cricket has been affected by the presence of overseas players is to make a comparison between the number of appearances made by overseas players for each county and the average ranking that county has attained in the county championship between 1968 and 1992.

Number of appearances for county by overseas players		Average ranking in championship table 1968–92	
1	Gloucestershire = 1,085	1	Essex
2	Warwickshire = 1,007	2	Middlesex
3	Glamorgan = 950	3	Surrey
4	Worcestershire = 933	4	Kent
5	Surrey = 921	5	Leicestershire
6	Northamptonshire = 901	6	Hampshire
7	Leicestershire = 879	7	Nottinghamshire
8	Essex = 870	8	Worcestershire
9	Nottinghamshire = 865	=9	Warwickshire
10	Hampshire = 864	=9	Northamptonshire
11	Kent= 852	11	Gloucestershire
12	Middlesex = 770	12	Somerset
13	Somerset = 768	13	Yorkshire
14	Sussex= 665	14	Lancashire
15	Lancashire = 622	15	Sussex
16	Derbyshire = 595	16	Derbyshire
17	Yorkshire = 16	17	Glamorgan

No clear pattern appears from this comparison, except towards the bottom of the two tables. The five least successful counties in the championship correspond almost exactly to those that have relied least on overseas talent. But what are we to make of the presence of Glamorgan at the bottom of the county table, a county which has had considerable help from overseas players.

   Is Glamorgan's lowly position down to the relatively poor performance of its overseas players when compared to those representing other counties? An (admittedly vague) clue to this conundrum is provided by examining the average number of appearances overseas players made for each county. Essex, for example, have employed 9 overseas players and Middlesex just 7, but few would argue that these players were less valuable to their side than the 15 Glamorgan have employed over the last 25 years. And in theory the average appearances should provide a guide to form, as unsuccessful players do not tend to be retained by counties for very long.

Average number of appearances by overseas players for first-class counties

1	Surrey = 132	10	Sussex = 83
2	Leicestershire = 126	11	Lancashire = 78
3	Warwickshire = 101	12	Middlesex = 77
4	Gloucestershire = 100	13	Somerset = 70
5	Essex = 97	14	Northamptonshire = 64
6	Kent = 95	15	Glamorgan = 63
7	Nottinghamshire= 87	16	Derbyshire = 60
8	Hampshire = 860	17	Yorkshire = 16
9	Worcestershire = 85		

   This table seems to go some way towards solving the riddle of Glamorgan's poor showing in the county table and again there is a similarity between those counties that have performed badly in the county championship and those that have had relatively little assistance from overseas players. However, the above table again reflects the dichotomy between Middlesex's championship success and the apparent lack of influence on its performances by overseas players.

   An answer to this last question possibly lies in the fact that the bulk of Middlesex's county championship success came in the late 1970s and early 1980s. During this time Wayne Daniel helped the county win three championships and teamed up with Vincent Van der Bijl to capture a fourth. Gomes and Featherstone were to play a part in the 1976 victory, but Middlesex had little success before 1976 and the contribution from their overseas players was correspondingly poor.

   If Middlesex are the county whose performance appears to bear the least relation to the contribution of its overseas players, then Derbyshire's record shows the greatest consistency. The relatively few number of appearances by overseas players, combined with the fact that those employed by the county have not always lived up to expectations, ties in closely with the county's poor county championship performance since 1968.

   In fact Derbyshire, apart from Yorkshire, is the county to have suffered the sharpest reversal in fortunes following the introduction of immediate registration. A comparison of the average position attained by each county during the period 1968–92 with the position it achieved in the post-war period 1946–67 hints one more time that it is the counties with the least overseas input that have suffered the most, while those that have taken to the new development with a will have not necessarily prospered.

Change in average ranking in county championship table 1968–92 compared with 1946–67

1	Essex	+14	=10	Worcestershire	−2
2	Leicestershire	+11	=10	Warwickshire	−2
=3	Nottinghamshire	+10	=10	Gloucestershire	−2
=3	Kent	+10	=10	Sussex	−2
5	Hampshire	+6	14	Glamorgan	−7
6	Middlesex	+3	15	Lancashire	−10
=7	Surrey	−1	16	Derbyshire	−11
=7	Northamptonshire	−1	17	Yorkshire	−12
=7	Somerset	−1			

Here, perhaps, is the clearest indication of the impact of overseas players on English domestic cricket. All 6 counties which have significantly improved their performance over the last 25 years have employed effective overseas players on a regular basis. The four counties that have all suffered a noticeable fall in their fortunes are those which have either experienced problems with their overseas players, or fought shy of recruiting foreign talent to a lesser or greater degree. As an aside the table also shows that the south-east has been the area of the country in which to follow successful teams over the last quarter of a century. Likewise, it must have been 'grim up north'.

However, for the first nine seasons following the introduction of immediate registration, it was far from clear that any county (apart obviously from York-shire) was going to suffer or benefit unduly from the flood of overseas players.

In county cricket's post-war period (1946–67) two sides had dominated the championship contest, winning the trophy in 15 of the 22 seasons. Yorkshire were, as usual, top dog – winning the championship eight times. Surrey came next, thanks to an unprecedented run of success in the mid-1950s, with seven. Middlesex and Worcestershire won twice, and Hampshire, Warwickshire, Lancashire and Glamorgan once each. The remaining nine counties did not get a sniff of the trophy. Many have argued that it was this dominance of the championship (which for most of the period was the only competition in English domestic cricket) by a few counties, that drove increasingly picky crowds away from coming to watch less successful sides. For much of the immediate post-war period players and spectators often expressed a kind of fatalism over the likely identity of the championship winners. Most years it was not a case of whether Surrey or Yorkshire would clinch the trophy, but when.

That this tedious and damaging arrangement was turned on its head follow-ing the arrival of an army of overseas players seems too much of a coincidence.

In the nine seasons from 1968 to 1976, the championship was won by nine different counties. Admittedly, in 1968 Yorkshire again came first (for the last time to date), but they were knocked off the top of the table by Glamorgan in 1969, giving the Welsh county only its second championship after a gap of 20 years. In 1970 Kent secured their first championship for 57 years, then it was Surrey's turn, followed by Warwickshire (first triumph for 21 years) and Hampshire (first for 12 years). In 1974 Worcestershire took the title after a nine-year break; Leicestershire scored its first ever championship victory in 1975; and Middlesex began the most successful period in its history by picking up its fifth championship after 29 years.

After the upheaval of this 9-year period the county championship seemed to settle down and, in the 16 seasons between 1977 and 1992, two sides emerged to exert the kind of dominance over the championship previously enjoyed by Yorkshire and Surrey. Middlesex followed up its 1976 victory by sharing the title with Kent. The North London county then went on to win the trophy four more times during the last decade and a half. But Middlesex, in turn, were overtaken in terms of county championship success by Essex, which won its first championship in 1979 and then went on to secure five more victories. In the remaining seasons Kent came first in 1978, and later in the 1980s Nottinghamshire and Worcestershire won two championships apiece.

One of the reasons behind the free-for-all which existed in the first nine years following the introduction of immediate registration was the fact that many counties often fielded three or four overseas players. The rule changes of 1979 meant that those counties who had registered two youngish overseas players before the watershed had the advantage over their rivals whose overseas bowlers were coming to the end of their careers. It also boosted the chances of counties, such as Essex, Middlesex and Worcestershire, which were able to establish a strong squad of English qualified players.

The new rules governing the registration of overseas players read as follows.

1 For the seasons 1979, 1980 and 1981 – each county will be allowed to play two 'non-qualified for England' cricketers, irrespective of whether or not they were registered (or negotiations were in progress) prior to 28 November 1978.

2 From seasons 1982 onwards, a county may only play two such cricketers in a match if both of them were registered (or negotiations were in progress) prior to 28 November 1978. Otherwise they may play one such cricketer.

The change in fortunes brought about by the registration changes is clear from the following analysis.

Average ranking in the county championship

1968–78		1979–92		+/– change in ranking
1	Kent	1	Essex	+6
2	Hampshire	2	Surrey	+6
3	Leicestershire	3	Middlesex	+3
4	Warwickshire	4	Nottinghamshire	+12
5	Middlesex	5	Leicestershire	−3
6	Essex	6	Worcestershire	+6
7	Surrey	7	Hampshire	−6
8	Yorkshire	8	Kent	−8
9	Northamptonshire	9	Northamptonshire	
10	Gloucestershire	10	Derbyshire	+8
=11	Somerset	=11	Gloucestershire	−2
=11	Worcestershire	=11	Sussex	+6
13	Lancashire	13	Warwickshire	−10
14	Glamorgan	14	Somerset	−4
15	Nottinghamshire	15	Lancashire	−3
16	Sussex	16	Yorkshire	−9
17	Derbyshire	17	Glamorgan	−4

Of the seven counties that saw their performance improve from 1979 onwards, three of them owe much of their success to the fact that the new registration rules allowed them to play two overseas players well into the 1980s. Rice and Hadlee, McEwan and Phillip, and Imran Khan and Le Roux often proved too much for county sides with only one overseas player.

Of the four remaining successful counties, Middlesex and Derbyshire had in the past employed relatively few overseas players and those whom they did select had often proved less than world beaters. With the arrival of Daniel and Van der Bijl at Lords, and Kirsten and Holding at Chesterfield, things began to look up, especially for Middlesex who had just discovered an impressive group of young home-grown players. Surrey's performance improved as the overseas players they hired increased in quality and effectiveness, while Worcestershire's rise owed as much to the standard of the English-qualified players they developed or acquired from other counties as it did to the arrival of Hick.

Excluding Yorkshire, 7 of the 8 counties that saw their performance decline over the 14 seasons between 1979 and 1992 had the number of overseas players they could field severely restricted by the new regulations. Worst affected was Warwickshire, which had regularly fielded three overseas players during the early 1970s. This was eventually reduced to one during the 1980s and, until Alan Donald's arrival, the county struggled to find an overseas player to match Kanhai, Gibbs or the young Kallicharran. Hampshire had a similar problem in that they had in the past regularly fielded three overseas players, including Barry Richards who (because he was South African) was never away playing for his country. Marshall and Greenidge were a duo to be respected, but they could not do the work of three players and were on demand for the West Indies every fourth English summer.

Lancashire, Leicestershire, Gloucestershire and Kent were able to go on using two overseas players for some time into the 1980s, but the players signed in the 1970s (Lloyd, Davison, Zaheer, Asif Iqbal and Shepherd) were all getting on in years and those recruited to help out during the 1980s proved only a mixed success. Glamorgan was the only county to get caught absolutely cold by the new regulations and was restricted to fielding one overseas player by the early 1980s. For the county circuit's weakest and unluckiest team this was a typically cruel trick of fate and a virtual guarantee of failure.

Somerset actually had the most successful period in their history during the late 1970s and early 1980s, but a rapid decline in performances during the mid to late 1980s resulted in the comparative drop in the rankings.

Of course, the dominance that any one county could exert over the domestic cricket scene was also dramatically reduced by the introduction of the three one-day competitions, giving every county four chances of glory each season.

In the limited-overs game it was the period immediately following the 1968 season which saw two sides dominating the one-day competitions. In the period 1968 to 1976, Kent and Lancashire won six one-day trophies each and it is worth noting that both counties boasted two or three overseas all-rounders (Lancashire – Lloyd and Engineer; Kent – Shepherd, Asif and Julien) during this period.

All-rounders are considered by many to be particularly effective in one-day games as the matches do not last long enough for any deficiencies in the players' batting or bowling to be exposed. A hard-hit 30 and half a dozen tight overs are worth their weight in gold, and these five players (who formed the nucleus of their county's one-day sides) were capable of one or other of these tasks, and usually much more. During the last 16 seasons, every county except Glamorgan has at least one limited-overs title, with Middlesex, Somerset, Essex and Hampshire being the most successful sides.

At first glance an examination of the 17 counties' success in one-day competitions does not seem to give any particular clue as to the possible influence of overseas players.

Number of limited overs competitions won by counties 1968–92

1	Lancashire	10	=9	Yorkshire	3
=2	Middlesex	7	=9	Warwickshire	3
=2	Kent	7	=9	Nottinghamshire	3
4	Hampshire	6	=13	Gloucestershire	2
=5	Somerset	5	=13	Northamptonshire	2
=5	Essex	5	=13	Derbyshire	2
=5	Leicestershire	5	=13	Surrey	2
8	Worcestershire	4	17	Glamorgan	0
=9	Sussex	3			

However, a closer look reveals that the majority of the seven most successful one-day sides captured the bulk of their honours at a time when their overseas players were contributing most. We have already seen that Lancashire and Kent each won six of their trophies while benefiting from the presence of overseas players whose game was apparently suited to this form of cricket.

Middlesex won five of the seven of its one-day trophies when its overseas players were making a significant contribution: Vincent Van der Bijl was to the fore in the 1980 Gillette Cup triumph; Daniel was one of the driving forces behind securing the Benson & Hedges Cup in 1983 and 1986, as well as the Nat West in 1984; and Haynes batted consistently through Middlesex's 1992 Sunday League campaign. Essex, meanwhile, secured all five of its one-day victories while Ken McEwan was playing for the county and the first two – the Benson & Hedges Cup in 1979 and the Sunday League in 1981 – while Norbert Phillip was also available to the county and firing on all cylinders.

The most obvious case of one, or in this case two, overseas players powering a county to a series of one-day success came during Somerset's cup-winning run of the late 1970s and early 1980s.

Somerset won the Sunday League and the Gillette Cup in 1979, and then picked up the Benson & Hedges Cup two years running in 1981 and 1982, before finishing the run by winning the Nat West trophy in 1983. Although there were considerable heroics from both Richards and Garner, as well as Somerset's home-grown players, in the campaign to win all five titles, the details of the finals show just how great an influence the two West Indians brought to bear. Richards scored 117, 132, 51 not out and 51 in the four cup finals to record the highest match score on each occasion. Garner was both meanness personified and deadly with it. In the four cup finals the tall West Indian took 16 wickets at a ridiculous average of just 4.43 runs.

Never was it better demonstrated how commitment could combine with an overseas player's talent to dominate matches between two English counties. Unfortunately for Somerset, Richards and Garner unsurprisingly found it hard to maintain this almost superhuman level of performance in later seasons.

Leicestershire won four of their five one-day trophies over a five-year period, during which the overall strength of the team was considerably improved by the presence of three overseas players. Garth McKenzie was considered past it by his country when he played county cricket, but his penetrative and above all accurate seam bowling played a part in the Benson & Hedges triumphs of 1972 and 1975, as well as the Sunday League championship of 1975. Brian Davison was another key part of these three campaigns and also helped Leicestershire to its second Sunday League triumph in 1977, this time assisted by fellow Zimbabwean, all-rounder Paddy Clift.

Hampshire have spread their one-day successes over a greater time span, but many of their triumphs do contain significant contributions from overseas players. These contributions were sometimes from surprising quarters as in the 1988 Benson & Hedges Cup final. South African paceman Steven Jefferies was enduring a difficult season with Hampshire and was to spend only one more summer with the county. But he did have one moment of glory as Derbyshire were put in and the cloudy atmosphere allowed Jefferies to swing the ball to devastating effect. Derbyshire struggled for just over three hours but were eventually dismissed for 117: Jefferies, 10 overs, 3 maidens, 5 for 13. In 1991 Hampshire won the Nat West trophy, despite a rather lacklustre performance from Pakistani pace bowler Aquib Javed, but a year later Malcolm Marshall played a large part in beating Kent and securing the Benson & Hedges Cup for Hampshire for the second time.

The influence exerted by overseas players on English domestic cricket was of course dependent on how effective their particular skills were in the context of the playing conditions they found and the make-up of the teams in which they played. Because of this, the long-running debate over what type of overseas player is of the most use in English county cricket is a particularly relevant one.

When it comes to shopping for an overseas player, English counties appear to have kept their priorities pretty consistent. On top of the wanted list is usually an effective pace bowler, and if he is astonishingly quick, has a mean streak a mile wide and is capable of putting the wind up the opposition on a regular basis then so much the better. Forty-eight (34 per cent) of the 142 overseas players employed by English counties since 1968 have been pace bowlers and a further 25 (18 per cent) have had enough batting talent to be classed as all-rounders. Next on the wanted list are batsmen. Fifty-three (37 per cent) of the overseas players have been picked because their respective counties believe that they will strengthen the batting line-up. At the bottom of the counties' priorities are spin bowlers, even those who can bat. Just 15 (11 per cent) of overseas spin bowlers have played for English counties and only Bishan Bedi can be said to have been a consistent success.

If we consider Farokh Engineer as primarily an all-rounder, then the West Indian Deryck Murray can claim to be the only overseas player picked for his wicket-keeping skills alone. And, even so, there are those who claim that Murray's most important task was providing company and encouragement for his West Indian and Nottinghamshire captain, Gary Sobers.

However, these 25-year totals can be misleading. The pattern of employment of overseas cricketers by English counties has changed significantly since 1968. Overseas players can be divided into seven main categories: batsmen; West Indian fast bowlers; West Indian pace bowling all-rounders; pace bowlers from other countries; other pace bowling all-rounders; spin bowlers; and spin bowling all-rounders. An examination of those players registered by English counties other the last 25 years shows how the fortunes of some types of players have increased and others declined.

Types of overseas players 1968–92

	Bats	WI	WI(AR)	P	P(AR)	S	S(AR)
1968	14	1	3	1	1	2	2
1969	15	1	3	4	1	2	3
1970	15	1	4	4	1	3	3
1971	18	2	4	2	2	5	4
1972	19	2	4	2	2	6	5
1973	19	3	5	2	2	7	4
1974	20	3	6	3	2	5	5
1975	19	3	5	3	4	4	5
1976	16	1	5	3	4	3	5
1977	19	6	4	3	4	3	3
1978	19	6	2	4	7	2	3
1979	17	7	2	5	8	1	2
1980	15	8	2	5	7	2	1
1981	17	9	3	2	8	1	1
1982	15	11	3	1	7	–	–
1983	10	10	3	1	7	–	–
1984	10	9	2	3	8	–	–
1985	12	11	3	–	9	–	1
1986	8	12	2	2	8	–	1
1987	7	13	2	3	6	–	2
1988	7	8	1	3	5	–	1
1989	6	10	1	1	5	–	1
1990	7	9	1	3	4	–	1
1991	4	2	2	5	3	–	1
1992	7	5	1	4	2	–	–

Key: Bats = batsmen; WI = West Indian fast bowlers; WI(AR) = West Indian pace bowling all-rounders; P = pace bowlers from other countries; P(AR) = pace bowling all-rounders; S = spin bowlers; S(AR) = spin bowling all-rounders.

From the viewpoint of the early 1990s the first reaction to this table is twofold: first, surprise at how many overseas spin bowlers were employed during the early 1970s; and, secondly, a rueful recognition of how English counties over the last decade and a half have sought to employ almost anybody hailing from the Caribbean who could, or said he could, bowl fast.

From this end of the telescope it is incredible to think that in 1972 and 1973, there were 11 overseas spin bowlers playing in county cricket (and only 5 West Indian pace bowlers). This was mainly due to the fact that, in Gibbs, Bedi and Intikhab Alam, world-class spinners were available for hire and partly because at that time wickets were left uncovered. It was also the case that many of the 'bits and pieces' employed by counties as their second or third overseas player were spin bowlers of varying degrees of skill. Later in the decade, wickets were covered and the supply of spin bowling talent dried up to the extent that there was only one overseas spin bowler (Abdul Qadir) who was considered a match winner at test level. This sharp reduction in available talent also coincided with a switch in policy by the counties (encouraged by developing one-day tactics) to employing pace (as opposed to spin) bowling all-rounders, especially those from South Africa.

The recruitment of Caribbean fast bowlers really took off after the West Indies' 1976 tour of England. This was the first chance for UK cricket watchers to see the Windies' four-man pace attack in operation and it had a galvanizing effect on the English counties. Everybody wanted a piece of the action and, as in the late 1960s, most of the counties tried to secure a part of the Windies' reflected glory, this time personified in the world's fastest bowlers.

The desire to have a West Indian fast bowler on your playing staff was most prevalent in the mid-1980s. In the three seasons 1985, 1986 and 1987, there were either 14 or 15 West Indian pacemen playing English county cricket. Many counties, restricted to fielding just one overseas player, were even employing two Caribbean quicks so as always to have one fresh and raring to go.

This particular tactic, as well as the employment of West Indian fast bowlers, reached its peak in 1987. Gloucestershire with Walsh and Greene, Surrey (Clarke and Gray) and Leicestershire (Ferris and Benjamin) were able to play a fully-fit overseas quick bowler in at least 20 of their first-class games. The tactic paid off for Leicestershire, who rose from seventh to third place in the county table, but Surrey dropped one place to fourth and Gloucestershire plummeted from second to tenth.

Elsewhere Tony Merrick and South African Alan Donald were taking turns to bowl the new ball for Warwickshire, and Winston Davis, Michael Holding and Eldine Baptiste had their load lightened by Roger Harper, John Wright and Roy Pienaar, respectively. There was a real belief on the county circuit at that time, that to be without a fast bowler (i.e. somebody who could 'dish it out') a county would simply not be taken seriously by its opponents and that morale among the county's English players would crumble.

Three other counties, Middlesex, Hampshire and Lancashire, also regularly fielded West Indian fast bowlers during 1987, but none of the ten counties with a Caribbean quick on their books won anything that year. Lancashire came nearest, finishing four points behind Nottinghamshire in the county championship as Patrick Patterson, unaided by any other overseas player, took 52 wickets at 26.13. Northamptonshire also came close, fighting their way to the Nat West final against Nottinghamshire, only to lose by three wickets.

The demise of spinners and the rise of West Indian fast bowlers apart, the other big change in the type of overseas players taking part in English domestic cricket has been the sharp deduction in the number of foreign batsmen employed by the counties. In the mid to late 1970s, almost every county (apart of course from Yorkshire) had an overseas batsman on their books.

The decline in their numbers was sparked by the change in the regulations governing overseas players. Asked to reduce their overseas players from two to one, most counties ditched their batsmen. Studying the table it is clear that the number of overseas bowlers in English county cricket remains virtually unchanged as the new regulations come into force, but that the employment of overseas batsmen is cut back sharply. In 1978, for example, the year before the new regulations were agreed, there were 19 overseas batsmen and 24 overseas bowlers. Ten years later, with the new regulations implemented, the number of overseas batsmen had dropped 63 per cent to just 7, while the number of bowlers had actually climbed by 8 per cent to 26.

In the last two seasons under review, we can see a new pattern emerging as every county is allowed to register, as opposed to play, just one overseas player. There now appears to be a neat division with a third of the counties each choosing to employ either a batsman, a West Indian fast bowler or pace bowler from another test playing nation. This said, it is worthwhile noting, and applauding, Somerset's decision to employ Pakistani leg-spinner Mushtaq Ahmed, the first overseas specialist slow bowler to play for an English county since Dilip Doshi in 1981, 12 seasons ago.

Although fast bowlers, in recent years at least, have proved the most popular choice for English counties seeking an overseas player, it is worth noting that the most successful sides of recent times have tended to rely on high-class overseas batsmen. Former Northamptonshire captain Geoff Cook speaks about the benefits of developing a 'five-man attack'. This 'positive option' as he describes it has been most successfully followed by three counties over the last ten years.

But Essex, Middlesex and Worcestershire have built up their bowling attacks without resorting to importing overseas talent. Middlesex, after saying goodbye to Daniel in the mid-1980s, have managed to maintain their challenge by developing a bowling attack featuring Cowans, Williams, Fraser, Emburey and Tufnell – all England test players. Worcestershire captured their two championship trophies in 1988 and 1989, with a bowling line-up consisting of Dilley, Newport, Illingworth, Botham and Radford – again all England players. The most successful modern county side of all, Essex, has regularly fielded a highly effective English-qualified attack permed from Lever, Foster, Pringle, Childs, and Ilott or Andrew. All the counties also had useful English-qualified seamers, such as Lampitt and Topley, waiting in the second team to take the place of injured first stringers.

With the effort to develop a high-class home-grown bowling attack having paid off, the counties were then free to recruit a high-class overseas batsman. Not only did this complete the balance of the side, it brought added advantages. In the eyes of most counties, successful overseas batsmen tend to be greater crowd pullers than bowlers and also are able to contribute more significantly to one-day games in which bowlers are only allowed to bowl a set number of overs.

Mark Waugh, Salim Malik, Graeme Hick and Desmond Haynes have all demonstrated recently how signing an overseas batsman can help a county achieve success, but still the belief persists that employing a West Indian quick is the surest way of securing glory. A look at the county championship winners over the last 25 years, however, shows that this is simply not the case.

County championship winners 1968–92

Year	County	Overseas players	Type
1992	Essex	M. Waugh	Batsman
1991	Essex	Salim Malik	Batsman
1990	Middlesex	D. Haynes	Batsman
1989	Worcs	G. Hick	Batsman
1988	Worcs	G. Hick	Batsman
1987	Notts	R. Hadlee/C. Rice	All-rounder/batsman
1986	Essex	A. Border	Batsman
1985	Middlesex	W. Daniel	Fast bowler
1984	Essex	K. McEwan/N. Phillip	Batsman/all-rounder
1983	Essex	K. McEwan/N. Phillip	Batsman/all-rounder
1982	Middlesex	W. Daniel	Fast bowler
1981	Notts	R. Hadlee/C. Rice	All-rounder/all-rounder
1980	Middlesex	P. Van der Bijl/W. Daniel	Pace bowler/fast bowler
1979	Essex	K. McEwan/N. Phillip	Batsman/all-rounder
1978	Kent	A. Iqbal/J. Shepherd	Batsman/all-rounder
1977*	Kent	A. Iqbal/J. Shepherd/ B. Julien	Batsman/all-rounder/ all-rounder
	Middlesex	W. Daniel/N. Featherstone	Fast bowler/all-rounder
1976	Middlesex	L. Gomes/N. Featherstone	Batsman/all-rounder
1975	Leicester	P. Clift/B. Davison/ G. McKenzie	All-rounder/batsman/ pace bowler
1974	Worcs	G. Turner/V. Holder	Batsman/pace bowler
1973	Hampshire	B. Richards/C.G. Greenidge/ D. O'Sullivan	Batsman/batsman/ spin bowler
1972	Warwick	R. Kanhai/W. Bourne/ A. Kallicharran/D. Murray	Batsman/all-rounder/ batsman/wicket-keeper
1971	Surrey	Y. Ahmed/I. Alam/ G. Howarth	Batsman/all-rounder/ batsman
1970	Kent	A. Iqbal/J. Shepherd/ B. Julien	Batsman/all-rounder/ all-rounder
1969	Glamorgan	M. Khan/B. Davis/ A. Cordle	Batsman/batsman/ pace bowler
1968	Yorkshire	–	–

*Joint winners

Treating each championship-winning side separately (ignoring the fact that players such as McEwan and Daniel played in more than one trophy-winning year), overseas players made a total of 50 appearances in those successful teams. Half of these were by batsman, 20 by pace bowlers, 4 by spinners and 1 by a wicket-keeper.

Of the 20 pace bowlers, 15 came from the West Indies, but Daniel apart, they have hardly been in the fearsome mould of present Caribbean quicks. Cordle,

Shepherd, Phillip and Bourne were essentially no more than highly competent 'English-type' seamers, while Holder and Julien, although sharp, were a yard or two slower than members of the post-1976 Windies' test attack, such as Marshall, Holding et al.

The majority of the West Indian fast bowlers who were part of championship-winning sides also had something else in common, being successful all-rounders, with only Daniel and Holder considered tail enders. In fact, this trend is also present in the five appearances accounted for by pace bowlers from other countries. Of the four bowlers involved, Hadlee and Clift were increasingly feared for their batting, while McKenzie and Van der Bijl were much less of a threat.

The cliché of an overseas fast bowler, blasting his way to the county championship has in fact happened only seven times during the 25 seasons since the introduction of immediate registration. Daniel led the way, bowling Middlesex to victory in 1977, 1982 and 1985, as well as teaming up with Van der Bijl to win the 1980 trophy. Hadlee comes next, bringing home the bacon in 1981, with considerable help from Rice, and in 1987. The remaining example was in 1974 when Holder took 94 wickets as Worcestershire secured the championship. The great majority of championship victories have been accomplished by sides with an overseas batsman, usually backed up by a competent, but not world-beating, pace bowler who could bat.

Incredibly in one-day cricket the trophy-winning success of overseas players follows almost exactly the same pattern as in the first-class games. Of the 120 individual appearances made by overseas players in cup or league-winning sides, 58 have been made by batsman, 35 by West Indian fast bowlers, 23 by pace bowlers from other countries and 4 by spinners. Of the total 62 appearances made by bowlers, 36 were by players considered to be all-rounders.

As we have already seen many counties have picked overseas batsmen in the belief that they would contribute more to the one-day game, while others have selected fast bowlers hoping for a shot at the first-class championship. The analysis of appearances by overseas players in sides that have secured the county championship or won a one-day competition seems to throw this widespread belief into considerable doubt.

Expressed in percentage terms the appearances of overseas players, by type, in the first-class and one-day championship-winning sides is as follows:

	Batsmen	WI fast bowlers	Other pace bowlers	Spinners
First-class*	50%	30%	10%	8%
One day	49%	29%	19%	3%

*The remaining 2% is accounted for by Deryck Murray, the wicket-keeper

The analysis of the contribution of overseas players also seems to give the lie to the often-heard belief that all-rounders are more effective in one-day games. Of the 24 appearances made by bowlers in county championship-winning sides, 71 per cent were by all-rounders. In one-day competitions, of the 62 appearances only 53 per cent were by all-rounders.

Studying the overseas cricketers who have played in championship and trophy-winning sides makes it possible to examine which type of players have been the most effective in English domestic county cricket. The results are surprising and challenge conventional thinking about the choice of overseas players.

First it is necessary to determine exactly how great or small is the percentage of overseas players of different types in English cricket over the past 25 years. Analysing the make-up of the overseas contingent by treating each season separately (taking full account of the foreign players who had lengthy careers in county cricket) reveals which type of player has had the greatest presence over the last 25 years.

Types of overseas player, season by season, 1968–92

Batsmen = 39%
West Indian fast bowlers = 18%
West Indian pace bowlers (all-rounders) = 9%
Other pace bowlers = 8%
Other pace bowlers (all-rounders) = 14%
Spin bowlers = 6%
Spin bowlers (all-rounders) = 6%

The next step is to compare this 'average presence' with the number of times players of a different type were part of a winning side.

Presence of overseas players in winning sides compared to total appearances in county cricket, 1968–92

	County championship	One-day competitions
Batsmen	+11%	+10%
WI fast bowlers	–8%	–4%
WI pace bowlers (all-rounders)	+11%	+6%
Other pace bowlers	–6%	–1%
Other pace bowlers (all-rounders)	–6%	–1%
Spin bowlers	–4%	–5%
Spin bowlers (all-rounders)	0%	–3%

Over the last 25 years the sides with batsmen as their overseas players seem to have benefited the most, in terms of trophies at least. Again, there seems little difference between the batsmen's relative performance in one-day and first-class cricket.

West Indian fast bowlers, the supposed kings of overseas players in England, come out of this analysis about even. But a closer look reveals a sharp division with the ranks of the Caribbean speedsters. Those Windies pace bowlers who could bat have had much more success than their compatriots who were fast-bowling specialists, the difference being particularly acute in first-class cricket. *In fact the specialist West Indian fast bowlers recruited by English counties have proved the least effective type of overseas player (when compared to their ubiquity) in terms of helping to win the four major domestic competitions.*

Pace bowlers from other countries also have a bad record, compared to their presence in English county cricket over the last 25 years. Again the difference is greatest in the first-class game, suggesting that in many cases those bowlers recruited were little more than superior English line and length merchants – a point supported when one thinks of players such as Corrie Van Zyl and Anton Ferreira. Spin bowlers also under-performed, but it is worth noting that this unenviable record is almost totally due to the poor record of the players considered tail enders, with the spin bowling all-rounders almost breaking even.

There are, of course, a great number of other factors, such as the ability of the other players in the side, which could lead to an overseas player becoming part of a winning team: Larry Gomes for example had little to do with Middlesex's triumphs of the mid-1970s. But it seems that – all other factors being equal – employing an overseas batsman is the best way to add to the silverware collection. Hiring a specialist West Indian fast bowler, on the other hand, might command 'respect' from other county teams, but is the least effective way of stocking up the trophy cupboard.

5 Overseas players and international cricket

The way in which overseas players have changed the face of English county cricket has led to much debate among the more dedicated followers of the game. But the effect that this mass migration of playing talent has had on the fortunes of England's test team is a subject which even the most casual cricket watcher is happy to give an opinion on. The belief that the presence of overseas players in county cricket has somehow contributed to the decline of English test cricket is, along with issues such as the football premier league and the poor quality of British tennis, one of central controversies in UK sport.

The roots of this widespread interest in the issue of overseas players lie in the early 1980s, when English test cricket entered its least successful period since international competition began. The inquest into why this should have happened immediately threw up the suggestion that the opportunities for young English test hopefuls were being restricted by overseas players. This belief quickly became received wisdom and was widely preached by many ex-players in the sporting media.

However, the way in which the performance of the English test team has been affected by the presence of overseas players is not as straightforward as these critics would like to suggest.

True, county cricket does seem to serve as a finishing school for young test hopefuls from overseas, often turning them from talented but inconsistent performers into world beaters. And it cannot be disputed that the presence of overseas players, certainly during the 1970s, restricted the opportunities for a number of promising young English players and sometimes forced them out of the game. But, on the other hand, it does not seem unreasonable to suggest that existing and potential English internationals will have learned much from playing day to day alongside and against the world's leading players. The overseas players may discover the weaknesses of their English rivals and team mates, but it should not be beyond the ability of English test players to carry out the same analysis on the foreign 'stars'.

The whole debate over whether or not the presence of overseas players is connected to England's poor test performances over recent years is further complicated by a number of other issues, such as:

1 the fact, as demonstrated in Chapter 4, that the arrival of overseas players created a greater equality among the counties and therefore created a

disposable wealth which directly benefited the development of English-qualified players;

2   the mass production of West Indian fast bowlers;

3   the growing professionalism and depth of talent in the test teams of countries (such as Pakistan, India and New Zealand), previously regarded as second-string cricketing powers;

4   the continuing relative decline in the popularity of first-class county cricket which provides the seed bed for the English test team;

5   the two rebel tours of South Africa which deprived England of some of its leading players at a time when the number of high-class cricketers available to the selectors seemed to be dwindling.

Because of all these factors, and a number of others, the much touted case that the introduction of immediate registration of overseas players has had an adverse effect on English test cricket is a hard one to prove outright. It is perhaps worth while starting to review the evidence for and against by considering, not how the system affected the English game, but what impact it had on the performance of rival test-playing nations.

West Indies   52 county cricketers

The West Indies have provided the greatest number of overseas players to have taken part in English county cricket during the last 25 years. Fifty-two West Indians (37 per cent of the total of overseas players) have played for English counties, including most of their leading players of the last three decades. The degree to which county cricket and the West Indian test team are inter-dependent can be gauged from how the number of overseas players on the county circuit dipped every time the Windies toured England. This was seen clearly in the 1976 and 1988 seasons, where the number of overseas players fell by 20 per cent compared to the preceding season, but most dramatically in 1991 when the numbers fell by 30 per cent to an all-time post-1967 low.

Excluding the touring years, the Windies have had at least a dozen players taking part in county cricket during each English summer from 1968 until 1987. In fact, if you include those West Indian cricketers banned because of their links with South Africa, the world's leading test team of modern times has had 16 plus players on the county circuit for 10 out of the last 25 years. Add the years in which the West Indies were playing a test series against England and it could be argued that the UK has hosted a full-strength West Indian touring party for 17 out of the last 25 years.

The number of West Indian players taking part in county cricket effectively enabled the Windies' selectors to treat the English domestic season as an extended test trial. The West Indian players on the fringe of the test side certainly recognized the importance of recording good performances in county cricket. Whenever Clive Lloyd or Viv Richards travelled to Lord's, for example, they could be sure of a fiery welcome from Wayne Daniel, who was determined to blast himself back into the Windies side. When the Windies' magisterial performance temporarily faltered during the early 1990s, voices were raised in the Caribbean identifying the relative lack of West Indian players in county cricket as the root of the problem.

Joel Garner at the start of his career had no doubt that he had to travel to England even to cement his place in the Barbados side. In his autobiography he remembers a piece of advice given to him in the mid-1970s: 'Bird, let me tell you something about Barbados that you don't seem to know. You could bowl you ass off for YMPC [Garner's local club] every Saturday and get the most wickets in the BCA and be the most promising youngster and all that. And still one of the professionals would come from the [English] Leagues or the Counties and walk into the team and you would be left on the outside. Barbados respects achievement overseas more than it does brilliance at home.' And research suggests that the attitude in the other islands from which the West Indies draw their team is very similar.

Current West Indian captain, Antiguan Richie Richardson, who made his county debut for Yorkshire in 1993, was in no doubt about what English county cricket means to Caribbean players, even those at the peak of their international career. 'Every youngster in the Caribbean wants to play county cricket. It's highly competitive and it attracts internationals from all over the world. It is a wonderful stage to prove your skills.'

One glance at the leading test averages for modern West Indies test cricketers confirms the link between the Caribbean side of the last 25 years and English county cricket.

West Indian test averages* (to the end of the 1992 English season)

Batsmen	Tests	Runs	Average	County appearances
I.V.A. Richards	121	8,540	50.23	223
G. St A. Sobers	93	8,032	57.78	107
G.C. Greenidge	108	7,558	44.72	275
C.H. Lloyd	110	7,515	46.67	219
D.L. Haynes	103	6,725	42.29	63
R.B. Kanhai	79	6,227	47.53	173
R.B. Richardson	63	4,693	47.40	–
A.I. Kallicharran	66	4,399	44.43	285
R.C. Fredericks	59	4,334	42.49	45
P.J.L. Dujon	81	3,322	31.94	–
H.A. Gomes	60	3,171	39.63	42
A.L. Logie	52	2,470	35.79	–
L.G. Rowe	30	2,047	43.55	17

West Indian test averages* continued

Batsmen	Tests	Runs	Average	County appearances
D.L. Murray	62	1,993	22.90	155
C.L. Hooper	32	1,409	28.18	21
C.A. Davis	15	1,301	54.20	–
S.F.A.F. Bacchus	19	782	26.06	–

Bowlers	Tests	Wkts	Average	County appearances
M.D. Marshall	81	376	20.94	197
L.R. Gibbs	79	309	29.09	109
J. Garner	58	259	20.97	94
M.A. Holding	60	249	23.68	73
G. St A. Sobers	93	235	34.03	107
A.M.E. Roberts	47	202	25.61	94
C.A. Walsh	51	178	24.96	122
C.E.L. Ambrose	34	148	22.43	42
C.E.H. Croft	27	125	23.30	49
V.A. Holder	40	109	33.27	181
B.P. Patterson	27	92	29.87	70
K.D. Boyce	21	60	30.01	211
I.R. Bishop	11	53	20.58	43
B.D. Julien	24	50	37.36	80
W.W. Davis	15	45	32.71	102
R.A. Harper	24	45	27.82	54
S.T. Clarke	11	42	27.88	160

*Excluding players who had finished their test careers before 1968

The message of these two tables is clear; a place in the West Indies test side and summer employment on the English county circuit go hand in hand. Twelve out of the 17 highest run-getters for the West Indies since 1968 have played county cricket, 10 of them finding employment for at least 2 seasons. But this symmetry between English and domestic cricket, and West Indian test success is most starkly highlighted by the bowlers' table.

Every single West Indian test bowler who has taken more than 40 test wickets since 1968 has played county cricket. Thirteen out of the 17 have played in the English game for the equivalent of three seasons, while just under half have made more than 100 appearances in county cricket.

The link is clearly established between English county and West Indian test cricket. The next question to ask is one normally associated with chickens and eggs. Did test success follow county glory, or were these 28 players international stars before they arrived in the UK? In other words, did English county cricket act as a proving ground for West Indian test cricket?

Given the amount of cricket played during an English domestic season, it is clear that most successful West Indian test cricketers of the last 25 years have played the majority of their first-class cricket in the UK. And as the only reliable way to improve your ability as a cricketer is to play cricket, then it can be reasonably argued that the West Indians have had their greatest opportunities to 'learn' the game while playing in England. But that conclusion goes out of the window if the player concerned is already an experienced player with confidence in his own ability to cope with different circumstances. It is highly doubtful, for example, that Alan Border or Jimmy Cook had much to learn from playing county cricket, especially compared to the knowledge they were able to impart to others.

The Windies have been impressively loyal to the players they believe have the talent to succeed in test cricket. The admirable consistency in their selection policy has in turn played its part in the Windies' unparalleled success since the mid-1970s. But the question remains, whose discovery were these players to whom the West Indian selectors have shown such loyalty? Was their talent confirmed before they left the Caribbean or did English county cricket do that job for the Windies' selectors? One way to answer the question is to examine the test records of the leading 28 West Indian county players before their first full season in the UK.

Many of the players who were picked up by English counties before making their international debut would have already made their mark in West Indian domestic cricket, but it is clear from these two tables that the UK clubs do not demand evidence of consistent performance at test level. Eighteen of the West

West Indian test records to 1992

Batsmen	Before county debut			Test record up to 1992		
	Matches	Runs	Av.	Matches	Runs	Av.
R.C. Fredericks	14	767	28.40	59	4,334	42.49
H.A. Gomes	–	–	–	60	3,171	39.63
C.G. Greenidge*	–	–	–	108	7,558	44.72
D.L. Haynes**	85	5,340	41.39	103	6,725	42.29
C.L. Hooper**	32	1,409	28.18	32	1,409	28.18
A.I. Kallicharran	–	–	–	66	4,399	44.43
R.B. Kanhai	56	4,685	48.30	79	6,227	47.53
C.H. Lloyd	8	596	54.18	110	7,515	46.67
D.L. Murray***	5	93	15.50	62	1,993	22.90
I.V.A. Richards	–	–	–	121	8,540	50.23
L.G. Rowe	11	1,131	70.69	30	2,047	43.55
G. St A. Sobers	65	6,059	59.64	93	8,032	57.78

*Greenidge moved to England when he was 14 and played for the national schools side
** Still playing
*** Murray played for Cambridge University in 1965 and 1966. His test record is measured up until his debut for the university

Bowlers	Before county debut			Test record up to 1992		
	Matches	Wkts	Av.	Matches	Wkts	Av.
C.E.L. Ambrose*	17	60	27.35	34	148	22.43
I.R. Bishop*	4	16	23.12	11	53	20.58
K.D. Boyce	–	–	–	21	60	30.01
S.T. Clarke	6	27	31.52	11	42	27.88
C.E.H. Croft	5	33	20.48	27	125	24.52
W.W. Davis	–	–	–	15	45	32.71
J. Garner	5	25	27.52	58	259	20.97
L.R. Gibbs	34	151	22.84	79	309	29.09
R.A. Harper	14	34	28.41	24	45	27.82
V.A. Holder	–	–	–	40	109	33.27
M.A. Holding	28	115	24.78	60	249	23.68
B.D. Julien	–	–	–	24	121	30.92
M.D. Marshall	3	3	88.33	81	376	20.94
B.P. Patterson*	–	–	–	27	92	29.87
A.M.E. Roberts	–	–	–	47	202	25.61
G. St A. Sobers	65	157	33.91	93	235	34.03
C.A. Walsh*	–	–	–	50	174	24.95

*Still playing

Indies' top test performers for the last 25 years have made their debut for an English county either uncapped at international level or having played in fewer than 10 tests. This is especially true when it comes to picking a West Indian fast bowler. Boyce, Davis, Holder, Julien, Patterson, Roberts, Walsh, Bishop, Clarke, Croft, Garner and Marshall – part of the greatest line-up of fast-bowling talent in the history of the game – have all made their debuts for English counties before they had played more than six tests. Of all the great West Indian fast bowlers of the last 25 years only Curtly Ambrose and Michael Holding have had to wait more than half a dozen tests before being picked up by an English county.

In practice the desperation of English counties to sign a West Indian fast bowler in the late 1970s and early 1980s led to clubs signing up players about which they knew next to nothing. So little was known of Croft, for example, when he joined Lancashire after playing just five test matches, that the majority of the club's officials and players believed him to be a left-arm bowler!

The mania for having a West Indian fast bowler as one of your overseas players reached its peak in the late 1980s. From a three-year period between 1985 and 1987, there were at least a dozen West Indian pace bowlers contracted to play for English counties. As they were employed at a time when the number of overseas players was declining from its late 1970s high, it meant that West Indian fast bowlers accounted for half the foreign recruits in county cricket during the mid to late 1980s.

There is no doubt that county cricket contributed significantly to the learning process of the majority of the West Indies' leading modern test players, but what of those ten players who arrived in English county cricket with an international reputation already established?

The West Indian test side of the early 1970s suffered from the extra burden that was placed on three of its leading players by county cricket. Sobers, Kanhai and, particularly, Gibbs all saw their record decline at test level after becoming county cricketers. Their advancing years would, of course, have played a part, but the ageing process, in sporting terms at least, must have been accelerated by having to push their 35+-year-old bodies around the county circuit. These are not the only West Indian casualties of county cricket. Lawrence Rowe's outstanding test record declined sharply after spending a disappointing season with Derbyshire, while Roger Harper saw his test career crumble as he tried to carry the Northants attack. Coincidence or not, it appears that county cricket does not agree with every West Indian.

On the credit side, Roy Fredericks' years with Glamorgan appear to have tightened the technique of the dashing opener and allowed him to double his test average. County cricket also appears to have done Curtly Ambrose no harm, his reputation growing with every passing year. The two West Indian late-comers to county cricket, Haynes and Holding, experienced as little trouble in adapting to English domestic cricket as you would expect from two acknowledged masters of their art.

South Africa   30 county cricketers (incl. Kepler Wessels)

Zimbabwe   8 county cricketers

Without the presence of South African and Zimbabwean cricketers in English county cricket, New Zealand and India would have been called on to provide many more overseas players. In this way the presence of overseas players from Southern Africa has assisted the English game by preventing young cricketers from those nations learning the game in England.

On the negative side, however, is the fact that overseas players from Southern Africa, who until recently had no test calls, and were therefore constantly available for county sides, played a greater part in reducing the opportunities for English-qualified players. The desire of Southern African cricketers to qualify for England and play test cricket has also helped disguise the paucity of young English players with test potential. Of the six test-class batsmen to make their debuts for England in the last decade, Lamb, Smith and Hick would have all played test cricket for South Africa or Zimbabwe given the chance, leaving England with Broad, Atherton and Stewart as the only likely successors to Gooch, Gatting and Gower.

Australia   **18 county cricketers (incl. Kepler Wessels)**

Australian cricketers have always tended to view English domestic cricket with some suspicion – there is too much of it and the quality leaves a lot to be desired. The ethos of the part-time cricketer also remains quite strong in Australia, many of its leading players still believing that it is impossible to retain your commitment to the game if you play it constantly and for a living. The Australians who did make the trip to England before 1968 tended to be forgotten as far as test selection went and this has led to the cricketers braving the journey post-1968 often being at the end of their careers and therefore less concerned about securing a test place.

Some Australians were tempted to become overseas players in the late 1960s and early 1970s. These were usually young players like Greg Chappell, O'Keeffe and Francis, or cricketers reaching their sell-by date at international level, such as Connolly and McKenzie. After this first rush, there followed a period of around ten years from the early 1970s when Australians were largely absent from English county cricket.

Of the players who made up the great Australian sides during this period, very few graced English county cricket. Greg Chappell had come, seen and was now returning at regular intervals to conquer; Lillee stayed away until he had announced his test retirement; Thomson came for one season and spent most of it on the physio's bench. Ian Chappell, Redpath, Walters, Walker, Marsh, Hughes, Yallop, Hogg et al. were happy to see the poms once every other year and not risk letting familiarity breed contempt.

The belief that playing county cricket is a dangerous pastime for young Australian players was still strong in the early 1980s. It is little remembered that a promising young fast bowler called Merv Hughes struggled with a recurring injury after spending a season with Essex in 1983. This was considered bothersome at the time, but had Australia's supporters realized how big, and how colourful, a part Hughes would have played in the national side during the late 1980s and early 1990s, their irritation might have turned to anger. Both Dennis Hickey and Glenn Trimble also faced serious injury problems after playing county cricket, and Bill O'Reilly, the greatest Australian slow bowler, specifically blamed the decline of promising leg-spinner Stuart Saunders on the season he spent with the Middlesex second XI in 1981.

The debate raged, with David Hookes claiming that the success of Crowe and Hadlee proved that English county cricket would 'not take the flair out of our promising players'. On the contrary he claimed it would 'add the dimension we see when the hardened county pro sets himself to do the job'. However, ex-pat South African Englishman Tony Greig countered by claiming that the intensive nature of English cricket would suck the flair from players such as Steve Waugh.

Despite the considerable reservations still held in Australia, the cultural boycott was broken in 1986 in the biggest way possible when Australian captain Allan Border agreed to play for Essex. In 1985 Border had led his country to a

3–1 defeat against England, but nevertheless had played so well and acknowledged defeat with such grace that he become hugely popular with English crowds, making his recruitment a major coup for the county.

With Border in the vanguard, the majority of Australia's awesome batting line-up of recent times have spent at least one season in county cricket. Border, Jones, Moody and the Waugh twins are providing the batting talent that English county cricket used to search Southern Africa for in the 1970s.

The Australians seem to have overcome their fear of county cricket's baleful influence and Jones for one was very clear that he considered playing county cricket to be the best way to polish his skills. 'I joined them for selfish reasons', he says. 'I had gone through a poor year in test cricket and wanted to play in England to check out my technique.'

Pakistan   14 county cricketers

Although slightly fewer in number than Australian county cricketers, Pakistani overseas players have had a far greater impact on the English game and vice versa. Of the 14 Pakistani players to have played regularly in county cricket, 4 have made over 100 first-class appearances in English domestic competitions and 6 over 200.

The commitment by Pakistani players to county cricket is without parallel from any other leading cricketers of a foreign country. Imran Khan played county cricket over 18 years; Mushtaq Mohammad and Asif Iqbal over 15; Sarfraz Nawaz and Zaheer Abbas over 14; Intikhab Alam over 13; and Sadiq Mohammad over 11. What is more amazing is that all these players, plus Majid Khan and Javed Miandad, were near or exact contemporaries who played against each other in county cricket during the English summer and side by side while on test duty.

The team that took the field to play against New Zealand at Karachi in Pakistan in October 1976 is typical. It featured current county players filling the first nine positions in the batting order. The two remaining players were both test débutants.

1   Sadiq Mohammad (Gloucestershire 1972–82)
2   Majid Khan (Glamorgan 1968–76)
3   Zaheer Abbas (Gloucestershire 1972–85)
4   Javed Miandad (Sussex 1976–9 and Glamorgan 1980–5)
5   Mushtaq Mohammad (Northants 1964–78)
6   Asif Iqbal (Kent 1968–82)
7   Imran Khan (Worcs 1971–6 and Sussex 1977–88)
8   Intikhab Alam (Surrey 1969–81)
9   Sarfraz Nawaz (Northants 1969–82)
10 Shahid Israr
11 Sikander Bakht

It is as if the Pakistani test team of the mid-1970s had decided *en masse* to seek employment in English county cricket.

This mid-1970s team was by far the strongest batting side in the world. Since that time Pakistan has produced two world-beating bowlers but only one batsman fit to rank with those of the mid-1970s vintage. Pakistan's opening batsman Mudassar Nazar has no doubt why that is the case:

Pakistan first-class cricket produced only two world-class players – Hanif Mohammad and Wasim Bari. In the 1970s, we produced top-class batsmen because of English county cricket and nothing else. You only have to look at Steve Waugh's performance to judge how much help county cricket has been to Pakistan cricket. One year of county cricket has turned him into a top-call test player. Unless we improve our first-class cricket, we shall find it very hard to produce top-class cricketers.

Imran Khan agrees: 'The Pakistani batting might of the 1970s was almost entirely due to team members playing for various counties who returned home and raised the standard of our domestic cricket.' He adds, 'We have so much talent, but our domestic cricket is of such a poor standard that it is impossible to polish it here in Pakistan.' No wonder then that Imran has gone to great efforts to secure a county place for both his young protégées (Wasim Akram and Waqar Younis). Imran's sharp eye can spot talent, but he also recognizes the best atmosphere in which to nurture it.

India   10 county cricketers

Indian cricketers do not appear to take to the seven days a week competition that English county cricket sometimes requires. Whereas Pakistani players have usually stayed with their adopted counties for long periods, the Indian players who have experimented with county cricket tend to spend only a few seasons in the UK. Farokh Engineer and Bishan Bedi are the only two Indian cricketers to have played successfully for English counties for an extended period of time and both were men of unusually outgoing personalities.

These two apart, the link between Indian cricket and the county game is a slender one, with no Indian batsman, for example, spending more than one season with an English county. The resulting influence on the Indian test side is also therefore relatively small and still shrinking. In the mid-1970s the high-class spin bowlers whom India provided for the county circuit took the opportunity to fathom the strengths and weaknesses of their English opponents. However, since Doshi was the last to leave at the end of the 1981 season, the Indian overseas players have only stayed long enough to get the most fleeting glimpses of their international rivals.

New Zealand   8 county cricketers

The whipping boys of international cricket, New Zealand have always had a few outstanding players. We have already seen earlier in the book how county cricket provided the impetus for Glenn Turner to expand his range of strokes. But up until shortly before the master batsman took early retirement, most of New Zealand's other test players were still too far below test standard to enable their country to win many games. The difference came with the rise to prominence of all-rounder Richard Hadlee. In the last decade of Hadlee's career, New Zealand became the last side to beat the West Indies in a series, defeated England both home and away for the first time, beaten Australia in Australia and proved difficult opponents for the other test nations. Once Hadlee had retired the country slipped back down the international pecking order.

When he joined Nottinghamshire in 1979 for his first full season with the club, Hadlee had been playing test cricket for seven years and had established a reputation as a wild but sometimes effective fast bowler. Facing the challenge of having to dismiss a new set of batsmen in every game inspired him to develop the control and the variations of swing and seam which turned him into the world's leading bowler. His test record at the start of his Nottinghamshire career was 89 wickets at 31.54, and when he left Trent Bridge ten years later it was 355 at 22.46.

Hadlee has no doubts about what brought about that transformation. 'What did ten years of county cricket mean? It was ten years which made me as a cricketer, a decade of county life which sharpened and refined my skills.'

He adds:

I owe the club [Notts] a great deal because they taught me the game. They taught me finesse. And that, in turn, has helped New Zealand cricket. It's unfortunate if it has sometimes backfired on England. But it is not a coincidence that New Zealand have enjoyed a lot of success first with Glenn Turner, then myself, and now Martin Crowe getting a good grounding in county cricket. Things may change following the new restriction to one overseas player per county, which I think is fair.

As Hadlee says, New Zealand would not have been able to raise their game at international level during the 1970s and 1980s without talent in depth. Like all bowlers Hadlee needed his side to score enough runs to enable him to put the opposition under pressure. This New Zealand were able to do, largely thanks to the efforts of John Wright, Geoff Howarth, Jeremy Coney, and Martin and Jeff Crowe. Wright and Howarth both played the majority of their first-class cricket for English counties, and the younger Crowe brother enjoyed three very successful seasons with Somerset.

It is unlikely that New Zealand would have displayed such unexpected resilience if their leading players had not been tempered by playing in English county cricket. But it is worth noting that Turner eventually decided to stop playing test cricket and concentrate on his county career, and Howarth had his development hampered by having to compete for a place with Intikhab Alam and Sylvester Clarke.

Overseas players and restricted opportunities

The West Indies (from the mid-1970s at least), Pakistan and New Zealand seem all to have benefited from having their leading test players take part in English county cricket. But what of the other side of the equation, the effect the presence of overseas players has had on the fortunes of the English test team? How much truth is there in the widely heard claim that the places given to overseas players in county teams stopped promising young Englishmen from playing and developing into test cricketers?

As usual with this debate, little conclusive evidence has been brought forward to either prove or disprove the theory that overseas players are bad for English cricket. For example, Christopher Martin-Jenkins writing in 1983 commented that Kim Barnett and Tony Pigott had only been able to establish themselves as potential test players when they no longer had to compete with Peter Kirsten and Imran Khan, respectively, in their county sides. Yet he also claims that Eddie Barlow, Mike Procter and Richard Hadlee all had 'a beneficial effect on the young English players around them'.

The last three decades of English county cricket are dotted with examples of promising players whose careers ended at a time when they were competing with an overseas player. But there are usually so many factors associated with a player's failure to make the grade that it is impossible to determine which was the major one.

One way to examine how great a part overseas cricketers play in this equation is to study a relatively short period of time. This enables other factors to be considered in detail and, where necessary, discounted. And, as the presence of overseas players is so closely associated with England's poor test record during the 1980s and 1990s, it seems appropriate to shine the spotlight on the darkest night of the soul suffered by English cricket during that period.

The seasons of 1988 and 1989 were difficult ones for English cricket. In 1988 the West Indies arrived in England and displayed some complacency in only managing to beat the home side 4–0, thereby failing to complete their third 5–0 'blackwash' in a row. The proposed winter tour to India was cancelled, because of the South African links of some of the English players. But after this pause there was to be no respite from the gloom as, in the summer of 1989, the Australians arrived to give the old country its second thrashing in two summers. English cricket was at its lowest ebb and as the inquisition began the usual suspects were rounded up.

The presence of overseas players was often cited as one of the prime causes of England's plight. Critics argued that overseas players were restricting opportunities for home-grown talent to establish itself in county sides and therefore come to the notice of the England selectors. But was this true?

In 1988, the restrictions on the number of overseas players in English county cricket introduced in the early 1980s had finally begun to take effect. Thirty-two overseas players had been employed by the counties in 1987, but a year later the number had dropped to 25. This new level was to be maintained for the next three years.

The end of the 1988 and 1989 seasons saw a total of 67 English-qualified players leave the county which had employed them during the previous 12 months. Twenty left to join other counties and a further 14 retired. But 33, half the number leaving their county, were quitting the game (for one reason or another) while still relatively young.

A pen picture of one of these 33 departees would run as follows: 25 years of age; in and out of first-class cricket since the age of 20; likely to have played more than 20 first-class games for their county and to have achieved reasonable success. Most (23 out of the 33) would either have had to compete with an overseas player of a similar kind during their last season or had one join the county in the season after they left.

Like most generalizations, this career profile can be misleading. But it does illustrate two points. The first is that young cricketers are usually given a reasonable length of time to prove themselves and the second is that the presence of overseas cricketers does pose a threat to the opportunities given to young English players.

With any cross-section of those players leaving a county at the end of a season there will always be a group of 'unknown quantities', players who had simply not played enough first-class cricket to prove conclusively either way whether they had the talent to make the top grade. For example, our group of 23 threatened by overseas players included Ian Redpath (Derbyshire), Steven Monkhouse (Glamorgan), Neil MacLaurin (Middlesex), Dean Hoffman (Northamptonshire), David Fraser-Darling (Nottinghamshire), Peter Heseltine and Julian Kimber (both Sussex), and Simon Myles (Warwickshire), all of who had played only a handful of first-class games.

Two players, Glamorgan's Philip North and Sussex's David Standing, failed to achieve any kind of track record despite being given ample opportunity. And two other players, Derbyshire's Roger Finney and Gloucestershire's David Thomas suffered recurring injuries that forced them from the game.

A further two had already had extensive county careers despite their relative youth. Alan Green, who had played for Sussex for 10 years despite being only 29, left the county in 1989 after seeing his form run down for the last two seasons and his place was only theoretically threatened by the presence of Tony Dodemaide. Likewise, 28-year-old Steve O'Shaugnessy, a highly promising all-rounder for Lancashire, found it hard to rediscover past glories for Worcestershire despite playing 10 championship matches during 1988, his first season for the southern county. Again, the theoretical argument that the presence of an overseas batsman counted against O'Shaugnessy's retention seems laughable alongside the Lancastrian's record of 18 innings and 142 runs in 1988.

However, the remaining nine players were all relatively young, fit and boasting promising track records over a reasonable period of time. It is worth examining their cases in detail.

Paul Roebuck

Roebuck, the brother of Somerset's Peter, was a Cambridge blue who played one season for Gloucestershire before arriving at Glamorgan at the age of 23. His first-class record was respectable (20 matches, 711 runs at 27.34) and he scored heavily in the county's second team during 1987. Yet, in 1988, despite Glamorgan finishing bottom of the table, Roebuck was given only two games in which he scored just 60 runs at an average of 15 per innings. The signing of Viv Richards for the following season, which in the event he missed through injury, helped close the door on Roebuck and he was released at the end of 1988.

Mark Harman

In 1988, Mark Harman had played a small but important part in Kent's county championship campaign. Picked for 10 games late in the season, he bowled his off-breaks with some skill to take 20 wickets for 26.85 and was instrumental in pushing Kent into the runners-up spot, just one point behind champions Worcestershire. It seemed that the next year, at the age of 22, he might consolidate his partnership with left-armer Richard Davis. Instead he played just one game, while the West Indian fast bowler Alleyne, the understudy for number one overseas player Roy Pienaar, appeared in five games taking just nine wickets. Tony Merrick, who joined the year after Harman left, was injured for most of the season and again only played five matches.

David Makinson

Makinson was one of the many promising all-rounders Lancashire were lucky enough to possess in the early to mid-1980s. With competition coming from Michael Atherton, who took 42 wickets in the 1990 season, Michael Watkinson, Steve O'Shaugnessy and Ian Austin, it was always likely that one of the five would leave the county. In fact, two of the group eventually left, O'Shaugnessy moving to Worcestershire and Makinson quitting the game altogether. Such was the level of competition that Makinson, after seeing his batting fall off sharply in 1986, did not play a single championship game in his last two seasons with the county. Makinson was the wrong player in the wrong place at the wrong time, but even he must have raised half an eyebrow on hearing the news that Lancashire's new overseas signing in 1988 was to be Wasim Akram, another seam bowling all-rounder, albeit a world-class one.

Jamie Sykes

Although Jamie Sykes left Middlesex at the end of the 1989 season after seven years with the county, he had not played more than a handful of matches since their championship-winning season of 1985. Even then his role as middle-order batsman and off-break bowler was not that productive, producing 149 runs from 12 innings and just 13 wickets from 176 overs. Sykes continued with the county for the next three seasons, making useful contributions to the county's one-day record, but only getting a first-class game in the case of injury and

The presence of overseas players in the 1980s has meant English cricketers having to combat the greatest concentration of fast bowling talent seen on the county circuit since Edwardian times. Leading the charge have been the high-quality fast bowlers produced by the West Indies over the last two decades. Patrick Patterson, Courtney Walsh and Malcolm Marshall (above) have kept county batsmen on the back foot since the early 1980s, and Ian Bishop (below) has proved that the next generation of Caribbean quicks are just as formidable.

The three overseas players at the centre of
Somerset's civil war: Viv Richards (far left); Joel
Garner (above); and Martin Crowe (left).

Few could have foreseen that when Clive Rice and Richard Hadlee (above) left Nottinghamshire in 1987 on another high note, their replacement overseas player, Franklyn Stephenson (below), would produce a performance worthy of his illustrious predecessors.

West Indian fast bowlers are the most sought-after overseas players, but records show that it is batsmen who have brought their counties most success. This has been particularly true over the last decade, in which players such as Graeme Hick (above) and Desmond Haynes (below) have both been members of county championship and one-day cup-winning sides.

The impressive Pakistani pace attack of the 1990s is largely a product of county cricket. Sussex veteran Imran Khan (above left) made sure that his two protégés, Wasim Akram (above right) and Waqar Younis (below left), were able to develop their prodigious talents on the county circuit. Imran had less to do with Hampshire's selection of Aquib Javed (below right), but the young bowler's experience during the 1991 season prepared Aquib perfectly for his support role to Wasim and Waqar during the following year's tour of England.

The Australians return. Alan Border (below) learnt to win at Essex, while Dean Jones (left) and Mark Waugh (bottom) grew in stature with every county attack they murdered.

A boy sent to do a man's job? Sachin Tendulkar belied his 19 years when he filled
the post of Yorkshire's first overseas player with dignity and professionalism.

emergency. When he left at the age of 24, he could look back on a county career in which it was the emergence of Tufnell, Hutchinson, Ramprakash and Rose-berry which had a greater influence on restricting his playing opportunities, rather than the presence of Wayne Daniel or Desmond Haynes.

Julian Wyatt

When Richards and Garner left Somerset in 1986, it was hoped that the county's impressive list of young hopefuls would finally get a chance to shine. Martin Crowe arrived back at Taunton and a more cohesive atmosphere held sway in the dressing room. This should have assisted in the development of young talent, but unfortunately the raw material proved to be wanting.

In 1987 Julian Wyatt, a free-scoring batsman, played in 8 championship matches and scored 250 runs at 22.72. The next year he was given a more exten-sive run, being picked for 14 games, but his 532 runs at 23.13 did not further his reputation at Somerset. In the 1989 season the arrival of Chris Tavare from Kent effectively reduced by one the number of places open to Somerset's young batsmen. Of the four under scrutiny – Wyatt, Harden, Hardy and Bartlett – it was Wyatt who had both been given enough rope and had managed to hang himself with it.

Before 1968, and the presence of players like Crowe, Steven Waugh and Jimmy Cook, Somerset would have probably persevered with Wyatt. But it is hard to see any county, at any time, giving employment to four young batsmen (who were all under-performing to some degree) for much longer than Somer-set actually did.

Nick Falkner

Unusually for the nine county outcasts, Nick Falkner tasted real success for at least one season. Playing for Surrey in 1986, he played 11 games, scored 567 runs, including a century against Middlesex, and finished third in the county averages as Surrey took third place. Unfortunately for Falkner the return of David Smith, and the development of Darren Bicknell, restricted his opportunities and in 1987 when they came in three championship matches, he could not grasp them, scoring only 47 runs in 4 innings. The following season Falkner moved to Sussex, and was given reasonable exposure in championship matches. Again he disappointed, managing only a single 50 in 14 innings, and in 1989 the young batsman was given only 2 games in which he scored 10, 17 and 1. Falkner had rested on his laurels too long, although it seems a pity that Sussex should have continued to employ Tony Dodemaide throughout this period when they had a number of promising young batsmen and badly needed a penetrative pace bowler.

Alastair Storie, David Banks and David Thorne

The remaining three players on the list all played for Warwickshire, and the story of their departure from the game and the influence on that move by over-seas players is far from straightforward. The three players, all batsmen, are

Alastair Storie, who left at the end of the 1988 season, and David Banks and David Thorne, who both left in 1989.

Storie was one of a long list of impressive young batsmen that Northampton-shire produced during the 1980s. He made his debut in 1985 against Hampshire by scoring 106 and finished the season on top of the county averages with 407 runs at 40.70. As usual, success during his second season proved much harder to achieve and 6 games brought him just 152 runs. Released, with what seems like undue haste, by Northampton, he joined Warwickshire in 1987. He became an automatic member of the first team and played in 15 championship games, but he achieved little and passed 50 only once. He found that 1988 was another year of slipping back and, after playing just eight games, he was dropped from the side for good.

David Banks's story is similar to that of Storie, although it takes place over a slightly longer time span. Banks made his first-class debut for Worcestershire in 1983 and scored a century in the traditional fixtures opener against Oxford University. At the end of the season he had played 6 more matches and scored 363 runs at 30.25. The next two seasons with Worcestershire saw Banks restricted to just 10 championship games in which he scored only 203 runs. The honeymoon was over and he left the county to play minor counties cricket for Staffordshire. Three seasons later he was signed up by Warwickshire and took part in the disaster that was Warwickshire's batting performance in the summer of 1988, during which Gladstone Small was the county's fourth most successful batsman. Six games brought just 134 runs for Banks and 1989 saw his playing opportunities restricted to 2 games in which he scored 0, 0 and 10.

Of the nine players assessed over the last few pages, David Thorne has by far the most extensive first-class career. He made his debut for Warwickshire at the age of 18 in the year before he went up to study at Oxford University. When he left the county at the end of the 1989 season, he had played in 69 first-class matches.

That Thorne had talent was obvious from the start. In 1984 he was the uni-versity's leading bowler with his left-arm medium pace and his batting was con-sistent if not hugely impressive. In 1985 he became the university's leading batsman, playing in all of the team's 11 games and scoring 849 runs at 56.60, with a century and 8 50s. He also finished high up in the national averages, announcing himself to the cricketing world. The year of 1986 probably saw the peak of Thorne's career. Appointed captain of the university team, he again dominated the batting, hitting 334 runs at 41.75. In the university match he waged a virtual one-man war against a much stronger Cambridge side. He scored 61 and an undefeated 104, as well as bowling 40 overs and taking 3 wick-ets, as his side lost by 5 wickets.

The big question was whether Thorne could translate his university success into consistent performances on the county circuit. The evidence of the 1987 season was a resounding 'no'. Thorne played in 9 championship games and fin-ished with the horrifying figures of 116 runs at 8.92. However, in 1988, Thorne appeared to be on the way back. He played in 14 games and scored 561 runs with 4 half centuries, finishing fifth in the averages. But in 1989 it seemed to fall apart again and 4 matches brought just 91 runs.

During the two seasons under investigation Tony Merrick and Alan Donald were Warwickshire's main overseas players. However, the county had another famous 'foreign recruit', Alvin Kallicharran, who also played regularly for the county. Set out below is Kallicharran's record over the two seasons, compared to those of the three county outcasts, whose career records appear in brackets.

	M	I	NO	HS	Runs	Av.	100
A.I. Kallicharran	24	40	2	119	911	23.98	2
A.C. Storie	8	16	2	68	233	16.64	0
	(45	75	12	106	1,350	21.42	1)
D.A. Banks	8	11	1	47	144	14.40	0
	(30	45	7	100	1,034	27.21	1)
D.A. Thorne	18	32	1	76	652	21.03	0
	(69	113	15	124	2,523	25.74	2)

During the 1988 and 1989 season Kallicharran was considered as 'English qualified' and it was hard to see him ever playing again for the West Indies given his involvement in the rebel tours of South Africa. However, Kallicharran was also never likely to play for England and considering that his performances over the two seasons in question were only marginally better than our three outcasts, his retention does seem somewhat short-sighted. This, of course, is slightly unfair to Warwickshire, in that Kallicharran had given sterling service to Warwickshire for nearly two decades and was therefore due some loyalty.

It could also be argued that the three English batsmen in question had all been given ample opportunity to make the grade and that Warwickshire could hardly be expected to continue to employ all of them. Certainly Banks, who was 28 at the time of his dismissal and had the least impressive track record, must have known that he had little chance of being retained. However, Storie and particularly Thorne had shown themselves capable of competing as first-class cricketers and were only aged 23 and 24 respectively at the time of their departure from the game.

Conclusion

Of these nine young English cricketers who left the game between September 1988 and September 1989, the presence of overseas players seems to have played an unquestionable part in the departure of just three, possibly six. Makinson, Sykes and Banks were either forced out by a preponderance of more talented English players or simply did not have the talent to compete at the highest level. Roebuck, Wyatt and Falkner may have all heaved a sigh of frustration at the selection policy of their former employers, but the choice of overseas player cannot be said to have been the biggest factor in their leaving first-class cricket.

It appears, however, that Harman, Storie and Thorne have a legitimate complaint with their former counties. Each one had his playing opportunities severely restricted by the presence of an overseas player who was not performing at a level that they, given the opportunity, could have matched. At Edgbaston and Canterbury insult was added to injury when the overseas players were retained after the English players were released and they still continued to under-perform. In the season after Storie and Thorne left Warwickshire, Kallicharran played 5 games scoring just 175 runs. In the same season Kent fielded a West Indian fast bowler, Tony Merrick, who broke down after 5 games and took just 13 wickets.

A piece of pure speculation

So, in the final analysis, what do we have? Out of a total of 33 players who left county cricket at the end of the 1988 and 1989 seasons, overseas players can be said to have played a part in the departure of 3, possibly 6 and perhaps even 14, if all those who played less than 20 games are included.

Extrapolating this analysis out across the 25 years since the introduction of immediate registration it is possible to make an estimate that overseas players have played a part in ending the careers of between 50 and 150 English players since 1968. As around one in 10 players who enter first-class cricket will at one time in their career be considered for international honours, the presence of overseas cricketers could have deprived England of at least 5 test hopefuls, possibly 15 if the theoretical influence of overseas players is widened to its greatest. Since England have selected just over 100 new test debutantes from 1968 to 1992, the influence of overseas players could be said to have reduced the choice open to England selectors by 5 per cent to 15 per cent.

The more these, already haphazard, figures are extrapolated the less reliable they get, but it is worth following through the analysis to its logical conclusion.

If we take a median of ten potential test players denied their chance by overseas players and speculate that half that number would have both been picked by England and made a success of their international careers, then it is not unreasonable to suggest that England's performance might have improved by 5 per cent over the 25-year period in line with the extra resources available to the test team. England have played 51 test series during the period 1968–92, including single match rubbers, and they have lost 24, won 24 and had 9 draws. A 5 per cent improvement would have turned one of the losses into a draw and one of the draws into a victory.

The timebomb effect

The consequences of restricted playing opportunities for young English players takes some time to feed through to international level. It is unlikely that a young English player deprived of a place in his first season of county cricket would have had any influence on the international scene for a number of years. Therefore, the presence of overseas players in English cricket is somewhat akin to a timebomb, exploding some time after its mechanism has been activated.

Most successful test cricketers of modern times usually play around three seasons of first-class cricket before making their mark on the international scene. Their international careers, given the demands of modern test and one-day cricket, usually last around ten years. If we take these two factors and relate them to the number of overseas cricketers playing in English cricket year by year, the influence of foreign recruits on the resources available to the English selectors might look something like the diagram overleaf.

So, if this analysis is right, although it was the late 1970s which saw the greatest number of overseas players in English county cricket, it was not until the mid to late 1980s that the opportunities they had denied to young players began to make a difference to the English test team.

A glimpse at England's performances at test level adds weight to this argument. In the season following the introduction of immediate registration, England drew two series against Australia (at home) and against Pakistan (away). These two rubbers were followed by five straight series wins, as England (in the absence of South Africa) became for the last time to date the best test side in the world. A losing series against India in 1971 heralded a period lasting around seven years in which heavy defeats (by Lillee and Thomson, and the 1976 West Indies) were counterbalanced by wins over the lesser test nations.

From the start of the 1977 series against Australia, England entered its second and last winning streak of modern times. Often, it must be admitted, against Packer-weakened sides, England won five series and drew two. This phoney war was shattered by the West Indies in 1980 when, in two back-to-back series, the Caribbean side beat England four times and usually had the better of the six draws. For the next few years, the status quo returned with England usually dispatching India and New Zealand with some ease (in England at least), and enjoying some good tussles with Australia and Pakistan.

At the end of the English season of 1983, England occupied much the same position it did in the late 1960s. Despite the South African defections, England was thought to have a solid enough side. It wasn't a match for the best of its opponents (Clive Lloyd's West Indians), but it would give Australia a fight for its money and look to achieve respectable draws away from home, while thrashing the weaker test sides during an English test summer. Despite 15 years of overseas players English test cricket appeared (without the benefit of hindsight) to be no worse off than in 1968, and had actually won 19 more tests than it had lost during the period. The balance was still in the black.

But not for much longer. The second half of the 1980s was the most disastrous period in English test cricket history. While the UK economy boomed, the stock of English test cricket crashed to an all-time low.

Influence of overseas players on the supply of talent to the English test team 1970-94

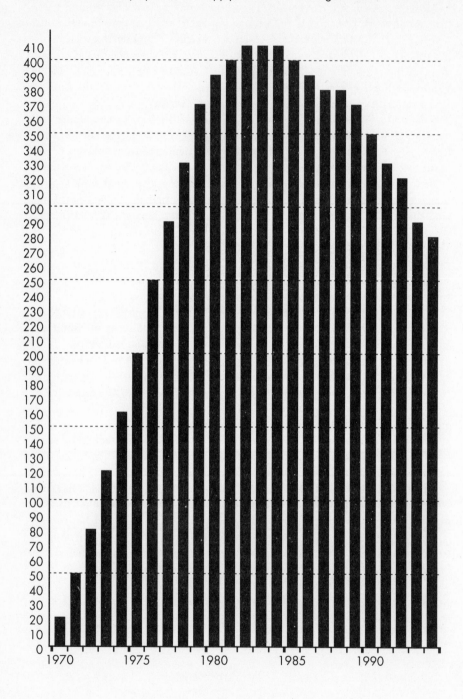

Table Key
The vertical index measures the influence of overseas players. It is calculated by counting the number of overseas players who took part in each English season between 1968 and 1992, and then extrapolating that influence out over the next 12 years – using 2 years to take account of the fact that most promising young English players do not come to the attention of the test selectors until they are into their third season of county cricket, and a further 10 to take account of the average length of an international career.

As the years progress, the influence exerted by overseas players during one season is added to by the number of foreign players employed in the following seasons. Therefore, since there were 24 overseas players employed by English counties in 1968, 29 in 1969 and 31 in 1970, the level of influence grows as follows: 1970 = 24; 1971 = 24 + 29 = 53; 1972 = 24 + 29 + 31 = 84; and so on. The 1968 figure of 24 is removed from the equation in 1980 because any English player of the late 1960s is likely to have ended his test career by this date.

England's test record, 1983/4 to 1989

1983/4	Lost 1–0 away to New Zealand
1983/4	Lost 1–0 away to Pakistan
1984	Lost 5–0 at home to the West Indies
1984	Drew with Sri Lanka in sole test
1984/5	Won 2–1 away against India
1985	Won 3–1 at home against Australia
1985/6	Lost 5–0 away to the West Indies
1986	Lost 2–0 at home to India
1986	Lost 1–0 at home to New Zealand
1986/7	Won 2–1 away against Australia
1987	Lost 1–0 at home to Pakistan
1987/8	Lost 1–0 away to Pakistan
1987/8	Drew with Australia in sole test
1987/8	Drew 0–0 away against New Zealand
1988	Lost 4–0 at home to the West Indies
1988	Beat Sri Lanka in sole test
1989	Lost 4–0 at home to Australia

Opponents	P	W	L	D
West Indies	15	0	14	1
Australia	18	5	6	7
Pakistan	11	0	3	8
India	8	2	3	3
New Zealand	9	0	2	7
Sri Lanka	2	1	0	1
Total	**63**	**8**	**28**	**27**

By the time Allan Border's triumphant Australians set sail for home at the end of the 1989 season, the balance of victories against defeats since 1968 had sunk into the red for the first time.

As early as 1981 the alarm bells were beginning to ring around the county circuit. The Test and County Cricket Board (TCCB) took the highly unusual step of issuing an official request that the counties appoint English-qualified captains so as to ensure that candidates for the leadership of the national side would have some relevant experience. The request was completely ignored, with Gloucestershire and Nottinghamshire confirming that Mike Procter and Clive Rice would continue to captain their respective county sides. Three counties actually replaced English-qualified captains with overseas players Clive Lloyd taking over at Lancashire, Asif Iqbal at Kent and Glenn Turner at Worcestershire. The English alternatives that the TCCB might have wished the county to choose instead included Gloucestershire's David Graveney (who ended up leading the county for much of the season after Procter was injured), Kent's Chris Cowdrey and Chris Tavare, and Worcestershire's Phil Neale.

Although, on the face of it, the attitude of the counties was a snub to the authority of the TCCB, the decision to appoint overseas players as captain was more a reaction to the demands placed on their leading English-qualified players by a crowded international schedule.

Ever since the introduction of one-day internationals and the prevalence of six test summers, the counties have become more and more reluctant to appoint their leading English-qualified players as captain. The prospect of their county captain missing around half the season through international calls, and the constant chopping and changing that would require, has led many counties to shy away from the idea. Overseas players, on the other hand, often have considerable experience of captaincy and are also available for the whole season.

In recent times only Essex and Middlesex have been able to develop an effective system of working around a captain who was also an England regular. And even these two teams have experienced seasons in which the strain between the needs of test and domestic cricket has begun to tell, usually to the detriment of both the national and county side.

In 1982 the county players, who had been strongly in favour of immediate registration during the late 1960s, began to change their tune as they saw their playing opportunities sharply restricted. As part of a poll conducted by *The Cricketer*, players were asked their views on overseas players. Sixty-seven per cent said each county should only be allowed to field one overseas player, but significantly 39 per cent wanted the employment of 'non English-qualified players' to cease once existing contracts had run out. This represented a dramatic swing in opinion from the enthusiasm displayed during the late 1960s.

A year later former Australian captain Bill Lawry was adding his weight to the growing concern over overseas players. Writing in the Melbourne *Sunday Observer* he claimed: 'English cricket is dying and may take decades to recover unless overseas internationals are immediately banned from county ranks. England must wake up before it's too late. A mediocre English test team will denigrate all test cricket. Australia must learn from their mistakes.'

By 1984, with the influence of overseas players at its peak, the issue was enshrined along with limited-overs matches as one of the prime evils of the English game. Writing in December 1984 *Guardian* cricket correspondent Matthew Engel set out a list of reasons why 'England after 13 test matches this year, have failed to win any of them'. Numbers three and four on his list are particularly relevant to this book:

3 The improvement of standards elsewhere in the world, helped by English professional coaching, the opportunities provided to foreign players by the English counties, better facilities (in most cases), a more competitive atmosphere and a more favourable climate.

4 The weakness of the mid-1970s intake into English counties, and the consequent absence of players who should now be at their peak.

Engel adds: 'The next generation should be better, partly due to Packerism (more money in cricket) and Thatcherism (fewer alternatives).' He might have added, 'and fewer overseas players restricting playing opportunities.'

As the rule changes of 1979 began to bite towards the end of the 1980s, sharply reducing the number of overseas players on the county circuit, the concern over their adverse influence began to slacken.

The English players on the county circuit certainly seemed satisfied with the presence of overseas cricketers. Another survey conducted by *The Cricketer* in 1989 showed that the percentage of those wanting overseas players banned had reduced from 39 per cent to 17 per cent. Eighty per cent of those surveyed claimed that one overseas player per county was the correct limit.

And, for a moment at least, the media pundits ceased their railing against the presence of overseas players as Graham Gooch led England back towards some sort of international respectability, if only temporarily.

The influence of overseas players should continue to decline for a number of years as an increasing number of promising young English players come through without having to battle for places with two or three foreign recruits. Nevertheless it will not be until early in the twenty-first century that the 'influence index' finally hits its lowest possible point obtainable under the present regulations. At that time the influence of overseas players on English national cricket should be at around half the level of what it was in 1983/4.

The generation gap

But is the huge influence that overseas players exerted on playing opportunities in the late 1970s and early 1980s a red herring? Could it be that the reason behind England's poor performance at test level during the 1980s was not that the national side was suffering from a lack of new talent, but that the established players (who had done their county apprenticeship in the early to mid 1970s) were simply not good enough?

An analysis of the test records of those cricketers making their debut during the mid to late 1980s seems to suggest fears over the paucity of young talent in county cricket was anything but a false alarm.

Playing records* of test débutants 1983/4–1989

	Matches	Runs	Av.	Wkts	Av.
A.C.S. Pigott	1	12	12.00	2	37.50
T.A. Lloyd	1	10	–	–	–
B.C. Broad	25	1,661	39.54	–	–
V.P. Terry	2	16	5.33	–	–
J.P. Agnew	3	10	10.00	4	93.25
R.T. Robinson	29	1,601	36.38	–	–
R.M. Ellison	11	202	13.46	35	29.94
C.S. Cowdrey	6	101	14.42	4	77.25
A. Sidebottom	1	2	2.00	1	65.00
L.B. Taylor	2	1	–	4	44.50
D.M. Smith	2	80	20.00	–	–
J.G. Thomas	5	83	13.83	10	50.40
W.N. Slack	3	81	13.50	–	–
B.N. French	16	308	18.11	–	–
M.R. Benson	1	51	25.50	–	–
N.V. Radford	3	21	7.00	4	88.75
M.D. Moxon	10	455	28.43	–	–
G.C. Small	17	263	15.47	55	34.01
P.A.J. De Freitas	31	527	12.54	93	32.44
C.J. Richards	8	285	21.92	–	–
J.J. Whitaker	1	11	11.00	–	–
N.H. Fairbrother	7	64	8.00	–	–
D.J. Capel	15	374	15.58	21	50.66
P.W. Jarvis	6	109	15.57	14	50.57
J.H. Childs	2	2	–	3	61.00
T.S. Curtis	5	140	15.55	–	–
R.A. Smith	36	2,645	50.86	–	–
R.J. Bailey	4	119	14.87	–	–
M.P. Maynard	1	26	13.00	–	–
K.J. Barnett	4	207	29.57	–	–
R.C. Russell	31	1,060	27.17	–	–
P.J. Newport	3	110	27.50	10	41.70
D.V. Lawrence	5	60	10.00	18	37.55
A.R.C. Fraser	11	88	6.76	47	26.70
M.A. Atherton	21	1,311	34.50	–	–
D.E. Malcolm	21	105	5.00	74	36.12
A.P. Igglesden	1	2	–	3	48.67

*Until the end of the 1992 English season

In the 6-year period between the close of the 1983 and the 1989 seasons, England blooded 36 new test players, an average of 6 a year. Of these players only Robin Smith (who was a South African and had entered English cricket as an overseas player) and Jack Russell (who as a wicket-keeper faced no competition from overseas players) managed to establish a regular place in the national side. Of the rest, Broad, Robinson, Ellison, French, Moxon, Small, De Freitas, Richards, Fraser, Atherton and Malcolm all had their moments of glory without answering all the questions over their ability at international level. This, however, still leaves 23 cricketers, two-thirds of the new intake, who made little or no impact on the international scene at all.

But what of the other side to our original question – could it be that the older players, those who broke into international cricket before overseas players established such a complete dominance over the English domestic game, were the problem?

The answer seems to be no. The impression that the stream of potential English test players almost dried up during the mid-1980s is reinforced by how England's leading test players of the late 1970s continued to dominate England's test team for much longer than would usually have been expected. Although their performances were often well below what might be expected from England's leading players, series after series showed the country's established test team unchallenged by younger players.

Analysing these averages displays just how unsuccessful England was in finding new talent during this period, especially among batsmen.

Six players stand out as the country's leading players of the mid-1980s; three batsmen and three bowlers. Of the batsmen, Gower did well in 9 of the 14 test series under consideration, Gatting 6 and Gooch 5, but no other batsman forced himself to the top of the averages in more than three series. Of these players, Lamb would certainly have made his test debut in the 1970s if it had not been for the fact that he was South African and had to serve a lengthy residential qualification period. Only the Nottinghamshire opening pair of Robinson and Broad can be considered selectorial successes of the mid-1980s (although Robin Smith, another South African, who made his debut at the end of the decade was to achieve great things during the 1990s).

In the bowling department England fared better, but only just. Of 3 leading bowlers, the most successful was Foster who made his debut in 1983 and found a place among the top 3 bowlers in half of the 14 series. But Dilley, who did well in six rubbers, and Edmonds, who achieved some sort of glory in five, both made their first appearances for England in the mid to late 1970s. Of the second-rank bowlers, those who made the grade in three series, only Cowans was a product of the 1980s. The other two, Botham and Emburey, already had at least five years' England experience behind them before the 1983/4 series against New Zealand.

The average age of England's leading performers during this period also hints at the lack of younger talent forcing its way into the test side. During this 5½-year period, the average age of England's most successful test cricketers was

Series averages 1983/4–1989 (top three batsmen and bowlers)

vs. New Zealand 1983/4

	Matches	Runs	Average	Age	Test début
C.L. Smith	2	148	74.00	25	1983
D.W. Randall	3	293	73.25	32	1976
I.T. Botham	3	226	56.50	28	1977
		Wkts			
R.G.D. Willis	3	12	25.50	34	1970
N.G. Cowans	2	5	30.80	22	1982
I.T. Botham	3	7	50.57	28	1977

vs. Pakistan 1983/4

	Matches	Runs	Average	Age	Test début
D.I. Gower	3	449	112.25	26	1978
G. Fowler	2	134	44.66	26	1982
V.J. Marks	3	218	43.60	28	1982
		Wkts			
N.G. Cowans	2	7	25.00	22	1982
N.G.B. Cook	3	14	31.71	27	1983
N.A. Foster	2	7	32.85	21	1983

vs. West Indies 1984

	Matches	Runs	Average	Age	Test début
A.J. Lamb	5	386	42.88	30	1982
I.T. Botham	5	347	34.70	28	1977
G. Fowler	5	260	26.00	27	1982
		Wkts			
P.J.W. Allott	3	14	20.14	27	1981
I.T. Botham	5	19	35.10	28	1977
D.R. Pringle	3	5	51.40	25	1982

vs. India 1984/5

	Matches	Runs	Average	Age	Test début
M.W. Gatting	5	575	95.83	27	1977
R. Robinson	5	444	63.42	26	1984
G. Fowler	5	438	54.75	27	1982
		Wkts			
N.A. Foster	2	14	20.42	22	1983
P. Edmonds	5	14	41.71	33	1975
N.G. Cowans	5	14	44.78	23	1982

vs. Australia 1985

	Matches	Runs	Average	Age	Test début
M.W. Gatting	6	527	87.33	28	1977
D.I. Gower	6	732	81.33	28	1978
R. Robinson	6	490	61.25	26	1984

vs. Australia 1985 continued

		Wkts			
R.M. Ellison	2	17	10.88	24	1984
I.T. Botham	6	31	27.58	29	1977
J.E. Emburey	6	19	28.63	33	1978

vs. West Indies 1985/6

	Matches	Runs	Average	Age	Test début
D.I. Gower	5	370	37.00	28	1978
G.A. Gooch	5	276	27.60	32	1975
A.J. Lamb	5	224	22.40	31	1982
		Wkts			
J.E. Emburey	4	14	32.00	33	1978
N.A. Foster	3	7	40.71	23	1983
R.M. Ellison	3	7	42.00	25	1984

vs. India 1986

	Matches	Runs	Average	Age	Test début
M.W. Gatting	3	293	73.25	29	1977
G.A. Gooch	3	175	29.16	33	1975
D.I. Gower	2	101	25.25	29	1978
		Wkts			
D.R. Pringle	3	13	23.23	27	1982
P. Edmonds	2	7	25.42	35	1975
G.R. Dilley	2	10	29.90	27	1979

vs. New Zealand 1986

	Matches	Runs	Average	Age	Test début
D.I. Gower	3	293	58.60	29	1978
G.A. Gooch	3	268	53.60	33	1975
M.W. Gatting	3	170	34.00	29	1977
		Wkts			
G.R. Dilley	2	9	19.88	27	1979
P. Edmonds	3	8	26.50	35	1975
G.C. Small	2	4	33.50	24	1986

vs. Australia 1986/7

	Matches	Runs	Average	Age	Test début
B.C. Broad	5	487	69.57	29	1984
D.I. Gower	5	404	57.71	29	1978
M.W. Gatting	5	393	43.66	29	1977
		Wkts			
G.C. Small	2	12	15.00	25	1986
G.R. Dilley	4	16	31.93	27	1979
P. Edmonds	5	15	35.86	36	1975

vs. Pakistan 1987

	Matches	Runs	Average	Age	Test début
M.W. Gatting	5	445	63.57	30	1977
R. Robinson	5	299	37.37	28	1984
C.W.J. Athey	4	186	37.20	29	1980
		Wkts			
N.A. Foster	5	15	22.60	25	1983
G.R. Dilley	4	14	27.71	28	1979
P. Edmonds	5	4	54.75	36	1975

vs. Pakistan 1987/8

	Matches	Runs	Average	Age	Test début
J.E. Emburey	3	207	69.00	35	1978
G.A. Gooch	3	225	37.50	34	1975
B.C. Broad	3	204	34.00	30	1984
		Wkts			
N.A. Foster	2	6	17.33	25	1983
N.G.B. Cook	3	7	27.85	31	1983
P. De Freitas	2	6	28.33	21	1986

vs. New Zealand 1987/8

	Matches	Runs	Average	Age	Test début
M.D. Moxon	3	208	69.33	27	1986
B.C. Broad	3	204	51.00	30	1984
J.E. Emburey	3	106	35.33	35	1978
		Wkts			
G.R. Dilley	3	15	14.00	28	1979
P.W. Jarvis	2	6	33.50	22	1987
P. De Freitas	2	4	43.75	22	1986

vs. West Indies 1988

	Matches	Runs	Average	Age	Test début
G.A. Gooch	5	459	45.90	35	1975
A.J. Lamb	4	254	42.33	34	1982
D.I. Gower	4	211	30.14	31	1978
		Wkts			
G.R. Dilley	4	15	26.86	29	1979
N.A. Foster	2	9	27.77	26	1983
D.R. Pringle	4	11	29.63	29	1982

vs. Australia 1989

	Matches	Runs	Average	Age	Test début
R.A. Smith	5	553	61.44	24	1988
R.C. Russell	6	314	39.25	26	1988
D.I. Gower	6	383	34.81	32	1978

vs. Australia 1989 continued

		Wkts			
N.A. Foster	3	12	35.08	27	1983
A.R.C. Fraser	3	9	35.88	24	1989
J.E. Emburey	3	8	42.75	37	1978

28.4 years. As would be expected, the average was higher among batsman (29.3), than it was among bowlers (27.4).

The relatively aged appearance of England's test team during this period would have been even more accentuated if cricketers such as Gooch, Boycott, Willey, Knott, Old, Emburey, Underwood and Lever had not been banned for taking part in the rebel tour of South Africa. With these players prevented from playing for England, the average age of England's leading test performers during the period between the 1983/4 series against New Zealand and the 1984/5 rubber against India was just under 27 years. In the remaining ten series up to the Australian tour of 1989, the average rose to 29 years.

From this great weight of evidence it is clear that England lost to everyone and anyone because the steady flow of talent that the county circuit had provided in the past had slowed to a trickle. And this slump in the lifeblood of English national cricket coincided, almost exactly, with the period at which the influence of overseas players was at its strongest. By the time the counties decided to restrict the number of overseas players allowed in the domestic competitions, the damage had already been done and, having sown the whirlwind, English cricket was about to reap the West Indian hurricane.

Home and away

Another way of testing the theory of how the influx of overseas cricketers has weakened England's position as a test-playing nation is to examine the side's comparative performance in home and away test series.

Playing in county cricket can be said to have three major advantages for overseas players. First, it improves their general playing ability by giving them the chance to compete with and against cricketers of a high standard six or seven days a week, secondly it allows them to get to know the weaknesses of test opponents, especially those from England, and finally it allows them the chance to master the sharply varying playing conditions that are only found in England.

The first two advantages would improve the chances of an overseas test team beating England wherever the match was played, but the third is only an advantage during a test series in England. This being the case, it is reasonable to suppose that England's test performances will have declined more sharply at home than during away series. It should also be the case that the overseas test players who perform the best against England in England will have had county championship experience.

If we take England's test performances between the end of World War 2 and the start of the 1968 English season as a benchmark, we can see that the test side performed much better on average at home than overseas. During this period England played 106 test matches at home and 95 overseas. Of these matches England won 36 per cent, drew 37 per cent and lost 27 per cent. But if the home and overseas series are examined separately, a clear split emerges. At home England won 45 per cent of their test matches, drew 34 per cent and lost only 21 per cent. Overseas the performance was much less praiseworthy, England winning only 25 per cent of its matches, losing nearly as many (24 per cent) and drawing just over half.

The ten year-period that followed the introduction of immediate registration showed a clear change in England's test fortunes, but a change nevertheless that was largely restricted to home series. Between the 1968 season and the 1977/8 series against New Zealand, England played 92 test matches, winning 29 per cent, losing 24 per cent and drawing 47 per cent. There had been a clear decline in the level of the test side's performance, with England winning 7 per cent fewer matches and drawing 10 per cent more (though in fairness it should be pointed out that defeats also fell by 3 per cent). However, there was no discernible change in England's performance level overseas, and the percentages of wins, draws and losses were almost exactly the same as during the immediate post-war period. Where things had changed were at home. In England victories had fallen by 12 per cent, defeats risen by 4 per cent and draws by 8 per cent.

The next ten years saw a further decline in England's fortunes with the percentage of victories holding up, but the number of defeats rising 6 per cent at the expense of drawn matches. Although England actually lost more matches than they won in this period, at least there was an increase in definite results. But any pleasure English cricket lovers may have drawn from this would have been tempered by a concern over a fall in overseas results, hot on the heels of the decline in performance at home in the previous ten-year period. As with the comparison of test performances overseas during the previous two periods, the percentages of wins, draws and defeats remained the same during the home series. Overseas, though, the picture was different with victories remaining at 25 per cent, but defeats ballooning to 35 per cent, a 12 per cent increase.

In the five years remaining between the West Indian test series of 1988 and the Pakistani triumph of 1992, England's test performances declined across the board. Of the 45 test matches played during the period only 22 per cent were won (a fall of 8 per cent on the previous period) and 38 per cent were lost (an increase of 7 per cent). The decline was obvious during both overseas and home series. Victories at home declined 9 per cent and defeats rose 16 per cent. Overseas England won 6 per cent fewer tests, but also lost 4 per cent fewer.

Two straightforward comparisons confirm the impression given by the detailed figures that England's test performances have declined more sharply at home than overseas during the last 25 years. First we need to look at the contrast between England's performances before and after the introduction of immediate registration for overseas players.

	1946 to 1967/8	1968–92	Change
Home wins	45%	31%	–14
Home defeats	21%	29%	+8
Overseas wins	25%	24%	–1
Overseas defeats	24%	30%	+6
Balance between wins and defeats			
Home	+14%	+2%	–12
Overseas	+1%	–6%	–7

The second telling comparison is between the balance of wins and defeats over the four distinct periods under review.

	1946–67	1968–77	1978–87	1988–92
Home	+14%	+8%	+8%	–16%
Overseas	+1%	+2%	–10%	–12%

The trend is there for all to see. At home the balance between wins and defeats has fallen by a much greater degree than the comparative results recorded overseas.

At an individual level the advantage of coming to terms with English conditions is clear. In the ten seasons between England's tour of Australia in 1982/3 and the series in Pakistan during 1992, overseas county players have performed significantly better in the UK than they have against England in their home countries.

A series by series breakdown, identifying the two leading overseas batsmen and bowlers in each rubber, shows just how clear the distinction is.

Top two players in batting averages against England in England, 1982/3–1992

NZ	WI	Australia	India	Pakistan
Hadlee*	Greenidge*	Border	Vengsarkar	Miandad × 2*
Edgar	Gomes*	Ritchie	More	Yosuf
M.Crowe*	Logie	S. Waugh*	Azharuddin	Salim Malik*
Bracewell	Dujon	Taylor	Shastri*	–
Franklin	Richards*	–	–	–
Wright*	Richardson	–	–	–

* = County player

Top two players in batting averages against England overseas, 1982/3–1992

NZ	WI	Australia	India	Pakistan
Smith	Haynes × 2**	Hughes	Azharuddin	Salim Malik × 2
Coney	Richards*	Hookes	Kirmani	Zaheer Abbas*
Greatbatch	Best	Jones	–	Aamer Malik
Wright × 2	–	Border*	–	–
M. Crowe*	–	Boon	–	–
–	–	Matthews	–	–

* = county players   ** = topped averages in one series before becoming county player

During this period England played 12 home series and 11 overseas rubbers. In England 11 (46 per cent) of the 2 most successful batsmen on each of the opposing sides had played in county cricket. But on overseas tours this number dropped to just 7 (32 per cent).

Top two players in bowling averages against England in England, 1982/3–1992

NZ	WI	Australia	India	Pakistan
Hadlee × 3*	Marshall × 3*	McDermott	Singh	Imran Khan*
L. Cairns	Garner*	Lawson × 2	Sharma	Wasim Akram × 2**
Bracewell × 2	W. Benjamin*	Alderman*	Kapil Dev*	Waqar Younis*
–	Ambrose*	–	Hirwani	–

* = county player
** = topped averages in one series before becoming county player

Top two players in bowling averages against England overseas, 1982/3–1992

NZ	WI	Australia	India	Pakistan
Hadlee*	Garner*	Thomson	Sivaramakrishnan	Qadir × 2
Boock	Marshall*	Lawson	Yadav	Sarfraz Nawaz*
Chatfield	Ambrose*	Reid × 2	–	Iqbal Qasim
Morrison	Bishop*	Sleep	–	–
Su'a	–	McDermott	–	–
Patel*	–	–	–	–

* = county player

In this comparison the difference between home series and overseas tours is even more stark. Out of the top 24 overseas performers in England, 14 (58 per cent) had already played county cricket. Abroad, however, the ratio is just 6 out of 22 or 27 per cent.

A comparative failure

Yet another way of plotting the impact of overseas players on the performance of the English national team is to examine its comparative record against each test side. Of the test sides playing since 1968, the West Indies have contributed the most overseas players, followed by Australia, Pakistan, India and lastly New Zealand. This being the case it would be reasonable to expect England's record to decline most sharply against the West Indies and least against New Zealand. The truth is slightly more complicated.

**Percentage difference between test victories and defeats,
England 1968–92**

	1946–67	1968–77	1978–92	1968–92	Change between 1946–67 and 1968–92
Pakistan	+46	+7	–4	0	–46
West Indies	–8	–19	–56	–44	–36
India	+33	+19	0	+7	–26
New Zealand	+61	+46	+27	+48	–13
Australia	–22	–6	+2	–1	+21

The expected decline against the West Indies is clearly shown accelerating throughout the last two and a half decades, while England's performance against New Zealand, although getting weaker, still puts the 'old country' on top. Where things do not seem to fit is with England's test record against Pakistan and, particularly against Australia.

In both cases the causes of these anomalies are not difficult to discover. Both Pakistan and Australia saw a dramatic change in the strength of their test teams during the last 25 years. Pakistan began to play test cricket in the mid-1950s in the years following partition. For some time the country struggled to establish itself as a modern nation and luxuries such as playing cricket for your county went by the board. As things stabilized, English county cricket played an important part in transforming the talented but inconsistent leading Pakistani players into hardened competitors at test level.

Australia, too, owed their change in fortunes to the relative strength of their pre and post-1968 teams, although this time it was a relative decline in strength which occurred. The Australian test team of the late 1940s and early 1950s was a great one by any measure, but its record against England was considerably aided by the fact that the UK was still recovering from the after-effects of World War 2 and had to endure rationing (and therefore a poor standard of national health) for many years after the cessation of hostilities. As with Pakistan and England, the better standard of living enhanced Australia's performance in the immediate post-war period.

When immediate registration was introduced in 1968, Australian players did not flock to the UK. They rightly concluded that there was little the English game could teach them which their own well-established and highly competitive domestic cricket season could not. Therefore, unlike the other four test-playing nations, the overseas player explosion did not aid Australia.

In the late 1970s the Packer revolution seriously weakened the national side and the 1985 touring team lacked a number of players who had signed up for a rebel tour of South Africa. It was the combination of these three factors – the great strength of the Australian team post-war, the relative lack of impact of overseas playing opportunities and the reduction in resources during the late

1970s and 1980s – that produced the sharp decline in Australia's performances against England.

Australia's fate also demonstrates both how playing county cricket does not necessarily improve players who already have a superior domestic competition of their own and that the performance of the test nations must be viewed against both the relative strength of the opposition and its own playing resources.

The statistical evidence assembled in the previous two chapters clearly indicates that the introduction of immediate registration and the resulting flood of overseas playing talent has had a significant impact on both English county cricket and the balance of power among the test-playing nations. But, as always, statistics only ever tell part of the story. There are areas of the game, both at domestic and international level, over which overseas players can exert considerable influence. Over the next two chapters these issues are considered, starting with an episode which encapsulates all the drama and controversy associated with the arrival of overseas players in English county cricket.

6 Somerset's Greek tragedy

If Vic Marks and Peter Roebuck were the brains of Somerset's impressive late 1970s and early 1980s team, and Ian Botham was the sinew, then Viv Richards was the heart. Never before had English cricket known an overseas player with such a burning ambition to elevate not only himself but his Cinderella of an adopted club to new heights. Richards gave Somerset the unforgiving pride which it needed to win its first ever trophies, and during the late 1970s he felt victory and defeat as keenly as any of Somerset's English players. Yet in 1986 Richards and his fellow West Indian Joel Garner were summarily dismissed from Somerset for reasons which amounted to accusations of 'not trying' and 'being a disruptive influence'.

The story of Richards and Garner's time with Somerset, and particularly the events leading up to the 1986 flash point, give the clearest possible example of what good overseas players can bring to an English county, and what harm.

The Somerset that Richards joined in 1974 was on the brink of its most successful period in both three-day and limited-overs cricket. During the seven years between 1976 and 1983 Somerset, so often the make-weights on the county circuit, became respected, even feared opponents.

In the course of those seven seasons, Somerset finished outside the top half of the county championship only once, the longest such run in their history, and were fourth twice and third once. After narrowly missing winning their first trophy by occupying the runners-up spot in both the John Player League and the Gillette Cup in 1978, the county won both competitions in the following year. The year of 1980 was a fallow one, with both Richards and Garner touring England with the West Indies, but in both 1981 and 1982 Somerset were to carry away the Benson & Hedges trophy. Finally in 1983, supporters' disappointment that Somerset had slipped to tenth place in the county championship was largely displaced by the capture of the Nat West Cup.

Although Somerset were to win the Sunday competition only once during their trophy-grabbing run, they dominated the league during the late 1970s and early 1980s by finishing runners-up on no less than four occasions between 1978 and 1983.

The end of Somerset's glory days coincided with Brian Rose's decision to retire and hand over the captaincy to Botham. The England all-rounder kept the position for two years before being replaced by Roebuck. After the bloodletting of 1986, Roebuck continued for two more years and then handed over to long-serving off-spinner Vic Marks. His retirement saw Kent-import Chris Tavare take over from the 1991 season.

This period of change spanned eight seasons, the same period of time that Somerset – along with Middlesex and Essex – had previously dominated the county circuit. But despite the efforts of all four captains and the overseas batting talents of Martin Crowe, Steve Waugh and Jimmy Cook, Somerset averaged fourteenth place in the championship (compared to sixth during the halcyon days of the late 1970s). Fourth was the highest position achieved in the John Player or Refuge Assurance League, while the one-time masters of the one-day cup competitions had only 2 semi-final appearances to show for 16 attempts at the Benson & Hedges and Nat West trophies.

The 'official' story of Richards and Garner's dismissal comes in Peter Roebuck's 1991 history of Somerset CCC, *From Sammy to Jimmy*. It is a strange and engrossing book. As the author reaches the period with which he has been involved, the text takes on a denser and more complicated character as Roebuck attempts to explain the forces which made and then destroyed Somerset's cup-winning side.

According to Roebuck, the club's administration during the early 1980s seems to have been beset by in-fighting and this in turn appears to have led to a situation in which it was impossible to provide a smooth transition between the ageing and successful Somerset of Rose, Denning and Dredge, and the new and unproven intake of players such as Wyatt and Felton.

The first rumblings of discontent began in 1983 when Rose was retained as captain, despite some objections. Botham took over in 1984, but he was another disputed choice, and was immediately afflicted with problems both on and off the field. The dressing room soon developed cliques, and Somerset lacked an undisputed leader and a clear sense of direction.

In 1984 both attributes were provided for Somerset's confused younger players by the arrival of Crowe, ironically hand picked by Botham to replace the touring Richards and Garner. Crowe was then only 21 years of age and had played, not too successfully, in just ten test matches. But he had one performance of note to his credit and it was just the sort of back-to-the-wall feat that was likely to impress Botham.

During the summer of 1983, England had defeated New Zealand by three tests to one with Crowe scoring only 163 runs at 20.37. In Wellington, New Zealand, at the start of the first test in the return series it at first appeared as if the same script would be required for this rubber as well.

New Zealand had scored just 219, with Crowe being bowled by Willis for 13 and Botham taking 5 for 59. England were in equal trouble until Botham and Randall came together at 115 for 6. In a gloriously entertaining stand they added 232 and finally gave the visiting side a lead of 244. In the second innings Crowe came to the wicket with New Zealand 2 wickets down and still 165 behind. Batting with classical simplicity, Crowe finally began to reveal his true worth and by the time he was dismissed (by Mike Gatting!), he had his maiden test century and had broken the spirit of England's previously dominant bowling attack. New Zealand finally totalled 537 as Jeremy Coney (174 not out) and Lance Cairns (an explosive 64) took advantage of England's tiring bowlers. England's superiority had been effectively challenged and in the next test New Zealand thrashed England by an innings and 132 runs, despite scoring only 307.

Crowe arrived at Somerset in 1984 determined to make the most of his big chance. He played in every first-class match, scored 1,870 runs at 53.42 and took 44 wickets at 30.75. Just as important was what Roebuck describes as his 'Messianic streak' which saw him take Somerset's dangerously long list of young, inexperienced players and instil in them a will to perform at their best. This was not done purely by example, but by collecting Popplewell, Wyatt, Davis, Felton, Palmer, Booth and Davis into an informal yet close-knit group which provided mutual support and set high standards.

With Richards and Garner away, and Botham available for only 11 of the 24 championship games, much depended on how the young players performed. Thanks largely to Crowe they all played their part and the happy atmosphere that this engendered helped Somerset rise from tenth to seventh in the championship table. As Crowe departed at the end of the season there were many at the club, both players and officials, who realized just how much he had done for the county, and there more than a few of these who wished he was coming back again in 1985.

In 1985, Richards returned in majestic form, which was matched on his rare appearances for his county, by Botham. But Richards and Garner had stayed on in the Caribbean after the test series against New Zealand, a decision made even more doubtful by Marshall and Greenidge's prompt return to Hampshire. Somerset's home-grown players could not recapture the consistency of 1984. The county came bottom of the county championship and nowhere in the one-day tournaments. From this season onwards a real concern in some quarters that the two West Indians were hampering the chances of the county's success began to take hold.

Upon being removed from the captaincy after the 1985 season, Botham informed Richards that he would be leaving the county at the end of the 1986 season. After Roebuck's intervention the threat seemed to recede for a while, but after returning from his drugs-linked playing ban and being told that he would have to play a second XI match to prove his fitness, he once again said he would leave, and this time take Richards and Garner with him.

Such threats can only have given ammunition to those among the club's administration who were plotting to replace Richards and Garner. 'Was it not obvious', they may have argued, 'that Viv and Joel show greater loyalty to Botham than they do to Somerset?' And given the fierce loyalty shown by Botham towards the overseas players when they were sacked it would not be surprising if the two West Indians privately argued that the great England all-rounder deserved their loyalty more than the club which was eventually to dismiss them in such a cursory manner.

According to Roebuck, Somerset in 1986 was:

A hotchpotch of men from the same generation, men used to success and now, experiencing failure, of inadequate cricketers mostly signed when hubris began around 1982, and of bewildered, intimidated youngsters who enjoyed the sense of private danger in the air and yet could find no advance in their careers. Ever more Richards and Botham were living in a world apart, and scarcely hiding their contempt for officials and some colleagues.

Roebuck admits that Richards was angered by playing in a team which contained so many poor performers and was unnerved by rumours of a plot to unseat him. The former Somerset captain is also hard on himself, claiming that if he had been 'a man of diplomacy' these pressures could have been managed. But instead he found himself 'caught between two warring factions for neither of which he much cared' and the disintegration of the county side carried on unchecked.

It was not inevitable that the frustration in the dressing room should have spilled out into the public sphere during 1986. The crisis was only brought to a head when, during late July, Essex asked for permission to sign Crowe for the 1987 season as a replacement for Australian captain Allan Border who had decided not to fulfil the second year of his contract.

Somerset's position on Crowe had been an unanswered question during most of the season. David Foot claimed that this uncertainty had affected Richards's batting, with the West Indian champion appearing 'preoccupied at the crease'.

And Richards did have real cause for concern. Earlier in the season Somerset chairman Michael Hill had approached Richards and asked him, not too subtly, if he was not a little 'tired'. Richards asked why and was told that Crowe was eager to know whether he had a future at Somerset. The volatile West Indian exploded, shouting, 'I put up these four walls and you come asking me shit about Martin Crowe?'. Somerset chairman Brian Langford was forced to deal with the situation by telling Richards he would be offered a contract for the 1987 season.

A meeting of club officials to discuss Essex's approach, quickly transformed into an outpouring of concern over the situation. It was clear that Somerset could not hope to employ Crowe as well as Richards and Garner in 1987, and Hill was determined that it would be the New Zealander who got the vote.

President Colin Atkinson and Langford were unsure of the wisdom of dismissing Richards and Garner, and three committee members were also against the move, but after a month of secret meetings the decision to sack the two West Indians was announced in late August with what appeared to many of those concerned to be a complete lack of any warning.

On hearing the announcement Ian Botham declared his decision to leave the county and six general committee members resigned. A powerful rebel faction, including former players such as Peter White, Roy Kerslake and Peter Denning, organized a vote of no confidence in the committee scheduled for November.

Attacked publicly and privately by Botham, as well as by many die-hard Somerset supporters, Roebuck was forced to defend his support for the club's decision. The captain's argument was simple: 'Somerset had finished seventeenth in 1985 and sixteenth in 1986. Membership was dwindling, young players were failing and new ones could not be signed. Evidently the chemistry was wrong and a majority had decided it was time for change.'

With this argument accepted by the majority of club supporters and by many observers, there was a last-minute attempt to argue that Somerset needed a fast bowler more than a batsman and therefore Garner should be retained. Roebuck appears to make an important point when he suggests that although there was no doubt the retention of the two players should have been treated separately, it was the 'disruptive' Richards rather than the amenable Garner who had 'given much more of himself' to Somerset.

As for the argument that Somerset needed a fast bowler, Roebuck claimed that the side actually needed four new bowlers and that a class batsman would 'prop up the side until these men were found', as well as giving the county a greater chance in the three one-day competitions.

The 'no confidence' meeting, held on Saturday 8 November 1986, at the Bath and West Showground in Shepton Mallet, was a heated affair attended by over 3,000 and with the decisive contribution coming from Nigel Popplewell. The 28-year-old Somerset batsman, who had retired at the end of the 1985 season after coming fourth in the batting averages behind Botham, Richards and Roebuck, made clear his disillusionment with the leading figures of the county side. Speaking with an eloquence suited to a Cambridge graduate he claimed that the atmosphere in the Somerset dressing room had been 'awful' and that whereas Richards and Garner expected '110 per cent' from the other players at all times, they were only prepared to try when it suited them. He pointed out that in the 1983, 1985 and 1986 seasons, Somerset had won a total of just seven county championship matches, while in 1984 alone (with Crowe on board) it recorded six victories. Popplewell had written to the Somerset chairman in 1984, but nothing had come of his concern.

Against this heavyweight contribution, the rebels' tactics of cutting strips from banknotes to show what they believed the county was giving up, appeared exactly what it was, an empty gesture. Even support from as influential a figure as Lord Rees-Mogg, who has since said that Roebuck shares John Major's fear of flair or anything which challenges a preferred grey mediocrity, was of no use. The no confidence motion was defeated by 1,828 votes to 798 and a second motion demanding the committee's resignation by 1,863 to 743.

Kerslake attempted to find some compromise solution that would have seen Crowe playing first-class cricket, while Richards and Garner occupied places in the one-day side. But the proposal was obviously an unsatisfactory half-way house and the idea soon slipped away.

The two doyens of south-western cricket journalism, Alan Lee and David Foot, both expressed qualified support for the decision to release Richards and Garner. Lee claimed it was 'basically sound but sadly botched', while the more cautious Foot wrote: 'Ordinary players, lesser mortals, have confided that there have been too many disruptive elements [in the county side].'

Middlesex medium pacer and media pundit Simon Hughes backed Popplewell's disillusioned view of Richards. He was one of many to remark that Richards's egocentric view of the world often led to the West Indies captain making mountains out of molehills. A piece of advice not taken or a request turned down and Richards would sulk like a county freshman, often letting a grievance mature into a long-standing grudge. Arrogance is a valuable attribute in a world-class sportsman because it fosters self-belief, but it becomes destructive if it is not mitigated by maturity, and the realization that the ability of a leading player to set an example can be just as important as scoring runs and taking wickets.

There was a time, a period of four or more years, when Richards's burning pride in himself and, let's not forget, in Somerset as well, was channelled into inspiring and glorious performances. When, after Somerset's failure to win either the 1978 Gillette Cup or the John Player League, he took the bat that had destroyed England's bowling attack in 1976 and smashed it in two, it was not a brattish display of bad temper; the bat smashing was seen by all the Somerset players as an eloquent demonstration of Richards's belief that all the good work of the season was still not enough.

Before Richards's arrival, the disappointments of 1978 could, and would, have led to the county sinking into despondency and apathy during 1979, but thanks to the West Indian's eloquent gesture, Somerset's young players knew exactly what was expected of them when they turned up at the April nets the following season.

The counterargument to the claim that Richards and Garner 'did not try', was that the rest of the Somerset side was so weak that even if they did it made little difference. In a letter to *The Cricketer*, R.C. Townley of Devon cites this argument claiming that with Botham often away playing for England it was the limited skills of the home-grown playing staff that really lay behind the county's lack of success and therefore the perceived need to 'make changes'. He wrote: 'Constantly playing day after day with such an ill equipped and unbalanced team, must have a gradual detrimental effect on morale.'

Townley gives the example of a match in September 1986 when, after Richards had scored a century, Somerset's last five batsmen were required to make just 20 for victory – and managed only 10. The weakness of the county's English players was the problem, claimed Townley, not the personality of the two overseas stars. He suggested that if Richards and Garner had played for Hampshire, and Greenidge and Marshall for Somerset, the same problems would still have arisen.

Townley's claim appears to be well made and deserves some examination. Was the Somerset side during 1985 and 1986 so weak that, regardless of

Richards and Garner's contribution, it was bound to fail, and how did the county's and its overseas stars' performance compare with Hampshire's and that of its two West Indian recruits?

Both Richards and Garner played relatively full seasons during 1985 and 1986, but after the good showing in 1984's county championship, with Martin Crowe standing in for the touring Richards and Garner, the county slipped back badly during the two years, finishing bottom in 1985 and sixteenth in 1986.

During 1985 Richards played in 19 of Somerset's 24 county matches, scoring 1,836 runs at an average per game of 76.50. He was the leading run scorer by over 600 runs and only Botham, who scored 1,211 runs at 100.91, topped him in the averages. Somerset scored an average of 395 runs in each game, while Richards's individual average match score was 97, around one-quarter of the total. In 1986 Richards played 18 out of 23 matches but only managed 1,174 runs at 43.48. Roebuck scored more runs, while he, Marks, Rose and Botham all had higher averages. Somerset fell only one run short of their 1985 match average, but Richards's average was only 65, just 16 per cent of the total. In total for the two seasons Richards contributed just under 21 per cent of Somerset's runs in the county championship.

Garner played 15 times for Somerset in the county championship during 1985. Taking 31 wickets at 23.83, he was second to Vic Marks (67) in terms of wickets taken and behind Coombs (16.75) in the averages. The county's paper-thin bowling attack took an average of just nine wickets per match and Garner himself managed just two, 22 per cent of the total. In 1986 Garner equalled his record of 1981 and turned out for 18 games, heading the averages with 47 wickets at 23.21. Marks with 57 was the only bowler to capture more victims. The leap one place up the county table was evidenced by the fact that the number of wickets taken by bowlers during each game rose to ten. Garner's average was 2.6, a quarter of the total. The total for the two seasons shows that Somerset captured an average of 9.5 wickets every match, of which Garner accounted for 2.4 or 25 per cent.

That Hampshire did not win the county championship during the mid-1980s was a cause of constant surprise. In the two years under consideration they finished second and sixth, with their two West Indian stars playing a full part in the championship challenge.

In 1985, Gordon Greenidge played in 19 of Hampshire's 24 matches and hit 1,236 runs at 41.20. He was second in the averages behind Chris Smith, but both Smith brothers topped his tally of runs. Amazingly for championship contenders Hampshire only scored an average of 404 runs a match, of which Greenidge contributed 65 or 16 per cent of the total. In 1986 the West Indian had a better season, scoring more runs (1,916) at a higher average (68.42) than any other Hampshire player. He played in 19 of Hampshire's 23 games and supplied an average of 101 runs, a third of the county's surprisingly low overall tally of 333. Over the two seasons, Hampshire averaged 369 runs a game and Greenidge supplied 83, 22 per cent of the total.

By the mid-1980s Malcolm Marshall was the most feared bowler on the county circuit and his performances over the two seasons under investigation were outstanding. In 1985 he played in all but two of Hampshire's matches and dominated the bowling averages by taking 95 wickets at 17.68. He took an average 4.3 wickets in each match, 31 per cent of the county's match average of 14. A year later, Marshall was in even more brilliant form, playing in all of the championship matches and again putting all other Hants bowlers in the shade by taking 100 wickets at 15.08. His dominance was such that he again took 4.3 (33 per cent) of the 13 wickets Hampshire were averaging in every match. During 1985 and 1986 Hampshire's bowlers captured an average of 13.5 wickets per match, Marshall alone averaging 4.3 or 32 per cent of the total.

This rather tortuous but nevertheless revealing analysis does not seem to support the argument put forward by Mr Townley or other pro-Richards and Garner campaigners.

During the period covering the 1985 and 1986 seasons, Hampshire and Somerset seem to have had batting line-ups of equal strength. Similarly the two counties' overseas batsmen appeared to have contributed to their team's performance to almost exactly the same extent. Since both Greenidge and Richards's playing records were pretty much on a par during the 1985 and 1986 seasons, a relatively poorer Somerset batting performance would have seen the Antiguan's contribution correspondingly higher in percentage terms, but that is not the case.

On the bowling side, there is no doubt that Hampshire's attack was considerably stronger than Somerset's. Hampshire's bowlers captured 637 wickets over the two seasons, which was 30 per cent higher than Somerset's 447. But with Marshall and Garner's figures removed from the analysis the difference shrinks to just 17 per cent. And, again, if Somerset's home-grown bowling attack was that much weaker than Hampshire's, it would not be unreasonable for Garner to make at least as great a contribution to the average number of wickets taken in a game as his West Indian colleague. But, as we have seen, Garner was able only to take an average of 25 per cent of Somerset's wickets in each game that he played, and Marshall's average over the two seasons was 7 per cent higher.

The difference between Hampshire and Somerset during 1985 and 1986 had as much to do with the performances of their respective West Indian fast bowlers as it had with the different quality of the county's home-grown players. Of course, on purely technical grounds, it is highly unfair to compare Marshall in his pomp to the ageing Garner, but sympathy for giants of the past will always sit uneasily with county committees charged by the members to facilitate good results and a healthy bank balance.

A comparison with three other overseas fast bowlers of similar age who had to shoulder the same heavy international workload puts Garner's performance over the two seasons in a better light. Michael Holding, Richard Hadlee and Imran Khan all led county bowling attacks during the 1985 and 1986 county seasons which were stronger than Somerset's. Holding was also able to stay fresher than his West Indian colleague as he played only half of Derbyshire's county games, New Zealander John Wright filling in for the rest.

In terms of games played, Garner did as well as Holding (considering the playing restrictions operating at Derbyshire) and much better than the injury-hit Imran. However, all three were overshadowed by the performance of Hadlee, who turned out for 33 county games, despite missing half of the 1986 English season while touring with New Zealand.

Comparative performance Richards/Greenidge–Garner/Marshall, 1985 and 1986

	Runs	Runs/game	Team total/game	%
Richards	3,010	81.35	395	21
Greenidge	3,152	82.95	369	22

	Matches	Wkts	Wkts/game	Team wkts/game	%
Garner	33	78	2.36	9.49	25
Marshall	45	195	4.33	13.51	32
Holding	24	102	4.25	11.17	38
Hadlee	33	116	3.52	13.29	26
Imran	23	81	3.52	11.48	31

Since this analysis has shown that it was Garner and not Richards who contributed least to Somerset's performance in the two seasons before their dismissal in the late summer of 1986, it is worth shining the spotlight on the fast bowler's county career to set these figures in context.

At first Garner was unsure whether or not to commit himself to Somerset. During 1976 and 1977 he played for the Littleborough club in the Lancashire Leagues, turning out for Somerset during mid-week matches. Brian Close, then captain of the county, remembers that the agreement reached with Garner was that the West Indian would phone the county every time he was available. There was no telephone in Garner's Lancashire digs and the county only received three calls during the entire season. By the start of 1979, when he signed a full contract after hearing that Michael Holding was interested in joining the county, he had only played nine matches for Somerset.

But for the next two seasons in which he played the county were to receive more than their money's worth from the giant fast bowler. In 1979 Garner was to play a vital part in both Somerset's one-day triumphs. The quarter final of the Gillette Cup saw Garner dismiss Kent for 60 by taking 5 wickets for 11 runs. During the semi-final he took 4 for 24 to help defeat Middlesex and it began to become clear that Garner's ability to make the ball rear, delivery after delivery, from a full length posed a near unsolvable problem for batsmen intent on anything more than defence.

The Gillette Cup final was against Northants and after Richards with 117 and Denning with 90 had shot Somerset to 269, Garner bowled Wayne Larkins for a duck. Allan Lamb appeared to be rebuilding the innings, but after scoring

78 he was dismissed by Richards. Garner returned to the attack and swept away the tail, capturing 6 for 29. The very next day he was again among the wickets as Somerset beat Nottinghamshire by 56 runs and clinched the John Player League. It is no surprise that Roebuck claims that without Garner, Somerset's trophy cupboard would probably still be bare.

Garner was also a force in first-class cricket. His appearances were restricted by the 1979 World Cup but he still managed to take part in two-thirds of Somerset's county championship games. As ever he was irresistible, taking 55 wickets at the ridiculous average of 13.83. In 1981 he did even better; playing 18 out of 22 championship games, he took 88 wickets averaging 15.32. Driven forward by these efforts, and Richards's 1,718 runs at 57.26, Somerset won 10 games and finished third behind Nottinghamshire and Sussex who each won 11.

The last time that Garner was to have a strong influence on Somerset's performance in first-class games was in 1981. In one-day matches he was still master. From 1981 to 1983, Somerset appeared in three consecutive Lord's cup finals. During those games Garner returned spells of 5 for 14, 2 for 13 and 2 for 15.

Despite this success and his growing number of test wickets, Garner contributed little to Somerset during county matches after 1981. In the four seasons in which he played for Somerset between 1982 and 1986, Garner was to turn out for only 53 of Somerset's 96 championship matches. He still topped the county's averages every year, but took only 146 wickets in the 4 seasons, the 47 he captured in his last summer with the county being the highest annual total.

In the five full seasons that Garner played for Somerset between 1981 and 1986, the fast bowler played 18, 10, 10, 15 and 18 games respectively. He was 29 in that first full season, which is getting on for a fast bowler, and unsurprisingly the wear and tear of playing seven days a week had a proportionately greater damaging effect on Garner's huge frame. He was never the most athletic of the West Indian pace quartet and, unlike Curtly Ambrose for example, his size seemed a barrier rather than an aid to bowling fast. His stiff-legged run and ponderous, almost slow-motion action, all seemed forced and when he broke down time and time again during the long England season no one was that surprised.

But motivation has got a lot of cricketers through the pain barrier and on to the field before, and it does seem doubtful, though perfectly understandable, that Garner was able to produce the same sort of commitment to Somerset as he was to the West Indies. This possibly being the case, it is worthwhile, though hardly conclusive, to compare Garner's fitness record in test cricket against that during his Somerset career.

The 'Big Bird' made his international debut against Pakistan in the West Indies during the 1976/7 tour. Playing in all five tests, he spent the English summer playing for Littleborough and Somerset, before being signed to play in the inaugural season of Kerry Packer's Circus. Early in 1978 Garner left Australia to take part against the Aussies on their tour of the West Indies. The first two games passed off without incident, but the decision to drop three Packer players for the third test led to a boycott of the match by the other World Series Cricket (WSC) players including captain Lloyd and Garner.

The rift between the WSC players and the West Indian Board of Control lasted until the 1979 World Cup, spanning the remainder of the 1977/8 home series and the 1978/9 tour of India. But from the West Indian tour of Australia in 1979/80, Garner was a regular fixture in the strongest international side of the 1980s. With one exception he played in every match for 6 consecutive rubbers, notching up 21 tests in three years. Only once did he lose his place, dropped to make room for a spinner on the Windies 1980/1 tour of Pakistan.

During this period Garner played 14 games for Somerset in 1979, despite having half the season occupied by the World Cup, missed the 1980 season through the Windies tour of England, played 18 out of 22 games in 1981 despite 'feeling wretched' and only 10 out of 24 in 1982 as a knee injury required surgery.

The operation was a success and Garner joined the West Indian team which was to contest a home series against India during the 1982/3 season. He played in the first four tests, but as Garner explains he was becoming worn down by the demands of round-the-year cricket. 'Bowling had become a chore', he claimed. 'My heart was there, but the body [was] weak and there was nothing I could do to motivate myself to reach the levels of performance that I knew the rest of the side demanded of me.'

Garner was not surprised when he was dropped for the fifth test, replaced by the young Winston Davis who had taken 33 wickets in that season's Shell Shield competition. Garner resolved to fight his way back into the West Indian side, which perhaps had more fast bowlers of high class to call on than any other in the game's history. Exercising every available minute, and working on recurring knee and shoulder injuries, he played only intermittently for Somerset in 1983 (10 games out of 25), missed the 1983/4 tour of India, but was finally reinstated in the West Indian side during early 1984.

This marked the beginning of Garner's second and last continuous occupation of a place among the most fearsome fast-bowling quartet of all time. In around 9 months during 1984 Garner played in 15 tests, of which the Windies won 13, drew 1 and lost 1.

What is more Garner had recreated himself as an out-and-out fast bowler, taking the place of the ageing Holding. To his accuracy and deceptive bounce was now added an element of unbridled pace and aggression which almost matched that of his opening partner Malcolm Marshall.

Two more full test series followed against New Zealand in 1985 and England in 1986. He was rested at his own request during the three-match away series against Pakistan, claiming to have feared damage to his digestive system more than any playing-related injury. Garner's last test series was against New Zealand early in 1987, when he played in the first two games until injury and age ended his test career.

The second stage of Garner's test career over-arched his performances for Somerset in 1985 and 1986. In the first season he arrived late in the country due to the death of his beloved grandmother and an unspecified recurrent injury meant that he played in only 15 of the county's 24 games. In 1986, a relatively injury-free season, he played 18 out of 23 games.

During Garner's international career the West Indies played 79 tests. Garner was a member of the side for 58 or 73 per cent of them. If the eight matches missed because of his membership of WSC and the one match in which he was dropped for tactical reasons are discounted, the percentage rises to 83 per cent. And of the other 12 games, although physical fitness played its part in his non-appearance, it was only during his very last tour that his omission from a test was due to a specific injury.

Garner's comeback to head the West Indian pace attack during 1984 shows that the man was capable of impressive feats of will. However, it also appears as if he was one of those high-class cricketers whose appetite is dulled by constantly playing for club and country. Greg Chappell was another, as is David Gower. Richard Hadlee and Graham Gooch, on the other hand, positively thrive on a heavy work rate.

It is not suggested for one moment that Garner invented injuries and aches and pains where there were none, but it does seem reasonable to suggest that niggles that would have been ignored on the eve of a test match seemed that much worse on a cold Tuesday morning at Taunton. Roebuck, though hardly a disinterested observer, has remarked on Garner's 'over-fondness for his arm-chair at home', but it was no great secret during Garner's last few seasons at Somerset that he would have preferred to turn out only for one-day games.

Garner, by all accounts a highly affable man, was shocked and deeply hurt by Somerset's decision to release him. He displayed considerable indignation over the accusation that he did not 'try' while playing for Somerset, and instead puts forward a complex conspiracy theory to explain the county's decision to dismiss Richards and himself.

The claims, surprisingly ignored by the sporting press, come in the postscript to his autobiography *Big Bird, Flying High*. In a 'self-interview', a technique he might have picked up while exploring the possibility of becoming a social worker after his playing days were finished, he makes the astonishing claim that the club actually made a conscious effort to reduce his effectiveness and therefore provide an excuse to sack him.

Garner the interviewee claims that Somerset deliberately prepared lifeless wickets, telling Garner the interviewer:

If I'm your best bowler and you tell the groundsman to shave the wicket or make it white, it means that you don't give a damn about your bowlers. And wickets have been shaved on more than one occasion.

He also claims that officials tried to present Garner and Richards as indistinguishable trouble-makers. In Garner's eyes these slurs were used to suggest that the West Indians were getting in the way of Somerset's 'team-building', an allegation which he counters by saying:

The arrogance at Somerset came more from another clique in the side . . . Everyone forgot that the thing was about playing cricket. As far as building a team was concerned the coach should have been doing his job. The overseas players didn't stop him from doing his job.

He also claims that the club blamed Garner and, particularly, Richards for Botham's much-publicized drink, drugs and sex problems.

These came to a head during the summer of 1986. Botham had been banned from first-class cricket for two months after he admitted smoking pot as a teenager in an interview with the *Mail on Sunday*. The article was not a piece of Bothamesque bravado, but a quid pro quo to settle a legal action with the paper. Botham had just returned from England's disastrous tour of the West Indies, where he had been besieged by tabloid reporters, and beset by sex scandals involving tell-tale models and collapsing beds.

Garner claims that those wanting to see the back of the two overseas players:

succeeded in building up this image of Viv Richards' influence on Botham; so that when Both had his problems with the media during the West Indies tour, it would look like Viv Richards and the West Indians were making a mess of the blue-eyed blond.

Garner rejects this allegation, pointing out that 'Botham is his own man', but alleges that 'somewhere behind the committee's decision lies the feeling that if they got rid of Richards and Garner, the Botham problem would go away'.

Hill was later to apologize to Garner for being 'coupled with Viv and Ian' as a disruptive element in the dressing room, but at the time these accusations were made, the fast bowler appears to have been in no mood to forgive or forget.

But Garner's most startling and worrying claim is that he and Richards were victims of the widespread racism he claims is still abroad in English cricket.

It's a clear warning. If two of the best players in the world can be sacked at their peak, it tells the younger lads: 'we don't care how good you are or of what ability or promise you have. You are dispensable.' It should speak volumes, not only to West Indian professionals, but also to men like Cowans, Slack, Small, Butcher and others like Mark Alleyne now coming along. The whole establishment of English cricket seems about to fight a rear guard action against certain players maintaining permanent places at the top. Look at Cowans, I've seen situations where he took eight wickets in a match and then be refused the new ball for the following game.

He reiterates the West Indian test team's often heard complaint that their success has bred a 'jealousy and selfishness' among English commentators and officials which results in the efforts of black players being constantly denigrated. As far as Somerset goes, Garner remembers that Hallam Moseley was 'got rid of' after 12 or so years with Somerset 'with the same absence of ceremony' as that which accompanied Richards's and Garner's departure from the club.

Roebuck was later to accept much of the blame for the tragic way in which the affair was handled and Garner is happy to let him take the blame. The West Indian quick claims that it was Roebuck who was the most disruptive element in the Somerset dressing room. Echoing the opinion of Rees–Mogg, Garner describes Roebuck as a man of poor playing ability and a worse captain who was, 'representative of that force in English cricket that is seeking to drag down others in order to accommodate itself instead of raising standards'.

Perhaps surprisingly Richards appears to have a more straightforward view than Garner of their dismissal from the club.

The former West Indian captain paints a familiar picture of Somerset CCC in his autobiography *Hitting Across the Line*. He claims that the club, after tasting continued success for the first time, was beset by accusations of self-importance. It has been well documented, by those on both sides of the argument, that during the early 1980s Somerset club officials were concerned about the amount of power the players seemed to be wielding, while the cricketers themselves thought that some of the administrators were not giving them the respect they felt they had earned. Richards puts forward the simple explanation that these 'arrogant types, who thought they were special' had enjoyed Martin Crowe's more deferential approach to the club, and had decided that they would do everything in their power to make sure he replaced Richards and Garner.

Unlike Garner, Richards does not simply dismiss allegations that he sometimes failed to make sufficient effort during county games. With refreshing and typical honesty he says: 'There are always times when you are going to have your indifferent days and, yes, I did suffer periods like that at Somerset. I do not deny that in the later years, my concentration did suffer a bit.' But despite these admissions Richards rejects claims of 'cricketing apathy', which he says 'almost destroyed me at the time, much more than all the back-stabbing which went on behind the scenes'.

He adds:

We did come into a very lean period at Somerset, but I'm telling you it was never through lack of trying. If my record is examined critically it will show that most of the time I did fairly well. My record for the county stands up along side other test player's records for their counties. It seems to me that some of the less knowledgeable people expect you to become a run machine.

A random comparison with Richards's contemporaries seems to reinforce his claims. In terms of average he is second only to Turner, an unashamed 'run machine'. But, perhaps more importantly, his runs and games per season average bear close examination. Considering that Richards played most of his cricket in the late 1970s and early 1980s, a time in which the average number of championship games was decreasing, and that he had to contend with the demands of international cricket, which Rice and Davison did not, the West Indies skipper does not seem to have been a shirker.

Leading overseas batsmen – a comparison

	Career	Matches	Runs	Average	Games per season
Turner	1967–82	284	22,298	52.09	18
Richards	1974–86	191	14,698	49.82	15
Greenidge	1970–87	275	19,840	45.40	15
Lloyd	1968–86	219	12,764	44.94	12
Rice	1975–87	283	17,503	44.29	22
Kallicharran	1971–90	285	18,157	43.75	16
Davison	1970–83	303	18,537	43.11	22
Asif Iqbal	1968–82	243	13,231	37.06	16

The two West Indians have obviously spent some time discussing the issue and Richards echoes Garner's comments about Botham being responsible for his own actions. He also reiterates the allegation that it was some of the senior English-born players who were the disruptive influence within the Somerset dressing room. The former West Indies captain also hits out at the accusation that he was a 'money-hawk'. He claims that he was well into his Somerset and test career before he asked for a pay rise, and that then he wanted only £12,500 for the full England season.

Finally Richards makes another surprising admission by claiming that he might have been prepared to share the Somerset dressing room with Crowe. He claims that he would have accepted the plan to sign Crowe as long as his own contract was honoured. He says: 'Maybe I would not have been happy playing second fiddle to Crowe. But surely after eleven years' service you deserve a little honesty'. If Somerset ever countenanced the cost of employing three overseas players, it would seem that Crowe, with Essex's no strings attached offer on the table, was the one who had the reservations about sharing the limelight.

As the start of the 1987 season approached, with the rebels finally defeated, and Richards, Garner and Botham all departed, it was time for Roebuck to demonstrate that the new spirit he hoped to install in the Somerset dressing room was worth the all the anguish undergone during the preceding six months. It was also down to Martin Crowe to prove, for the second time, that he was a worthy replacement for the two West Indians.

But the glory days did not and have not returned to Somerset. Since the great upheaval of 1986, the county has never finished higher than eleventh in the county championship. It has sat stolidly in the middle of the Sunday League and never got past a one-day cup semi-final. The county's overseas players were not responsible for this lack of success, but the replacement of Richards and Garner with such down-the-line team men as Crowe, Steve Waugh and Jimmy Cook may have raised team morale, but did little in terms of improving the county's on-field performance.

In 1987 Crowe was in masterful form. In 18 first-class games he scored 1,627 runs at 67.79, equalling his 1984 record of 6 centuries. Unfortunately injury and the demands of international cricket had reduced the effectiveness of his bowling, so that he only sent down 33 overs in the whole season. Roebuck had another good season, but the captain's hope that the younger players would flourish once they no longer had to cope with the unrealistic expectations of the three superstars, proved unfulfilled.

Jon Hardy stood still, playing in 7 more matches and completing 1,000 runs in a season for the first time, but not managing to get his average above 30, Neil Felton also had more playing opportunities, but failed to rise to the challenge and establish himself with Roebuck and Crowe as a reliable county batsman. Richard Harden actually slipped back from his respectable performance of 1986 (1,053 at 33.96) to make just 568 runs at 23.66. The fast left-armer Mark Davis, who had promised so much in 1984, when under Crowe's guidance he had taken 66 wickets, could not be revived a second time and was released by the county at the end of the season.

Off-break bowler Mark Harman played only six games and took just seven wickets, before joining Kent for the 1988 season. Richard Bartlett saw his record of four games in 1986 reduced to one sole appearance, in which he made a duck.

The greatest impetus to Somerset's improved performance – they rose from sixteenth to eleventh in the county championship – came from three bowlers imported from other counties. Neil Mallender from Northants, Graham Rose from Middlesex, and Adrian Jones from Sussex, were three of the four bowlers that Roebuck had been looking for. They arrived knowing little of the pressures that had played on the minds of the Somerset players over the last two seasons and took 147 wickets between them – Rose also scored 470 runs at 24.73. However, as they were newly arrived at Somerset, their performance cannot be attributed to an alleged greater sense of well-being brought on by the departure of Richards and Garner.

Even Neil Burns, who made a good job of taking over the wicket-keeping duties from Trevor Gard, was imported from Essex. Of the 1986 squad, only Palmer, Foster and Wyatt were able to demonstrate moderate improvement.

Roebuck admits that Richards's lack of faith in his Somerset team mates was proved by events to be correct in most cases and it is no surprise that he gives the final chapter of his Somerset history the unassuming title, 'Having a go'. The Somerset captain admits that 1987 was not the new dawn he had hoped for and that 'players who had complained bitterly about Richards performed no better in his absence'.

Another clue to Somerset's failure to recapture the spirit of 1984 may have stemmed from Crowe's attitude to the game. By the start of the 1987 season he had established himself as New Zealand's leading batsman, having played 36 tests and hit 7 test centuries. When he arrived in Taunton he was no longer the wide-eyed kid ready to make the most of every experience, but was learning to cope with the year-round grind of international cricket and readying himself to take on the burden of the New Zealand captaincy. Still only 24, he had become a more complete player and a more complicated character.

Looking back on his time at Somerset, Adrian Jones does not remember Crowe in a particularly good light, claiming: 'As a team man, in terms of creating an atmosphere that inspires us, Cook is better than Crowe, who became aloof in his latter years here.'

It is also interesting to compare Roebuck's description of Crowe in 1984, full of 'vitality' and 'innocence', to his farewell passage on the New Zealander, which notes:

Crowe was obliged to return to New Zealand [during the 1988 season] for a period of rest and recuperation. Batting was never an easy matter for him, for he was an analytical man who could play to his best only after summoning a depth of commitment, mental and physical. Being capable of such commitment he was inclined to dismiss those around him whose approach was more carefree, believing their sacrifices were too small, for which their team suffered. As an acknowledged test batsman of high calibre Crowe was not as easy a companion as in 1984...

The style and source of the commitment may have been different from that which drove Richards, but the similarities to the forces which charged the West Indian's character and people's perception of it are unmistakable.

Yet another possible factor behind Crowe's transformation from the inspirational player of 1984 to the introverted loner of 1987 were the malicious and unsubstantiated rumours circulated by those who had wanted Richards and Garner to remain. Crowe, it was claimed, was a closet homosexual, an unsettling and damaging lie, especially in the macho world of county cricket dressing rooms. Crowe, ever since he emerged as a test cricketer, has shown himself to be a sensitive and temperamental man. It was this facet of his character that his enemies seized upon and, helped by widely held misconceptions about gay men, managed to use as 'evidence' for the claims.

These claims have continued to dog Crowe throughout his playing career, with his enemies in New Zealand cricket adding to the controversy by falsely suggesting that he developed AIDS during the late 1980s.

In 1988, Somerset once again threw the weight of their expectations on the shoulders of a young test batsman. The comparisons between Steve Waugh and the Crowe that Somerset first got to know were obvious, as both were in their very early 20s. batted with an easy classical grace and bowled useful seam-up. In late 1987 Waugh had played four county games and summoned up images of Somerset's first import, Greg Chappell. Waugh had gone to the wicket 6 times, remained undefeated on 3 occasions, hit 2 centuries and scored 340 runs at 113.33. In 1988, after Crowe had flown back to New Zealand, Waugh took up where he had left off, stroking 1,286 runs at 80.37, with 6 centuries.

Disagreements with the committee led to Roebuck's resignation as captain at the end of the 1988 season and Waugh was wanted on Australia's 1989 tour of England, so Somerset entered a new era. The new captain was Vic Marks and the replacement overseas player, 36-year-old South African batsman Jimmy Cook – a sharp contrast in age and experience to the last two holders of the position. With the prolific and steady Cook leading the batting order and Marks, and later Tavare, captaining the side in a low-key manner, Somerset entered a period of quiet achievement, appearing to have given up trying to regain the holy grail of a return to the late 1970s.

Somerset's history from the mid-1970s to the early 1990s contained many of the elements of a Greek tragedy. It also provides a number of object lessons in the advantages and disadvantages of employing one kind of overseas player instead of another, as well as throwing up some interesting dichotomies around the making of that decision.

The strongest message that emerges from a close analysis of Richards' and Garner's last few years with Somerset is just how inevitable the bust-up was between the overseas players and the county. Once the two returned from the West Indies at the start of the 1985 season, it was soon clear that Richards's temperament and Garner's inability to shoulder the workload asked of him were going to give rise to acute problems.

Let us first examine the claims against the two overseas players, the first being that they only tried when it suited them. In Richards's case this is patently untrue. His performance in terms of quantity and quality was usually all that could be asked of an overseas player.

As for Garner, the accusation of 'taking it easy' while playing for the county does seem to carry some weight. But Garner's attitude to seven-day-a-week cricket was never any secret and, if we are to believe the fast bowler, constantly being asked to bowl on pitches that were shaved to protect Somerset's often unreliable batting line-up was bound in the end to reduce his level of commitment.

However, in the final analysis it seems that his commitment was at least equal to that of other fast bowlers of his age and workload on the county circuit. Garner, for example, was asked to play more games than those other ageing overseas fast bowlers charged with carrying a weak attack (Holding/Imran). In this context, the disappointment over his relatively poor performance in the county championship over his last two years with Somerset could just as easily be attributed to the unrealistic expectations placed on him by the county.

Perhaps the Somerset committee were too distracted by events at nearby Bristol to think straight. At Gloucestershire, Courtney Walsh, Garner's successor as the West Indies' stock bowler took 200 first-class wickets during the 1985 and 1986 seasons. Gloucestershire, with a weaker batting side and a bowling attack which (Walsh apart) was no better than Somerset's, finished third and second in the county table – 14 places higher than their West Country rivals.

The second main allegation, that Richards and Garner were disruptive and had a bad effect on morale, is perhaps more true than not. However, the reasons behind the deterioration in team relations appears in hindsight to have been inevitable.

Richards, like many great sportsmen, is a complex and at times highly difficult character. His contribution to team morale was always going to lie in the high standards which he set himself. Those colleagues who consistently failed were never likely to receive anything more than dismissive contempt. The young Somerset players of the mid-1980s may have needed more specific guidance than Richards had provided in the past, but it was always doubtful whether he would have thought that this sort of 'nannying' was his job.

In the end Richards had little respect for most of the players in the Somerset side and he had too much pride in the performance of any team he was associated with to hide it. The lack of commitment he seems to have displayed to the team's performance (as opposed to his own, which did not waver) could really only have been raised by improving the quality of the Somerset squad. The club, of course, tried to ensure that its new recruits were of a high quality, but when it failed Somerset's relationship with Richards was headed straight for the rocks.

Any negative effect that Garner had on team morale simply stemmed from the fact that other counties had West Indian fast bowlers with better fitness records and Somerset's players resented having to 'take it' from opposing overseas quicks while not being able to 'dish it out' to the other side's batsmen.

Questions of morale and a lack of effort apart, there was a third (and often hidden) factor behind Somerset's falling out with its overseas stars. Despite the one-day success enjoyed by Somerset during the early 1970s, it was the prospect of the first county championship title that loomed largest in the minds of most Somerset players, club officials and supporters. The trophy cupboard may have been packed with one-day silver, but when the county failed to clinch a championship title and started to slip down the table, the seeds of dissent which were later to flower into internal rebellion started to be sown.

Yet the club's administrators presumably knew what they were doing when they hired their overseas professionals. They chose with open eyes and continued to employ for 12 years a batsman who thrived on the large crowds which were only likely to be found at one-day or test matches, and a bowler who made no secret of his preference for limited-overs cricket, in which he had few equals (see table below).

J. Garner's playing record for Somerset, first-class and one-day compared

	Matches	Wkts	Av.
First-class	94	338	18.11
Sunday League	81	101	18.99
Gillette/Nat West	26	65	10.50
Benson & Hedges	21	40	13.02

It is generally accepted that to win the modern county championship, a club needs to find a bowler capable of taking 100 first-class wickets. If no home-grown player is available, then one must be recruited from overseas. If one-day success is the priority then a hard-hitting batsman is the best option. Unlike a bowler, who is only allowed to bowl a specified number of overs, a batsman has no artificial restrictions placed upon his involvement in limited-overs games.

Somerset obviously made their choice, for not once during the 15-year plus period in question do they appear to have sought the services of a player like Malcolm Marshall, Richard Hadlee, Courtney Walsh or Alan Donald who, given sufficient support, could have won the championship for the county. Under these circumstances it seems a bit rich to criticize Richards and Garner (as well as Crowe, Waugh, Cook and Gavaskar) for failing to secure a county championship when they were, in effect, hired to do another, completely different, job.

Two possible reasons lie behind Somerset's selection policy; one obvious, the other more subtle. The first reason, of course, is money. As Lancashire discovered in the early 1970s, continued one-day success is much more lucrative than the odd championship title. There are also at least three one-day competitions and just one first-class competition.

The second reason is allied to the first in that the money that enabled Somerset to become a modern cricket club was provided in the main by casual supporters who preferred 'results-in-a-day' cricket. However, power within the club rested mainly with members who still carried a torch for first-class cricket. If the club officials and committee members were to keep their positions, then both groups needed to be pandered to. Viewed in this light it is possible to see the dismissal of Richards and Garner as a sacrifice to the members, and the hiring of Crowe, Waugh, and even Cook and Gavaskar as offerings to the supporters.

It is clear that Somerset, as almost everyone involved with the saga now admits, could have handled the dismissal of Richards and Garner in a much more sympathetic manner. The time to tackle the problems posed by the club's continued employment of Richards and Garner was in 1984, not 1986. Admittedly, with the glory days of the late 1970s and early 1980s still fresh in their minds, it would have been hard for the county club administrators to start thinking in terms of problems – especially when those involved had contributed so much and had such a high profile. However, the warning signs were there in the form of Popplewell's letter and the spirit engendered at the club by Crowe in 1984. Steps to tackle the concern over Richards and Garner should have been taken much earlier than they were.

But what steps? Even in hindsight it is impossible not to conclude that Somerset's continued employment of Richards and Garner broke one of the fundamental rules underpinning the selection of overseas players. They were the wrong players for the county's needs at that time – Richards for temperamental reasons and Garner because Somerset, with its weak bowling attack, needed a fast bowler young and hungry enough to perform way beyond the call of duty (or the terms of his contract).

In 1992 the saga of Richards' and Garner's dismissal from Somerset, and the recriminations and ill-feeling it created, finally came to something approaching a satisfactory end. Somerset offered the two West Indians, as well as their great supporter Ian Botham, life membership of the county and, to the surprise of many, all three accepted. The offer had been made once before, in 1989, and refused. Richards said that he had thought long and hard about the decision to accept the second offer.

Garner was already back in Somerset cricket, although not at first-class level, playing club cricket for Glastonbury, and perhaps both he and Richards shared the view of once arch-enemy Roebuck who responded to the news of the county's move by saying:

It's an unchallengeable fact that we came bottom of the table with these great players in our side. Things obviously weren't right. But I accept that Somerset's decision to make them life members is an appropriate recognition for their magnificent service to the county. You get to a stage in life where you want to remember the good times.

7 The players' view

The drama accompanying Somerset's dismissal of Richards and Garner reflected the often fierce argument that was raging at the time over the employment of overseas players. But the circumstances surrounding the county's controversial move were naturally specific to the time and place in which they happened. The true impact of overseas players has taken place over a much longer period of time, nearly three decades, and has spread throughout the world.

This chapter represents a, necessarily shallow, trawl through this vast store of experience in an attempt to discover how the arrival of overseas players in English cricket has affected the modern cricketer. As such it seems appropriate that we start by seeking the opinions of two long-serving county pros, representatives of the group who have been at the centre of English cricket's love/hate relationship with overseas players.

Alastair Hignell, Gloucestershire 1974–83

When overseas players began arriving *en masse* during the late 1960s they brought about one of the most profound changes in English domestic cricket. Suddenly, almost from nowhere, there were 40-odd world-class players helping counties compete for domestic honours. The reaction from English cricketers ranged from relief that the domestic game was being given a much needed shot in the arm to feelings that bordered on xenophobia. Twenty-five years later the debate has ranged back and forth throughout county dressing rooms, while overseas players have carved a niche for themselves in the day-to-day life of the county circuit. Overseas players have become part of the English game, but the opinions on how valuable or damaging their role is differs even between the overseas players themselves, and certainly among the English professionals who are their colleagues and rivals.

Alastair Hignell played 170 games for Gloucestershire between 1974 and 1983. An England-capped rugby player who captained Cambridge University at both games, he was an integral part of Mike Procter's exuberant young Gloucestershire side.

Brimming over with the self-confidence that comes from an Oxbridge education and the ability to play most sports to a very high level, Hignell displays no outward signs of envy towards the overseas players who occupied three of the first four places in the Gloucestershire batting order during his time with county. His instructions at the start of every season were to bat at number five or six behind Sadiq, Zaheer and Procter, and to 'throw himself around in the outfield'. With the winter holding the promise of international recognition on the rugby field, he admits it was the perfect way for a young athlete to spend his summers.

Like most sportsmen who have succeeded at the highest level Hignell believes that if a player is good enough he will achieve prominence almost regardless of the barriers placed in front of him. As far as his own cricket career goes, he blames nobody but himself for the failure to translate his success as a schoolboy cricketer into the adult game and once again mentions that furthering his highly successful rugby career naturally took up much of his time. Hignell also recognizes that with a Gloucestershire side 'full of number 11s', it was only the presence of three overseas players that allowed him such a relatively long county career as a specialist fielder and middle-order hitter.

Claiming that 'life is too short to have any regrets', he does admit that other Gloucestershire players might have had playing opportunities denied to them by the overseas trio. But thinking about this for a while Hignell can only come up with the names of Chris Broad and Phil Bainbridge, and he notes that even they played the bulk of their cricket for the county after Sadiq's departure had created an opening at the top of the batting order.

But, in any case, the restriction in playing opportunities caused by regularly playing three overseas players was far less important in Hignell's eyes than the way in which they re-established Gloucestershire as a force on the county circuit. When Hignell played his first few games for Gloucestershire, the county was seeing its stalwarts of previous years retire almost in unison. Losing players of the calibre of Milton, Nicholls, Mortimore, Smith and Meyer within a few seasons would normally have meant waiting years for another strong county team to emerge. The arrival of Sadiq and Zaheer meant that the transformation was achieved almost immediately. As well as putting their not inconsiderable talents at the county's disposal, the three overseas players installed both the will to win and the winning habit into the club's English-qualified cricketers. Gloucestershire's home-grown bowlers even started taking more wickets, as batsmen, forced to defend against Procter, began to take more risks at the other end.

But it was not just the playing ability of the three overseas players that made the difference. According to Hignell, each overseas player presented a model of how to get the most out of a game both for them themselves and for their team.

Procter led from the front and was an inspiration, Sadiq was the least talented but was among the hardest workers on the county circuit and Zed refused to blame anyone but himself for his dismissal, knowing that for him to worry aloud about the bowler or the pitch would affect the confidence of the whole side.

Hignell admits that his county tended to rely rather too heavily on their overseas players and that, for example, Gloucestershire's English batsmen particularly were very rarely in a position to learn how to build an innings. But, according to Hignell, this dependence arose from the fact that the two Pakistanis and the South African were such good team players. 'We never developed a Somerset atmosphere, because we always felt that Sadiq, Zaheer and Procter were trying.'

Unsurprisingly Hignell does not believe that the employment of overseas players is detrimental to the state of English cricket and would actually amend existing legislation so that each county could play two overseas players, one batsman and one bowler. The secret, he claims, of making sure that overseas players become a positive influence is to find a foreign recruit who is able to contribute both on and off the field. This means a good player, who will improve morale while helping his colleagues develop their talents.

This criteria needs to be reviewed every season according to Hignell, citing the example of Majid Khan who, after a successful career with Glamorgan, was given the captaincy, only to let the team drift out of control. As far as the state of England's test side is concerned he argues that there are around 350 English-qualified cricketers available each season for the test selectors to choose from and that should be enough.

On a personal level Hignell has no doubt that batting against Hadlee and Imran 'sharpened you up' as a player and that there was much to learn by watching Zaheer concentrating through an innings.

Hignell also believes that most overseas players enjoy becoming part of the county circuit. Even Zaheer, who arrived in the UK with very little English, was able to fit in quickly as he had the more worldly Sadiq already resident at Cheltenham and willing to show him the ropes.

Though they came from different castes the experience of being two Pakistani players in English county cricket brought them together. Few would have recognized it, but Sadiq and Zaheer's friendship was very unusual. Hignell confirms that even when they were abroad the caste system continued to operate among the Pakistani cricketers playing for English counties. Members of a high caste such as Imran and Zaheer would have an unspoken hold over lower caste members such as Sadiq.

Not that this unduly worried Sadiq according to Hignell, who would simply make the most of his fame among English cricket fans to make sure his ego stayed healthy. For Sadiq, who sometimes had to fetch and carry for his Pakistani colleagues of a higher caste, having his bags lugged into the dressing room by helpful school kids was more than a convenience.

Hignell says that Sadiq came into his own during his own benefit season, with his mobile phone clamped to his ear, wheeling, dealing and mobilizing the local Pakistani community. Consequently, his benefit brochure was one of the fattest ever. Sadiq was also, unlike many of his countrymen, willing to put up with the sort of practical jokes beloved of English county professionals. The ability to laugh off itching powder in the jockstrap or a bar of 'dirty soap' is an important part of becoming 'one of the boys'. More significantly Hignell remembers Sadiq fondly for helping him develop his technique against fast bowling.

In his domestic life too Sadiq appeared to have little trouble in finding ways of making his time in England as comfortable as possible. Hignell recounts 'an apocryphal story' which is nevertheless illustrative of the Pakistani's ability to make the most of his circumstances.

Sadiq, so the story goes, on arriving in England at the start of the season, would rent an unfurnished house. He would then contact a local furniture warehouse and tell them that he was about to open a retail outlet, but that as his premises were not yet ready could they deliver the merchandise to his home address. Come the end of the season, he would then contact the warehouse again, explain that his venture had been a commercial failure, and would they please come and collect the unsold furniture.

Zaheer, according to Hignell, was a much more reserved character than Sadiq and claims that he revealed much more about the strength of his sporting ambition than he ever did about his character.

Hignell remembers batting with Zaheer during the second innings of a county match at Canterbury. The Pakistani had scored a century in the first innings and was fast approaching his second as Gloucestershire drew close to winning the game. With time running out Zaheer came down the wicket and to Hignell's amazement asked him to block the next few balls. When asked why, Zaheer told him 'I must score this century'. Hignell blocked and the next over Zaheer hit three fours, winning the game and reaching his century. Once back inside the dressing room, Hignell learnt what Zaheer had known all along, that by scoring two centuries in the match, the Pakistani had now accomplished this feat more times than any other batsman.

It was this relentless search for records that drove Zaheer, and Hignell got used to attempting short runs of the fifth or sixth ball of the over. Zaheer also liked to experiment with calling, sometimes doing it in Urdu, especially when batting with Sadiq, or switching the meaning of words so that 'yes' meant 'no' and vice versa. But despite this desire to occupy as much space in the record books as possible, Hignell remembers Zaheer as a helpful batting partner whose fierce concentration was an example to every other member of the side. 'If he was less helpful to younger players off the field than Sadiq was, this was probably because he was so wrapped up in perfecting his own game.'

Interestingly, former Gloucestershire captain David Graveney has a more positive view of Zaheer's approachability. Graveney claims that 'Zed' was 'always willing to assist young players and it is shame that many did not take advantage of talking to the great man.' Graveney also paints a picture of man at ease in the county dressing room, passing on culinary hints and gladly accepting racing tips.

According to Hignell, when it came to organizing his life outside cricket, Zaheer was much less methodical. His benefit season for example was 'totally disorganized'. When asked how he planned to raise the money during the year he answered, 'I will tell them that I am the best batsman in the world and they will give me money.' In the end this proved to be an accurate prediction and without much apparent effort on Zaheer's part, the cash began rolling in from as far away as Dubai.

Zaheer himself had no doubt about the debt he owed to county cricket. Speaking in 1982, 13 years after making his test debut, the Pakistani batsman claimed he was still learning from English cricket. 'I owe everything to Gloucestershire and to the county game over here', he claimed. 'Wherever a cricketer comes from in the world, I don't believe he can do better than play county cricket in England. It teaches you so much.' He added: 'When I scored that double century for Pakistan at Birmingham in 1971, I was still a baby. I have broadened my cricket education through playing for Gloucestershire ever since.'

Procter had no trouble fitting in at the county and a broad interest in rugby among the Gloucestershire players soon proved a useful touchstone for the South African. Although according to Hignell he was sometimes prone to drift off during a game, fed up with another meaningless county contest, Procter oozed confidence. He was one of the first captains to popularize declaration bowling and demanded the same high standards of his players that he asked of himself. Hignell admits that this last quality was sometimes a bit of a strain as Procter appeared to be able to perform wonders without needing any practice.

Hignell has no doubt that West Indian fast bowlers are the most useful type of overseas player: 'You must have somebody who can get two wickets early and then blast out the tail.' It was the failure to have somebody like this waiting in the wings after Procter's retirement that Hignell identifies as one of the side-effects of having three high-quality overseas players available over an extended period. 'The presence of Procter, Zaheer and Sadiq had made the county complacent and the team went through a particularly sticky patch after Procter's retirement in which our opponents took great delight in getting their own back.'

Hignell reinforces the widely held view that Procter's contemporary Barry Richards was unable to motivate himself against all but the strongest of county opposition. (He had a fondness for Kent, Hignell remembers.) Most of the overseas professionals were seen as successful buys for their county, although Hignell remembers Derbyshire's choice of Venkat and Rowe as particularly questionable and that 'no one rated Larry Gomes'. Hignell also thought that of all the other overseas players of his time only Middlesex's Norman Feather-stone was thought to be blocking the development of young English players.

Tim Curtis, Worcestershire 1979 to present

Worcestershire captain and Cricketers' Association chairman Tim Curtis has been one of the county circuit's leading batsman for the last ten years. He has played five times for England during the dark days of the late 1980s and as an opening batsman was on the receiving end of the West Indian assault of 1988. As his Cambridge education and nickname of 'The Professor' suggest he is also one of the deepest thinkers on the game still taking an active part in first-class cricket. For Worcestershire he has opened the batting with Glenn Turner, shared many stands with Graeme Hick and watched Kapil Dev struggle to establish himself in county cricket. All in all Curtis stands four-square in the middle of the modern English domestic game with a perfect viewpoint from which to reflect on the influence of overseas cricketers.

Curtis made his debut for Worcestershire in 1979 at the age of 19. His successful university cricket career, as well as his studies at Durham and then Cambridge, meant that he had little time for county cricket and did not often have to compete for a place with New Zealand legend Glenn Turner. He remembers early on in his career batting at number six in each of the four appearances he made for the county that year. Turner opened the batting and in one match scored a century in both innings. In 1982, Turner's last season, Curtis played just ten first-class matches but did not clash with the New Zealander who had been forced out by injury after scoring 1,000 runs in May.

These circumstances led Curtis to declare that he felt no particular jealousy towards Turner. In fact Curtis was sensible enough to realize that Turner had brought success to Worcestershire and that success meant money, some of which was, no doubt, paying his wages. And beyond this pragmatic approach he makes it clear that the average English county pro is likely to have a lot of respect for an overseas cricketer, whose attitude and talent produce good results for both the foreign player and his club. In this category he places cricketers such as Jimmy Cook, whose enthusiasm to play county cricket in his late 30s endeared him to English players, and whose instant and all-encompassing success made him 'completely respected' throughout the circuit.

Curtis has no doubt that the arrival of overseas players has been good for the financial health of the English game, but also no illusions that it has also resulted in restricted opportunities for home-grown players.

On the positive side Curtis claims that, 'Back in the late 1960s domestic cricket in England was struggling financially and it was only things such as the televising of matches between counties and the International Cavaliers that kept the public's interest alive.' He also is in no doubt that playing standards have been raised by the introduction of overseas players, but he does suggest that this improvement may have simply been the product of importing dozens of high-class cricketers into the domestic game and not an overall increase in playing ability arising from competing alongside and against overseas players.

On the negative side, Curtis dismisses the argument that the hundreds of county places available to English cricketers means that those with talent will always succeed. Some players, he says, can fail dismally for a couple of seasons and display no signs of being able to do better, only to come from nowhere to take the circuit by storm.

As a case in point he nominates Lancashire batsman Nick Speak who played 17 championship matches in 1991, scored just 806 runs at 27.79 and looked unlikely to secure a contract for the 1992 season. But Lancashire kept faith, Speak was given another extended run and he made a massive improvement, hitting 1,982 runs at 57.33. Before this run feast, he had played for the county for 5 years, taken part in 31 first-class games and achieved an average of just 28.61 with just two centuries.

As Curtis says:

There was nothing in his previous record to suggest that Speak could bat as well as he did in 1992. The fact that overseas cricketers reduce the number of places available to English-qualified players means that there is intense pressure on young cricketers to produce immediate results in order to justify their position in a county side. This arrangement works against late developers like Speak.

Curtis is equally convinced that playing in county cricket allows overseas cricketers to become acquainted with English conditions and therefore perform better against the national side on tours of the UK. He refers back to the Pakistani tour of 1992 in which the two most successful batsmen (Salim Malik and Javed Miandad) and the two most successful bowlers (Wasim Akram and Waqar Younis) had all played county cricket. He also describes English county cricket as 'a good finishing school' for overseas players.

A season or two in English domestic cricket allows a young overseas cricketer access to the accumulated knowledge of those that have played on the county circuit, sometimes for decades. It is a thorough cricketing education condensed into the shortest possible period of time.

Curtis claims that county cricket experience is much prized abroad and mentions how established foreign test stars will attempt to find places for their protégés in county cricket. This desire seems particularly strong in the West Indian cricketing community, where moves such as Michael Holding introducing Ian Bishop to Derbyshire are encouraged by the never ceasing search for a high-class fast bowler pursued by English counties. However, the West Indies are not the only cricketing country to want to put a final polish on their young test hopefuls by having county cricket buff up their skills. Imran Khan, for one, saw a county place as vital in the development of both Wasim Akram and Waqar Younis's international careers.

After taking all the pros and cons into account, the Worcestershire captain is clear in his own mind that the introduction of overseas players has contributed to the decline of English test cricket and the corresponding rise in the fortunes of other test-playing nations. However, he perhaps sees this as a necessary evil, claiming that English cricket should be able to support 18 overseas players without further damaging its international strength.

Curtis rejects Alastair Hignell's suggestion that the quota should be extended back to two overseas players per county, one batsman and one bowler. This, he claims, would mean the leading role for each county in the game's most important categories being occupied by overseas players and county matches turning into tests of strength between these players. He believes that the situation in which Hampshire with Greenidge, Richards and Roberts would take on Warwickshire with Kanhai, Kallicharran, Murray and Gibbs to the virtual exclusion of the counties' English-qualified players was a dangerous and unwelcome one.

One of the great unanswered questions arising from the employment of overseas players by English counties over the last 25 years concerns Kapil Dev. The Indian all-rounder had already played a couple of unsuccessful seasons for Northants before he joined Worcestershire in 1984, the season in which Curtis had just established himself as the county's first-choice opener. Over the next two seasons Kapil Dev played just 24 championship games for this new county, scoring 1,456 runs at an average of 42, but taking just 72 wickets (although at an average of 22). The quality was obviously there, but the quantity of runs and wickets expected from an all-rounder of Kapil's abilities was lacking.

Curtis explains that Kapil's appearances were restricted by a series of injuries and by being summoned back in the middle of one season to take part in a series against Sri Lanka. But, perhaps more importantly, the Indian all-rounder's effectiveness suffered because he was 'very much a fatalist' which meant that injuries and other setbacks were simply accepted as 'meant to be' rather than fought against. This attitude towards county cricket was encouraged by his onerous role as both a shock and stock bowler within the Indian test team.

According to Curtis, Kapil was also afflicted by the curse of quality. 'Kapil as a bowler tended to get the best players out, his best deliveries were simply too good for tail enders to get an edge to,' claims the Worcestershire captain.

In Curtis's view the major reason behind Kapil's failure to make the expected impact on county cricket was that his style of playing was simply 'too English'. His swing bowling skills simply replicated, albeit at higher standard, those already on offer in an average English county side. If Kapil was put on from the end that most suited swing bowling then the county's English swing bowlers would have to make do with second best. Kapil's presence in a side duplicated a threat that was already present in most county attacks rather than creating a new one.

What an overseas player needs to provide according to Curtis is 'something different, something that little bit extra'. He paints a picture of the perfect overseas cricketer, a 6 ft 9 in West Indian fast bowler, who possesses a boundless enthusiasm for the county game and mixes deadly yorkers with a stock delivery on a West Indian length that is almost unplayable. A player like this is able to pose a threat when English-type bowlers are defeated either by the lack of swing or movement off the wicket. *They extend the threat* and it is for this reason that, as Curtis points out, there have been more out and out fast bowlers in English cricket over the last 25 years than at any time since the Edwardian golden age.

Curtis claims that a significant amount of coaching goes on between county colleagues of different nations. But he points out that there are always exceptions to this rule, such as Aquib Javed who arrived in the UK with instructions not to show his fellow Hampshire bowlers how the Pakistanis achieved extravagant swing with the old ball. Abdul Qadir, of course, was always wary of playing domestic cricket in England, claiming that a season in county cricket would give the leading batsmen of the world a chance to master his tricks and varieties.

Curtis believes that the rules restricting each county to just one overseas player has made selecting the right cricketer all that more vital to the team's fortunes. But, even so he believes that the average county dressing room is welcoming even to those overseas players who do not make an immediate impact.

Failure, it seems, is acceptable up to a point, but the reaction is usually different if the overseas player is perceived not to be making an effort. Curtis confirms that there are overseas players on the county circuit who have a reputation of 'not trying'. In Curtis's eyes the problem is mainly one of motivation and is particularly acute with fast bowlers, who fear the injuries that seven-days-a-week cricket can bring about.

Sometimes discovering the necessary motivation is simply a question of becoming used to the peculiar conditions that exist on the English county circuit. Curtis remembers young West Indian fast bowler Hartley Alleyne going missing before one match on a particularly bitter English spring day. He was eventually found swathed in sweaters and huddled in the drying room trying to keep warm. Curtis says it is this sort of 'home-sickness' that many overseas players suffer from until they find motivation both from personal ambition and a desire not to let their new colleagues down.

Rather than being motivated by any national or personal ambitions, it is Curtis's belief that even experienced overseas players become caught up in the particular 'dressing room atmosphere' which exists within their adopted county side and react to it accordingly. It is perhaps this reason why Essex, whose dressing room is renowned for its healthy balance between ambition and humour, have managed to take on a series of widely differing personalities as their overseas players and successfully incorporate them into the side. The end result is of course that, although these players sometimes only stayed for one season at a time, they almost immediately felt at home and began performing at their best.

Despite Curtis's preference for bowlers, Worcestershire, like Essex, have picked batsmen as their overseas players ever since the mid-1980s. This has a number of advantages in terms of 'value for money' according to Curtis. First of all batsmen are much less likely than bowlers to become injured during the season and to miss important games. They are also of more use in limited-overs matches because their participation is not restricted as it is with bowlers who are allocated a set number of overs. And, finally, as most spectators still prefer to watch their side bat rather than bowl, a high-quality batsman is more likely to draw the crowds than a bowler of equal talent.

In Worcestershire's case, Curtis admits that fortune played its part in the county's choice of its most successful overseas player. 'It was mainly luck that Hick ended up at Worcestershire and that he turned out to be a star in the making. Nobody realized quite how talented he was and he could have slipped through our fingers.'

Hick played his first championship game for Worcestershire in 1984 at the age of 18, batting once and scoring 82 not out. In 1985, with Kapil out of action, Hick played 10 games and scored 664 runs at 47.72. From there on in Hick, as Worcestershire's first-choice overseas player, came from virtually nowhere to score 1,934 runs at 64.64 in 1986; 1,868 at 53.37 in 1987; 2,443 at 76.34 in 1988; 1,595 at 53.16 in 1989; and 2,273 at 90.92 in 1990. He totalled over 10,000 championship runs in 6 seasons and all from a batsman who, before his debut for Worcestershire, had played just 6 first-class games and scored less than 200 runs. Good luck indeed!

Overseas players and . . . morale

Both Curtis and Hignell make it plain that the way in which overseas players approach becoming part of a county team can be as important as the numbers of runs scored or wickets taken. The behaviour of overseas players while on county duty is always scrutinized by their colleagues and opponents. Courtney Walsh, for example, is widely admired for not demanding that he, as the premier strike bowler, should deliver the first over. Former Gloucestershire captain David Graveney says that Walsh recognized how important it was for 'Syd' Lawrence's development that he should be given the ego boost of bowling first and often having the choice of the downwind end. Walsh has the experience and talent to cope with bowling upwind and is unselfish enough to realize that his young colleague needed to be treated like the true speedster he became if he was to realize his potential.

Another example of an overseas players having a positive influence on a county side came in 1980 when Vincent van der Bijl joined Middlesex. The big South African was a fine cricketer, but perhaps just as importantly he was a great soul who displayed a fierce commitment to his side both off the field as well as on.

During the early 1980s Middlesex were a highly strung, sharply critical team. Van der Bijl was able to defuse the self-destructive side to the prevailing dressing room atmosphere by blaming himself before anyone else for the team's few failings. A fractious inquest into a bad day in the field, with accusations and incriminations flying to and fro, would quickly be undermined by the big South African stating 'It was all my fault, I never should have bowled those two half volleys early on'.

That a player who was contributing so much to what would eventually prove a championship-winning season was prepared to examine his own performance in such detail before turning on others was a salutary lesson to some of the more cynical players of the side. He was also, by claiming an unfair share of the blame for a poor team performance, able to take the pressure off other Middlesex players less sure of their own talent.

And again, Peter Roebuck says that Somerset coach Peter Robinson was very pleased with the influence exerted by Sunil Gavaskar on the county's younger players. The flamboyant example set by Richards and Botham was tempered by Gavaskar's more discriminating approach.

Yorkshire captain Martyn Moxon also claims that his county have selected their first two overseas players as much for what they could contribute off the field as on. He claims that the advice and guidance that a player of Richie Richardson's experience can give to the younger members of Yorkshire's squad is invaluable.

This judgement is endorsed by Geoffrey Boycott, who talks of Richardson's 'presence' commanding respect and attention from those he has attempted to help. Richardson himself says that he always tries to set a positive example to his team mates and claims that one of his aims at Yorkshire is to help the county develop the same self-belief as drives the all-conquering West Indian team.

A final example of the way in which an overseas player can increase his value by showing a willingness to help out those less talented than himself came from Mohammad Azharuddin during his one-season sojourn with Derbyshire in 1991. He was taken on mainly for his vibrant batting skills, but he also impressed with his attitude to the game. Fellow Derbyshire batsman Chris Adams declared that the Indian captaining was 'simply the best around today', while spin bowling all-rounder Ewan McCray praised 'Azza' for in his own words being 'just an average human being who happens to play cricket'.

It is not essential that overseas players 'fit in', as 'Azza' or Van der Bijl did, when they join an English county. There can still be a distance between the foreign stars and the county pros without it necessarily adversely affecting the team's performance. Rice and Hadlee for example, despite playing for Nottinghamshire for a number of years never quite became 'one of the lads'. But, in some circumstances the mental well-being of overseas players can have a direct effect on the quality of their performances, and the most enlightened counties have realized this. One of the best examples of how complex this issue can become happened recently within the county that has developed the strongest reputation for quickly and successfully integrating overseas players into its side.

A belief has grown up around modern Essex cricket. It is a belief that the county's dressing room is somehow imbued with a magical quality which creates a harmony between whatever group of individuals are gathered together under the Essex colours. As noted in earlier chapters it is the most common explanation as to how the county has managed to employ overseas players one season at a time and instantly integrate them into the county side.

The truth, according to Essex wicket-keeper Mike Garnham, is considerably more complicated. He remembers that during 1991 Salim Malik hardly operated in a way conducive to building team spirit. The Pakistani batsman arrived in England with the novel idea of calling 'no' when he intended to run and 'yes' when he planned to stay put. This was a similar tactic to the one pursued by Zaheer Abbas, but unlike his countryman Salim would not always tell his partner of his plans. Even when operating 'normally' Salim would always advance a couple of steps down the wicket before calling. This sort of disregard for his team mates' well-being was always likely to upset the tight-knit Essex side. Eventually he was ordered to stop mucking about, but not before he had run out most of his team mates.

Salim was obviously having some difficulties coming to terms with the Essex way of playing its county cricket. This was reflected by the county's worry about how an overseas player from the Indian sub-continent, Essex's first, might fit into their side. Pakistani players were renowned for being difficult to incorporate into county sides, as (unlike West Indians, or South Africans) English was not their first language and they did not come from a Westernized culture. Gooch had picked out Malik to replace Mark Waugh, claiming that he was 'a top batsman' and 'seemed like a nice guy'.

However, once he arrived in Chelmsford the problems began. Apart from his calling, Salim was an enviable asset on the field, appearing in 22 first-class matches, scoring 1,891 runs at 78.89 and playing a major part in Essex's fifth county championship victory, but off the field it was a different matter. Gooch relates that Malik missed one practice session because it coincided with 'the Muslim Christmas' and that he had to be given a week off in the middle of the season to return home to visit his wife. In fairness, however, these 'complications' were unavoidable and during his week off, Malik missed only one Sunday League match and returned in time for Essex's next championship game, despite apparently not being booked on the only flight back from Pakistan during the period of his holiday.

At the end of season Garnham reports that the Pakistani 'left without saying goodbye, and with my best bat hidden in his kit'. More heinous still was the fact that he 'never bought a drink'. All this would seem to suggest that the Essex magic is no more than a well-publicized myth. However, considering the county's success during the 1991 season, it is in fact a testament to the resilience of the county's good spirits, that the players could continue to operate as an efficient unit around such an obviously difficult individual. More importantly Salim, or Slim as he was known at Chelmsford, was to return to Essex two years later with, by all accounts, a much improved attitude.

Educating Mr Border

A tale which demonstrates the level of commitment Essex usually manage to produce from their overseas players concerns Australian captain Allan Border.

When Border arrived at Chelmsford he was already established as his country's premier batsman, the one reliable player among a string of talented but inconsistent strokeplayers. He had been handed the captaincy of his country after Kim Hughes had resigned in tears and was beginning the tortuous task of draggingAustralia back to its former glory. Because of the Australian marketing men's love affair with one-day cricket he faced the most arduous international playing schedule of any player in the world. He had the hopes of an entire country resting on his already weary shoulders, so why should Essex expect anything more than for him to turn up, score some runs and go home?

But, Border did much more, far exceeding the expectations of most including Essex patriarch Trevor Bailey. The former England all-rounder remembers Border as a player 'with all the strokes', but more importantly a fierce pride in the county's performance. Bailey says:

I remember Border batting against Warwickshire on a difficult pitch. A ball flew and cut his face. It was a bad slash and they took him off to hospital to get it stitched. Nobody expected him to play again in the match, but he came out of the hospital, went straight back to the ground and at the fall of the next wicket resumed his innings, eventually scoring a century. You don't do something like that if you're just a hired hand; he was a great team player.

He also remembers Keith Fletcher claiming that Border was 'the best player he ever batted with', which as Bailey says, is 'not something he would say lightly'. Fletcher played with Border during the Australian's first season in county cricket and it is easy to see where the Essex captain's admiration comes from. Border played in 18 of Essex's 24 championship games, many of them taking place on the 'sporting' wickets prevalent during that season. As Essex collected their fourth championship title, Border scored 1,287 runs at 51.84. This compared with Graham Gooch's 778 runs at 37.04 in 13 games and Paul Prichard's 1,165 at 31.48 in 24.

Border, himself, declared at the end of the 1986 season that the English first-class game was superior to the Sheffield Shield competition, claiming that 'They play a really crafty game here. The bowlers think more, and they brood about getting you out.' Brood the English bowlers may have done, but they had very little success against Border and it would be interesting to get the Australian captain's views of county cricket after beating England in three consecutive series.

There is in fact a widespread belief that Border used his two trips to England as a scouting mission to make sure that Australia did not again suffer the series of embarrassing defeats inflicted by England in 1985. Playing with Fletcher, who was a walking encyclopedia of English players' strengths and weaknesses, Border certainly had a good opportunity to pick up plenty of inside knowledge. The Australian side of 1989 was certainly much more deliberate in its field placing than the 1985 team – the mid-on positioned 20 yards from the bat which so unnerved Graham Gooch when he faced Alderman's bowling being a case in point.

But, perhaps closer to the truth was the fact that Border, by playing for Essex, finally knew what it was like to be part of a winning side. Fletcher backs up this theory saying: 'He picked up the way we played our cricket. We never went into any match other than totally convinced that we would win and I think Border picked up on this.'

Border's captaincy in 1985 was characterized by a sense of drift. From 1989 onwards it was fiercely committed, taking every opportunity to grind the opposition into the dust and often batting on until the opposition faced final innings targets of 500 plus. Border himself was a man far removed from the friendly but diffident character who toured in 1985. In 1989 he positioned himself at silly mid-off and played a full part in the verbal and physical pressurizing of uncertain English batsmen. Sheer self-belief and a will to win marked out the Australians of 1989, and Essex's part in this transformation should not be under-played.

Overseas players and . . . coaching

It could be argued that Border received a master class in captaincy from Keith Fletcher while he was at Essex to the detriment of the English test side, but it is the other side of the argument, the coaching of young English players by overseas cricketers which is often put forward by their supporters as one reason for their presence in county cricket. Former England fast bowler Jonathan Agnew, for example, is steadfast in his belief that Andy Roberts 'taught me virtually everything I know'.

Over recent years there has in fact been a tendency to look overseas for coaching as well as playing talent, a trend reinforced by the belief that Australian coaches in particular are the best available. Bobby Simpson did not manage to do for Leicestershire what he accomplished for his country, but Western Australian coach Daryl Foster has revived Kent's fortunes.

During the 1980s Australia established itself as one of the world's leading nations in sports coaching and psychology, and this has rubbed off on the Aussie players who have come to England to play county cricket. Border, Steve and Mark Waugh, and particularly Dean Jones have all spread the word of Australia's new coaching creed.

Durham seamer Simon Hughes tells of how one young batsman from an opposing county who was struggling for runs was helped by Jones.

He [the young English player] tried adjusting his stance, grip, foot movement, even make of bat. It made no difference and his self-belief was seriously eroded. The arrival of Dean Jones with the visiting Durham second XI was the turning point. The batsman spent 20 minutes with Jones, who told him simply to fix his eyes on the seam of the ball as the bowler was running in and as it arrived down the wicket, instead of gazing in a general direction as most batsmen do. The player has not failed since.

Former Durham captain David Graveney agrees with Hughes's high regard for Jones, claiming that the Australian was 'absolutely fantastic'. 'I've never known a player with a more positive attitude and that has been especially valuable with so many inexperienced players in the squad', he claimed.

Graveney's impression of Jones is reinforced by the events of 1993. Durham did not renew Jones's contract after his first season because it was assumed that he would be part of the Australian team touring England in 1993. But much to the surprise of most in English cricket Jones was not selected and the Australian batsman applied for a work permit to rejoin Durham. When this was refused by the Home Office he flew to England and took up the role of an unpaid second team coach.

However, it seems that English players are not always willing to take up the opportunity of learning from overseas players. Richard Hadlee, for one, found it hard to understand that very few of his colleagues or rivals on the county circuit wanted to know 'how he did it'.

Speaking in 1990 he said:

In the ten years I was at Notts, only a couple of players ever approached me for advice. I find that amazing and it's an insight into the modern attitude. Maybe some guy has learned a bit from watching me, but as far as technique and attitude, forget it. Nobody ever wanted to know.

This attitude is particularly worrying as Dennis Lillee, for example, believes that the kind of perceptive but simple advice which Australian cricketers seem to be able to pass on is simply not available from English coaches. He points out that Andrew Caddick and Martin McCague, England's two most promising bowlers of 1993, both received their early coaching in New Zealand and Australia respectively.

Simon Hughes describes the new Australian coaching method as practised by Lillee everywhere from Northamptonshire to the Indian fast-bowling academy:

Confidence is the key to success. This is what Lillee is good at instilling. Instead of picking holes in your technique after a brief net sessions, he monitors match performances and highlights the assets. Not for him the obsession with foot and body positions, his concern is harnessing natural enthusiasm to the quest for runs and particularly wickets. It sounds simple, but so often coaches get bound up with technical perfection, quashing a player's spontaneity and confidence.

Hughes contrasts this approach with that of Surrey and England bowling coach Geoff Arnold, who would constantly insist on Devon Malcolm developing the outswinger, or 'shape' as he called it, rather than concentrate on helping the Derbyshire paceman bowl consistently at high pace.

Kent coach Daryl Foster, who is an associate professor of physical education at the University of Western Australia, perhaps best sums up the straightforward approach adopted by modern Australian coaches. Expressing disappointment at Kent's failure to make the most of match-winning positions during the 1991 season, he complained:

We've lost too many games by narrow margins – games we should have won. We even had the West Indies on toast and then lost. People came up to me and said, 'What a fantastic game of cricket.' It's only a great game when you've won – that's the spirit I'm trying to instil into this side.

It was, of course, also exactly the opposite of Kent's traditional approach to the game, which was, although tacitly, based on Kipling's belief that one should 'meet with Triumph and Disaster, And treat those two impostors just the same'. Foster was having none of that and developed a training regime that concentrated much more on physical fitness and mental preparedness, than cricketing technique. Every member of the Kent squad was presented with a book on developing mental skills, written by Foster and printed at his own cost.

Echoing Jones's advice to the young second XI left-hander, Foster describes his approach to the game.

Cricket is a lot of mini games contained in 100 overs. Each ball is a separate entity – so that's 600 games in day. The bowler has to channel his energies and concentrate on one ball at a time. He can't expect to take a wicket with every ball, so he has to set traps – and spring the trap when the batsman least expects it. Then he must switch off between balls; as he walks back to his mark he needs a focus – the flags or the dolly-bird in the bikini – to enable him to build up peak concentration for the next delivery. The skill is to limit concentration to those peak times.

Overseas players and . . . self-reliance

Foster's stressing of concentration highlights one of the commonest failings of English test cricketers during the 1980s and 1990s. The greatest contrast between the English and Australian teams in the last three series was not the talent of the players involved, but the level of determination they displayed. According to some, that lack of determination is 'taught' in county cricket with English players relying on their overseas recruits to win their matches for them.

New Zealand captain Martin Crowe certainly believes this to be the case:

I'm sure there should only be one registered non-Englishman per county. Steps have been taken in that direction but if you took more responsibility from the overseas guys, it would fall on the English players. In my experience, the home-grown lads have subconsciously said, 'Oh, he'll do it – he'll take the wickets and score the runs' – and it shows. From what I have seen, the overseas players outshine the English players not only in the terms of ability but in attitude and determination.

One of the clearest examples of over-reliance on an overseas player by a county side came in the 1993 Benson & Hedges Cup final. It was not just Wasim Akram's poor performance with the ball which helped Derbyshire win a tension-filled match, but also the way in which he let his anger at a pre-match controversy infect his performance and in turn that of the whole team.

The seeds of Akram's failure of temperament were sown during a county championship match a fortnight before the final. The game between Lancashire and Derbyshire was meandering towards a draw when Wasim took the ball and, swinging it sharply for the first time in the match, took six wickets to win the match for the Red Rose county. Coming in the wake of the 1992

Pakistan tour of England and the allegations of ball tampering by the tourists, there was much suspicious whispering in the press and around the county circuit.

These suspicions took on a great deal more weight when the ball was sent 'for examination' to the Test and County Cricket Board's (TCCB) HQ at Lord's. The TCCB claimed that in the interests of improving the quality of the balls used in the domestic competitions, examples of those that had 'worn badly' were regularly sent to them. They also pointed out that both umpires, as required by the new rules introduced after the controversy of 1992, had checked the ball at regular intervals during Akram's final devastating spell and had found nothing wrong. Derbyshire played down the matter, with captain Kim Barnett claiming that the decision to send the ball to Lord's was not 'a personal go' at Akram.

He added: 'We were concerned about the state of the ball and were within our rights to send it away. But, Lord's decided it was OK and that's fair enough.'

Lancashire and Akram, in particular. though were far from convinced by Derbyshire's bland protestations. The Pakistani captain and his team mates were in fact furious, believing that Derbyshire had deliberately tried to smear their dramatic county championship win, throw into question the methods employed by their leading bowler and, specifically, put him off his game for the final.

If the last tactic really was Derbyshire's aim, then it worked a treat. On the morning of the final Lancashire won the toss and put Derbyshire in. Akram came on to bowl after eight overs with Derbyshire already having lost Bowler and with De Freitas and Austin bowling well. Akram on the other hand bowled like a drain, and his direction went haywire as he strived for pace. He was lucky to dismiss Barnett as he bottom-edged on to his stumps trying to repeat the square cut for four he had played off the previous delivery. Chris Adams came in next and Akram, who had identified the Derbyshire batsman as the main instigator of the ball-tampering smear, redoubled his efforts.

Whether through malice or striving for pace, Akram thudded a chest-high beamer into Adams's back and Lancashire simply went off the deep end. What had previously been a tightly-fought game of cricket became a war and, as in most wars, reason vanished. Time and again one of the county circuit's best fielding sides let balls shoot through their fingers to the boundary. Those balls that were stopped were just as likely to be sent sailing past the stumps for over-throws, the result of ill-judged (and ill-tempered) attempts at run-outs. Derbyshire, reduced to 66 for 4 through an over-ambitious approach by their batsmen, were allowed to recover to 252 for 6 of their 55 overs. The pressure built up over the match's first hour evaporated and Dominic Cork (first with Tim O'Gorman and then Karl Krikken) was able to take advantage of a team motivated by a irrational desire for revenge, rather than a cool and focused desire to win the game.

Akram proved the most expensive of the 10 bowlers used in the match, his 4 spells being 3 overs for 17, 3 for 15, 2 for 7 and 3 for 26. When eventual man of the match Cork stepped briskly outside off-stump to send an Akram delivery through square leg for four off the penultimate ball of the Derbyshire innings, it was an eloquent summation of how badly the Pakistani and his team mates had let their anger adversely affect their standard of play and how well their opponents had exploited that failing.

Later in the dressing room Adams and Akram confronted each other, but both must have known that Derbyshire had already had the last word. It was also somewhat ironic that Derbyshire had overcome Lancashire and Akram without their own overseas player, West Indian fast bowler Ian Bishop, who missed most of the 1993 season through a recurring back problem.

This was not the first time that Akram's lack of temperament had affected the performance of his team mates. In 1991 he was fined £1,000 for swearing at umpire Nigel Plews, a penalty his team mates thought a massive over-reaction. The fine and the resultant press attention soured team morale and Lancashire opener Gehan Mendis commented: 'I hate to think that it had a bearing on our performances for the rest of the season, but I'm sure it did.'

Akram is a wonderful player and, as Lancashire captain Neil Fairbrother freely admits, the county's young team revere him for both his skills and his commitment. For example, when Akram was fined for swearing at Plews, his team mates (most on a much lower salary than the Pakistani) all chipped in to help him pay it. But at the time of the 1993 Benson & Hedges final Akram was still only 27 and described by one team mate as 'young for his age', as well as over-sensitive to criticism. This is a fragile base from which to construct team morale, and provides an object lesson in the dangers of introducing a powerful talent and explosive personality into a county club dressing room. Lancashire's opponents now possess the invaluable knowledge, 'upset Akram and the wheels start to come off'.

Overseas players and . . . life on the county circuit

This theory of over-reliance, like most issues in the overseas cricketers' debate, has a counterargument. A perfect example was that used by Mike Procter in an article defending overseas players. He takes issue with Alec Bedser's suggestion that Frank Hayes's career had been harmed by having to bat below Clive Lloyd and writes:

I would have thought it was easier for Hayes to follow Lloyd, because if he bats with Clive, there's no pressure on Hayes to get quick runs. Lloyd is such a good fast-scoring batsman that his partner just needs to chug along quietly, playing himself in and giving Lloyd as much of the strike as possible, then taking over when he gets out. Conversely, walking in to bat after the bowlers have been smashed around by Lloyd is surely an enjoyable prospect. The bowlers could well be demoralized after being thrashed around the park, and a talented player like Hayes would find them fairly undemanding.

Imran Khan is another who believes that overseas players have been good for English cricket. In his autobiography he exclaims:

I wish that in Pakistan we could have two world-class cricketers per first-class team. I am sure we would become unbeatable. We have so much talent, but our domestic cricket is of such a poor standard that it is impossible to polish it here in Pakistan. The young county cricketer has such an excellent opportunity to play with and against great players . . . If top players are not being produced within the [English] county system, then there has to be other serious structural deficiencies. It was their own fault if [English] youngsters could not learn from Rice and Hadlee and others of that calibre. The two English players who are kept out by overseas cricketers will probably be marginal players anyway, with no chance of ever representing England.

Imran concludes by making the persuasive point that if overseas players were harming the development of young English players, 'then Yorkshire should have supplied the bulk of the English test team [since 1968]'.

Richard Hadlee is another to come to the defence of his vocation, simply saying: 'It's the overseas players who have made the county game the commodity it is today; without those players, I dread to think what the standard would be like.'

Procter, Imran and Hadlee demonstrate some sensitivity in their comments and obviously feel that they were not always welcome everywhere on the county circuit, due to the belief that their presence was harming English cricket. But, there is a darker side to this 'lack of welcome' for overseas cricketers. Despite the fact that black and Asian cricketers form the majority of overseas players, rumours of racism still persist in the selection and treatment of foreign-born county players. In an earlier chapter we have seen how a considerable amount of racial tension surrounded Yorkshire's selection policy and that Joel Garner hinted at an inherent racism embedded in the heart of UK cricket. It is also possible that Gordon Greenidge might have chosen to play for England rather than the West Indies had he not encountered such a virulent 'anti-black' feeling while making his way as a schoolboy cricketer in the south of England during the late 1960s.

Allegations of racism were also made, albeit 11 years after the event, by Bishan Bedi concerning his dismissal by Northants. Bedi had taken part in the Packer Circus and the Midlands county had decided that this was a sackable offence. A legal challenge to the county's decision proved fruitless and Bedi believed that his claim that John Lever had been using Vaseline to shine the ball during the 1976/7 tour of India was behind the alleged witch hunt.

Speaking to *Wisden Cricket Monthly* in 1988 he described his reaction to his departure from county cricket:

[I was] bitter, very bitter. I was also a fool, I should never have gone to court. The TCCB, the MCC and the judiciary all ganged up against me during the proceedings. Later I could only laugh at my foolhardiness to seek justice from quarters where everything was alien.

Asked if he had any regrets he said:

The only regret was that I had bowled my heart out for that wretched club. They were most ungrateful in not allowing me to go through the course. I would have got my benefit – but didn't. It was evident from the moment I resumed in 1977 that they were hell-bent on getting me out. After all, I was an outsider.

In fact, I had got offers from two other county sides, but those two clubs were instructed to keep their hands off me. They [Northants] were quite determined to phase me out of county cricket. This is something I secretly liked about the English. They were quite determined to ensure that no black man earning his living in England could dare call the white man a cheat and get away with it. Had I been born white, things may not have worked out as they did. To prove this statement, let me tell you that Clive Rice was sacked by Nottinghamshire when he joined World Series Cricket. He not only went to court and won, but was reinstated as captain.

There is no love lost in my opinion. The only regret, let me repeat, is that I sweated blood for the county, joining them when they were in the dumps. I took nearly 500 wickets for them in six seasons, which most don't do in 12 years of county cricket. When Mushtaq Mohammad [who was known to be unhappy for much of his time with the county], Sarfraz Nawaz and I played for them, Northants were elevated to the top bracket.

It would be grossly unfair to suggest that the experience of playing county cricket is as painful for most overseas players as it eventually was for Bedi. The lifestyle of overseas players can differ dramatically depending on their salary, age and background. Many are left, for example, to find their own accommodation. This is a difficult enough task for an Englishman considering the current state of the private rented sector, but it is particularly onerous for an overseas player in his early 20s, living away from home for the first time, and having to cope with an alien culture and a very limited budget. But other overseas players have a much happier time of it.

Wasim Akram, starting his county career in 1988 with a six-year contract already signed, sealed and delivered, was in the best possible position to enjoy his time in the UK. In a 1989 interview with *Cricket Life International* he painted a picture of life as a 20-year-old cricketing bachelor that would have had most old county pros gnashing their teeth in envy.

After shivering his way through the English summer of 1986 while playing in the Lancashire Leagues, Wasim moved up in the world when he joined the county circuit. He said goodbye to the tiny flat he shared with fellow Pakistani pace bowler Moshin Kamal and moved to a four-bedroom house in the Cheshire Countryside. He also exchanged bus and train travel for a sponsored Rover 820 – a director's car as opposed to the sales rep's Ford Escort that most 20-year-old county players had to make to do with at the time.

But the most enviable aspect of Akram's life arises, not from his county employment, but from being a cricketing hero in an area with a large Pakistani community. Not only is he able to provide a comfortable home away from home to those close to him, such as brother Nadeem and his old flat mate Moshin, but also such is his attraction to his cricket-loving countrymen living in the area that one actually agreed to move in and provide him with the fiery curries to which he is addicted.

Sunil Gavaskar in his stay with Somerset during the 1980 season also found England a pleasant place in which to work. Compared to Bombay, where his appearance on the street would signal the formation of a friendly mob bent on dogging his every footstep, the polite interest taken by Somerset's cricket lovers was a welcome relief. And, again like Wasim, Gavaskar was in no danger of feeling homesick as he arrived in England with wife, children, parents and a retinue of servants.

Overseas players and . . . a worrying lack of quality

Gavaskar's selection by Somerset as a one-season replacement for Richards and Garner was a legitimate one. The Indian batsman was a world-class player who, even during the course of just one season, could contribute a great deal to the club. But one of the most worrying, and damaging, results of the introduction of immediate registration has been some counties' desire to field an overseas player even when their choice can hardly be classed as a world beater. As was demonstrated when Daniel lost form and Middlesex were left without an overseas player for the 1988 season, many county players refuse to believe that their team will not be taken seriously without an overseas player. In Middlesex's case, this simply was not true as the county's good showing during the season displayed.

This phenomenon has became particularly acute over the last ten years. In seven individual cases counties have picked overseas players who were never likely to make the grade in English county cricket. Those players were as follows.

Player	County	Matches	Runs	Av.	Wkts	Av.	Season
J.A. Carse	N'hants	11	129	64.50	22	32.81	1983
D.J. Hickey	Glamorgan	12	19	4.75	17	58.58	1986
H.A. Page	Essex	12	201	16.75	25	33.56	1987
C. Van Zyl	Glamorgan	12	115	12.78	17	50.00	1987/8
P. de Villiers	Kent	12	264	22.00	25	39.68	1990
R.P. Snell	Somerset	16	436	27.25	27	44.22	1992
R.E. Bryson	Surrey	10	257	23.36	17	68.52	1992

Two things stand out from this list. The first is that all seven were pace bowlers, usually with ambitions to be considered as all-rounders. The second was that six of the seven were from Southern Africa.

Ever since the introduction of immediate registration the cricketing powers of South Africa have been very successful in marketing their players to English counties. Of course it did the apartheid regime no harm at all to have a large number of South Africans playing in English cricket, alongside players from

India, Pakistan and the West Indies. How, the apartheid apologists asked, could South Africa be such an awful place if players such as Viv Richards were prepared to take the field against Clive Rice and Mike Procter? This exercise in international relations was aided by the attitude of some counties, which – according to one county captain of the time – disliked employing black or Asian players. Garner and Bedi's fears, it seems, were not without justification.

Of course the South African players also had a genuine desire to take part in county cricket, robbed as they were of the chance to shine on the international stage. In the early 1970s, South Africa possessed some of the world's leading players and these naturally gravitated towards the highest quality (and best paid) cricket they could play.

Gradually, as time progressed, South African cricket, without the improving effect of international competition, began to produce fewer and fewer outstanding cricketers. But this did not seem to stop the flow of South African cricketers into English county cricket. 'Ordinary' players such as Anton Ferreira continued to come to the UK, usually to take on the role of the second overseas player allowed by the regulations until the late 1970s. In the 1980s, South Africa was no longer a world power, but still their cricketers were imported. Over the last 15 years only Jimmy Cook and Alan Donald have proved themselves to be wise overseas selections.

To a certain extent the international isolation of South African cricket has created an attractive mystery about the country's leading players. Very few English cricketers or county officials had seen much of South African cricket over the past 25 years, so the tales that have filtered up from the southern hemisphere about the prowess of Springbok cricketers could not be tested against more objective eye-witness evidence. The last meaningful contact England had with South African cricket was in the late 1960s when the Springbok team was the strongest in the world, creating the abiding impression of South Africa as a country of cricketing world beaters. Despite the continuing flow of South Africans into county cricket, that ceased to be the case in the early 1980s.

The cost of employing overseas players who do nothing to justify their salaries is disturbing enough, but perhaps more disturbing is the effect recruiting a below par overseas player can have on team morale. As was the case with Middlesex's employment of Alan Connolly, a far from poor cricketer, favourable treatment of an overseas player can disrupt even the most experienced team's equilibrium. And what were young bowlers such as Alan Walker, Steve Barwick, Simon Base, Philip North, Steve Watkin, Don Topley, Vince Wells, Mark Ealham, Adriannus Van Troost, Roland Lefebvre and Mark Feltham – all of whom had their playing opportunities reduced by these seven under-achieving overseas players – to think of a game which took more notice of advance publicity than on the field results?

Overseas players and . . . money

Money, of course, will always be a cause of tension between clubs and their players. And, because of the relatively higher salaries they command, overseas players often find themselves at the centre of disputes between English-qualified players and their county employers. For example, there was considerable bad feeling on the county circuit when a number of relatively highly paid overseas players stayed with their respective counties just long enough to earn a benefit and then refused to sign any further contract of employment. Barry Richards, for example, claimed that the established England test players in the Hampshire side he joined 'were unhappy at my intrusion on their salary scale'. Richards also admits that he did not make the situation any better by bullishly deciding that he would prove himself on the field without also taking a diplomatic approach in the dressing room.

Money certainly proved a sore point when Graham Dilley missed the 1984 season through injury. The neck problem which caused the lay-off had sprung up during England's 1983/4 tour of Pakistan and Dilley believed that he was entitled to £200 a week from an insurance policy organized by the TCCB. Unfortunately Kent believed that the money should go to them and gave Dilley the impression that if he disagreed he would find himself out of a job. When the English fast bowler found out that the county was allegedly using the money to pay Australian Terry Alderman's wages he was incensed and left to join Worcestershire soon after.

Overseas players and . . . respect

Unfair treatment of any kind is always likely to upset your average county pro, who usually does not need any encouragement to start developing paranoid thoughts. Overseas players tend to arrive in English county cricket with their reputation preceding them. This tends to encourage unequal treatment by officials (as was the case at Kent during 1984), captains and even, it seems, umpires. Adrian Jones claims in Rob Steen's *Spring, Summer, Autumn* that overseas bowlers have the reputation of being able to con umpires into responding positively to doubtful appeals.

Despite this allegedly unfair treatment, however, English county professionals appear to harbour very few grudges against overseas players. This was demonstrated when, during research for the *1992 Cricketers' Who's Who*, the 300 plus players and umpires on the county circuit were asked which cricketers they most admired. The results show a widespread admiration for the leading overseas players of the last 25 years.

Of the 25 'most admired cricketers', 13 were from overseas. Of those only Lillee and Graham Pollock had not had an extensive career in English county cricket. The lack of prejudice against overseas players is further highlighted by the fact that two of the 'Englishmen', Graeme Hick and Robin Smith, hail from Southern Africa and have been accused by some of taking test places away from cricketers born in the UK.

Most admired players, 1992

		Nationality	Votes
1	I.T. Botham	E	72
2	R.J. Hadlee	NZ	69
=3	I.V.A. Richards	WI	51
=3	M.D. Marshall	WI	51
5	D.I. Gower	E	40
6	D.K. Lillee	A	39
7	G.A. Gooch	E	27
8	A.P.E. Knott	E	23
=9	S.J. Cook	SA	22
=9	R. Smith	E	22
11	G. Boycott	E	20
12	R.W. Taylor	E	19
13	M.A. Holding	WI	18
14	G. St A Sobers	WI	17
15	A.R. Border	A	15
16	G.C. Greenidge	WI	14
=17	C.E.B. Rice	SA	13
=17	G.A. Hick	E	13
19	B. Richards	SA	12
=20	C. Lloyd	WI	11
=20	M.W. Gatting	E	11
=20	R.C. Russell	E	11
23	D.L. Amiss	E	10
24	J.E. Emburey	E	9
25	R.G. Pollock	SA	8

The overseas county players in the list divide neatly into two categories, the international superstars and the county stalwarts. The first category is by far the largest, but the players included in it all owe much of their recognition to their presence on the county circuit.

Hadlee, Marshall, Holding, Sobers, Border, Greenidge, Lloyd, and Viv and Barry Richards are all accepted as masters of their particular cricketing art, but so are Gavaskar, Greg Chappell and Kapil Dev. The fact that these three test stars only flirted with county cricket has counted against them in terms of recognition throughout the UK. It is hard to believe that Alan Border, for example, would have found such a lofty place in this list if he had not spent two highly successful seasons with Essex and established a reputation as a great team man who displayed an outstanding commitment to his adopted county.

The other two remaining overseas county players in the list are both from South Africa and therefore did not have the chance to shine at test level. That said, the reasons for their recognition are markedly different. Rice owes his level of admiration to a long and highly successful county career as one of the circuit's most respected players and captains.

Jimmy Cook, too, is widely respected as a player, but he managed to become one of the circuit's favourite players in just two seasons. When he joined Somerset in 1989, he had never played county cricket outside South Africa before. His massive success once he arrived in the UK, as well as the complete lack of airs and graces which accompanied his triumphant progress around the country, quickly endeared him to opponents and rivals alike. The county players' admiration for Rice centre mainly around his skill as a cricketer and the aura of success that surrounded Nottinghamshire in the early to mid 1980s; their votes for Cook were just as much a show of affection as they were a recognition of his great talent.

The above list is also interesting for the overseas county players who do not appear on it. Most notable perhaps is the omission of Imran Khan. He received just 5 votes from the 300–odd respondents to the survey; a low level of recognition given his record and length of county career which may possibly be a hangover from his controversial move to Sussex in the late 1970s and persistent rumours that he did not always 'try' while playing county cricket. Other surprising omissions include Martin Crowe, Mike Procter and Alan Donald who received just four votes each, as well as Wasim Akram, who got only three votes. Three of the longest serving overseas county players, Wayne Daniel, Joel Garner and Alvin Kallicharran, received just one vote each.

But perhaps the last word on the place overseas players occupy in English county cricket should be left to the people who pay their wages, namely the supporters.

Benefits tend to be the ultimate test of the degree of affection in which cricketers are held by their clubs' supporters. Two particular examples of benefits awarded to overseas players tend to suggest that, however great their contribution to the county has been, overseas cricketers are deemed not to be as worthy of reward as their English-qualified colleagues. Viv Richards and Malcolm Marshall, for example, were both highly successfully county cricketers and yet their benefits were nowhere near as successful as English-qualified players of similar standing.

In 1982 Viv Richards's benefit earnt him £56,440, but in 1984 Ian Botham made £90,822 and a year later Graham Gooch's benefit earnt him a massive £153,000. A similar scenario repeated itself in 1987. Malcolm Marshall, arguably the most effective overseas bowler in county cricket, gained just £61,006 from his benefit (a record for a West Indian county player). This compared to David Gower's £121,546 during the same year and to the 1988 benefits of Mike Gatting (£205,000), Alan Lamb (£134,000) and even those of Phil Neale (£153,005) and Arnie Sidebottom (£103,240)!

8 A self-inflicted injury

Has the presence of overseas cricketers in county cricket played a part in the increasingly poor results achieved by the English test side over the last decade? The answer to this must be yes.

It will be impossible ever to prove exactly how great an influence the presence of overseas players in county cricket has had on weakening the English test side and strengthening those of its opponents, but the weight of evidence presented over the last seven chapters leads to two main conclusions:

1 the decline of England as a cricketing power coincided with the number of overseas players in county cricket reaching its peak;

2 the success of rival test nations against England has usually coincided with periods in which many (if not most) of their leading players were employed as county professionals.

The first conclusion is supported by a number of findings within the preceding chapters. The most telling is that the poorest ever generation of would-be test cricketers (i.e. those making their debut in the mid-1980s) faced the greatest competition for places from overseas cricketers. England were a weakened side because of this lack of young talent, which meant that all other test sides stood a greater chance of defeating them.

For evidence to support the second conclusion it is not necessary to look further than the all-conquering West Indian side of the 1980s. Every single member of that team's fearsome and highly effective bowling attack, *every one*, honed his skills in county cricket, while the side's three leading batsman all had lengthy county careers. More specific examples are provided by Pakistan (whose batting strength of the 1970s and early 1980s was built entirely on county cricket experience according to Mudassar Nazar), New Zealand and Australia who all enjoyed most of their greatest successes while their leading players were taking part in English county cricket.

England's record against Australia in the 1980s and 1990s proves the best demonstration of the correlation between these two factors. In the three series covering the period 1981 to 1985, England won seven test matches against Australia and lost four. During the next three series they managed only two further victories and lost eight. At the time of writing, out of the 17 test matches vs.

England, Australia have won 11, drawn 5 and lost just 1 match. What could have brought about this reversal of fortunes? A number of factors spring to mind, but the one most relevant to this book is that most of Australia's leading batsmen of the last five years (Border, Jones, Moody, and Mark and Steve Waugh) have enjoyed highly successful, and confidence-boosting, county careers, while the Australian captain was given an extended lesson in winning cricket matches during his time at England's most successful county side, Essex. The Australian sides of 1981–5 possessed only two county cricketers, and one of those (Greg Chappell) had last played domestic cricket in England during 1969.

Apart from the Australians, now apparently extinct fear of playing English county cricket, leading players of all test nations have praised the way in which county cricket improves the playing standards of overseas recruits and have made every attempt to secure places for their promising youngsters. They, at least, have no doubts that the presence of overseas players in county cricket has increased the strength of other test-playing nations. They would also argue, however, that it has also had a positive effect on English-qualified players.

Since the mid-1960s, there have been two major changes to the nature of county cricket. The first was the introduction of three limited-overs competitions, and the second the introduction of immediate registration and the resulting flood of overseas players into the county game. Both have had an effect on the standards of first-class cricket in England (and the nation's decline as a test power), but one-day games are played the world over (if not to the same extent), while the significant presence of overseas players in domestic competitions is a factor exclusive to the UK.

This book has been an attempt to determine the influence of overseas players, both on the county game and on the fortunes of the English test team. Viewed from this perspective it now appears that there are a number of clear advantages and disadvantages to the presence of overseas players in county cricket.

Pros and cons of permitting overseas players to take part in county cricket

Pros

1 Coaching of young English players by experienced and highly talented overseas players will help them develop faster and to a higher standard. Overseas players can also help boost morale and instil the 'winning habits'.

2 The presence of overseas players 'takes the pressure off' young English cricketers, allowing then to develop their skills without feeling that every mistake would be highly damaging both to their county's chance of success and their chance of continuing employment.

3 Overseas players raise playing standards in the county game, therefore producing higher quality English test players.

4 A game featuring the world's greatest players becomes a bigger draw, both for spectators, and potential sponsors and advertisers. The money generated in this way can be ploughed back into the development of young English players.

5 An effective and successful overseas player can help weak teams win domestic competitions, therefore reducing the gap between richer and poorer counties, and creating a more equitable spread in cricketing opportunities across the UK.

6 Playing against overseas players on a regular basis allows those in and around the English test team to analyse their strengths and weaknesses.

Cons

1 The presence of overseas players restricts the opportunities for young county players and therefore hampers the flow of talent through to the English test side.

2 The dominant presence of overseas players has led to county players becoming less self-reliant.

3 The high salaries commanded by, often relatively inexperienced, overseas players can cause jealousy and disruption in the dressing room.

4 Overseas players taking part in county cricket can analyse the strengths and weaknesses of English test cricketers to the benefit of their countries' test sides.

5 Playing quality competitive cricket six days a week enables young overseas players to develop their talents. It also allows overseas players to come to terms with English conditions, a significant advantage in test series played in the UK.

On the face of it, the good and bad influences appear to more or less balance each other out. But a closer examination of each point produces a more worrying conclusion.

Coaching by overseas players can be highly advantageous to young English players and there are numerous examples of it taking place. But the actions of Dean Jones at Durham or Richie Richardson at Yorkshire are still unfortunately the exception. The blame does not lie exclusively with the overseas players (many, like Richards and Garner, believing that coaching youngsters was not part of their brief). English-qualified county professionals seem to be amazingly wary about asking for advice from overseas players (even those as highly skilled and admired as Richard Hadlee) and the county clubs themselves do not appear to make it sufficiently clear to their foreign recruits that they are expected to help the development of young players.

This haphazard approach to coaching by overseas players seems to be reinforced by the fact that their presence does not appear to have any real effect on the number of young England players that a county has produced. Yorkshire, Derbyshire and Lancashire (who have employed very few overseas players) might not have produced that many test players over the last 25 years, but then neither have Gloucestershire, Glamorgan and Warwickshire (who have employed dozens).

It is true, however, that the arrival of some overseas players has revived a county's fortunes, simply because they provide an example of excellence which others can begin to follow. In these cases, although the overseas player may never utter a word of technical advice, his presence can in itself produce an equally important boost to morale. This, for example, was the all-important role that Viv Richards played for Somerset in the late 1970s.

The idea, promoted first by former *Wisden* editor Sydney Pardon and most recently voiced by Yorkshire captain Martyn Moxon, that overseas players allow young English players to develop without constant and unrealistic pressure to perform also appears highly questionable. The argument goes that when a young player has developed his talent enough to shoulder his fair share of responsibility, he will emerge from beneath the protective umbrella provided by his overseas colleagues and be in a better shape to meet the demands of test cricket.

But this argument seems to fly in the face of common sense. How, without experiencing responsibility, will a young player ever learn to cope with it? The other side of the argument, advanced by Martin Crowe among others, that English players have become less reliant appears to carry much more weight. This seems especially true when considering that a worrying lack of fight seems to have characterized English test sides during the last ten years, with the honourable exception of periods during Graham Gooch's second stint of captaincy.

Alastair Hignell, one of the stoutest defenders of the presence of overseas players in county cricket, admits that young Gloucestershire players batting behind Sadiq, Zaheer and Procter rarely learnt how to build an innings. And how might Hignell himself, who displayed the ability to reach the highest level in one sport and admits that he did not fulfil his youthful promise as a cricketer, have developed if he had had to shoulder more responsibility while playing for Gloucestershire?

The lack of personal initiative or innovation has seemed particularly lacking among England's bowlers, and here the influence of overseas cricketers is particularly detectable. With a Waqar Younis or an Ian Bishop attacking from one end, all English bowlers need do is develop a good defensive bowling technique (encouraged in any case by the amount of one-day cricket which they play) and wait for the batsmen to make a mistake. This can be highly successful in county cricket, but once elevated to test level these bowlers are required to attack and find themselves unable to do so. Just examine the performances of England's attack during the 1993 test series against Australia to see how helpless county pace bowlers appear when they do not have somebody at the other end 'making something happen'.

Consider, too, the tactics adopted by English test teams against county players who are also internationals. In county cricket, the overseas player (whether batsman or bowler) will usually face defensive tactics while the opposition concentrate on attacking the weaker (English) members of the side. In test cricket, the same English county players facing the same overseas players are forced to develop attacking tactics from scratch or risk losing the initiative from the start.

It is also worth noting that there is a flip side to Moxon's claim that Yorkshire's young players were adversely affected by not having an overseas player to help them shoulder responsibility. Another county captain, Worcestershire's Tim Curtis, pointed out in Chapter 7 that competition from overseas players has meant that young English cricketers from other counties were under greater pressure to prove themselves almost immediately. Far from the presence of overseas players helping to ease them into the first-class game, young English cricketers had to battle from the word go to secure one of the remaining places in their county's first XI.

The third advantage, that overseas players have raised playing standards on the county circuit, is impossible to prove one way or the other. It seems very unlikely that the introduction of 20 to 40 high-class players on to the county circuit could have done anything but raise the level of skill on show, but there are very few county professionals, English or overseas, who believe that overall playing standards have risen during over the last 20 years.

It may be that the dynamics of the county circuit will only produce a set number of high quality cricketers and that, because they are usually players of test status, most of these are now provided by overseas recruits rather than English-qualified cricketers. This argument (advanced by Tim Curtis and Hadlee, among others) seems to be supported by the readiness of English county cricketers to sit back and let their overseas colleagues take the lead role. Certainly John Arlott's 1968 promise that 'Now higher standards are guaranteed' has turned out to be wildly optimistic.

Indeed, it could be argued that English county players now form a group whose most talented members are still second best to the overseas cricketers with whom they share a dressing room. This being the case, county form becomes no guide to the ability to compete at test level, something which might explain why most of the leading county players to have emerged over the last ten years have failed as internationals.

It would disingenuous, however, not to point out that a different conclusion can also be drawn from the evidence assembled in this book. The counter-argument is underpinned by plotting the numbers of overseas cricketers in county cricket against England's test performances since the late 1960s. As the numbers of overseas players increase towards a peak in the late 1970s and early 1980s, England continues to win more test matches than it loses. Once the numbers of overseas players begin declining around the mid-1980s, England starts to be beaten by every test nation and enters an unparalleled run of defeats which so far has lasted ten years.

The fourth and fifth advantages seem unquestionable. There can be no doubt that the influence of overseas players on the financial viability of the domestic game has been nothing but positive. The arrival of overseas players in England, together with the three limited-overs competitions, prevented county cricket becoming a sporting backwater in which many clubs would have struggled to survive. With most people now watching cricket via their television sets, the names of overseas test cricketers are now more familiar to them than many of the members of their local county side. Hearing that one of those test stars has joined that local team is likely to encourage many to climb off their couch and make their way down to the county ground.

More importantly it is also likely to attract the attention of sponsors and advertisers wanting to buy a share of reflected glory. However, this welcome source of revenue does carry some danger with it. If, as happened in Yorkshire before the 1992 season, a firm is persuaded to sponsor an overseas player to the extent that they are actually paying his wages, that firm may well begin to set down conditions on the type, nationality or even identity of the foreign recruit. Yorkshire TV stipulated that the county club sign a 'household name', and as there were no bowlers available who fitted that description, the club was effectively forced to choose a batsman, despite the belief of many at Headingley that it was the bowling attack which needed strengthening.

The presence of overseas cricketers has not brought crowds flocking back to watch first-class county cricket, but it has increased gate takings beyond what they would otherwise have been. And even if it is concluded that the presence of overseas players has weakened the England test team, the takings from test matches (on which the counties depend for much of their income) has still continued to rise. England may continue to lose but at least supporters can cheer the performances of their local overseas player.

If the extra revenue generated by the presence of overseas players has not been ploughed back into the development of young English talent, then that is hardly their fault.

Almost as important as the increase in revenue for the English game is the way in which the arrival of overseas players helped shake up the traditional power bases of English cricket. In the nine seasons following the introduction of immediate registration nine different counties won the championship and to date only Glamorgan have not secured a one-day trophy. Clubs such as Essex and Somerset (if only for a while) were no longer second-class citizens on the county circuit, as their teams earned respect, the clubs grew richer and more influential, and a greater spread of county cricket supporters across the country had something to cheer.

However, as the dynamics of the county circuit evolve and absorb the changes in the power balance produced by overseas players (while at the same time new rules restrict counties to one import each), it is again becoming clear that successful counties need to build from a strong base of home-grown players. It is no longer possible to build a team around three or four overseas players with

English-qualified cricketers filling in the gaps. Overseas players, while a barrier against failure (a lesson which Yorkshire, Derbyshire, Lancashire and Sussex took longest to learn), are no guarantee of success (as Gloucestershire and Warwickshire discovered).

As for the sixth advantage, very few players have adopted Aquib Javed's policy of keeping a few tricks up their sleeves for international matches, although some have been known to coast through 'unimportant' county games (Garner/Imran) and produce an altogether more challenging performance during test matches. English cricketers, *if* they have the have sense to observe and the skill to act on what they see, have had plenty of chances to work out what most worries the overseas players who are potential test rivals.

And what of the 'cons', the disadvantages of employing overseas players, how do they stand up to analysis? The first, that overseas players restrict opportunities for young English players, seems highly probable. Many argue, like Alastair Hignell, that the large number of places available within the UK's 18 first-class county sides is a virtual guarantee that those with sufficient talent will find a way of succeeding. There are no doubt cases where, despite the presence of overseas players restricting his development, a young English cricketer has fought his way through to international recognition. Evidence seems to suggest that most young county pros are not chucked on the scrap heap without a chance to prove themselves. But in the majority of cases, the presence of overseas players does seem to have been a real barrier to maintaining standards among England's young test hopefuls.

The poor quality of the mid-1980s intake while the influence of overseas players was at its height (23 out of 36 test débutantes between 1983 and 1989 making no impact on the test scene), the 'Speak syndrome' (in which a player can suddenly turn from no-hoper to test candidate), and the cases identified in the examination of the 1988 and 1989 seasons suggest that competition with overseas players has proved fatal for some promising young English players.

At the same time the very paucity of young batting talent has been disguised by the decision of a number of Southern African players such as Allan Lamb, Graeme Hick, and Chris and Robin Smith to qualify for England.

The third 'con' (that overseas players are a disruptive influence), however, does not seem to stand up to analysis. In some cases young English players have been dismissed because their prospective salaries were needed to create an attractive offer for an overseas player. But this has happened very rarely and one of the plus points of direct sponsorship of overseas players is that this difficult decision is now taken out of the county's hands.

Whether it be arguments over money or anything else, overseas players (with a few well publicized exceptions) do not appear to have been any more disruptive than your average English county professional. Players' anger, for example, at the amount of money the young Barry Richards was earning from county cricket quickly turned to admiration once they saw how he was blazing the path for other less talented cricketers to increase their earnings.

In any case the 'disruptive' overseas players can often contribute more to their counties' success than those who appear more amenable. This was one of the lessons of the Somerset affair.

As with the 'pros', the fourth and fifth 'cons' both seem unarguable. Allan Border worked out how to dismiss Graham Gooch during his time with Essex and exploited it mercilessly during the 1989 tour. There have also been plenty of other examples where overseas players have developed tactics to use in test matches against England while on the county circuit.

The improving effect that county cricket has on young overseas players is championed by those in the best position to judge; test stars such as Richard Hadlee and Zaheer Abbas who also enjoyed lengthy county careers. They, and others with the same experience, argue that an overseas player without the right level of natural ability and will to succeed will not be turned into a test player by county cricket, but those with the necessary attributes, however raw, can be polished up into the finished article. It is an unquestioned belief everywhere in the world (apart from Australia) that English domestic cricket is the fastest and most effective way of developing overseas talent, and promising young players aim for a place on the county circuit almost as soon as they decide to become first-class cricketers. Meanwhile their mentors (whether it be Imran Khan, Mike Procter or Michael Holding) fight to find a position for their protégés.

The West Indies, in particular, have recognized the importance of giving their young players county experience and 18 out of the West Indies' top 25 test cricketers of the last 25 years made their county debut before they had played 10 test matches, 11 before they had even received their first international cap.

But in one area this particular disadvantage was self-inflicted by English cricket. The number of fast bowlers, especially those from the West Indies, employed by counties since the late 1970s has been out of all proportion to their success on the county circuit. Marshall, Daniel and Clarke were all great bowlers and would take wickets in any conditions, but this was not true of the second string such as Patterson and Croft.

That these two bowlers, and many others not so talented, continued to be employed after it was clear that their style of bowling did not suit English conditions was down to the belief that even a weak county side with a West Indian quick would earn some respect – remember Ontong's threat to resign if Glamorgan did not re-sign Ezra Moseley and Tim Curtis's description of the perfect overseas player as a '6 ft 9 in West Indian fast bowler', despite the fact that he played for a highly successful county which has usually employed overseas batsmen. Curtis's view seems to stem from the fact that as opening batsmen he has to spend hour after hour fending off fast bowlers playing for opposing counties.

This book has demonstrated that specialist West Indian fast bowlers have been the least successful overseas players during the last 25 years. Few if any counties have won anything by employing second-string fast bowlers (though this cannot be said for batsmen and all-rounders of similar skill), indeed all that it has done is provide rival test nations, the West Indies especially, with a depth of well-trained, fast bowling talent.

Moseley, for example, played with Glamorgan until 1986. Four years later he made his debut for the West Indies against England, replacing an injured Malcolm Marshall, and dealt the decisive blow of the series by breaking Graham Gooch's hand. Moseley, already 32, was jettisoned by the West Indies after two tests, but thanks to English cricket it had a highly experienced fast bowler to call on when one of the first-line attack was unavailable. And the selection of Moseley was by no means an exception; to the list of English-trained stand-bys can be added Eldine Baptiste, Winston Benjamin, Winston Davis and Tony Gray, who between them played 38 tests and captured 109 test wickets.

England's declining performance at home over the last 25 years and the success of overseas county professionals in these rubbers also seems to confirm that competing against England in England is easier for those players who have come to terms with English conditions.

Of course, most of the alleged disadvantages associated with allowing overseas players to take part in county cricket derive their credibility from the fact that the English test side has, over the last ten years, experienced its worst run of results since the start of international competition.

So, how have the advantages and disadvantages stood up to analysis? Well, the evidence for the first three advantages seems slim at best, while the last three appear to be self-evident. As for the disadvantages, the allegation of disruption seems simply mischievous, but the other four all have the ring of truth and are backed up by a considerable weight of statistical and anecdotal evidence.

In the final analysis it is possible to conclude that while the importation of overseas players has been good for the county game in England, the only advantage it has given to English test players is the chance to suss out their overseas opponents before meeting them in international matches. Rival test-playing nations, on the other hand, have the advantage of competing against an England team which, because of the poor quality of its younger players and a general lack of self-reliance, is not as strong as it should be. They also benefit from an extensive knowledge of English players and of English conditions, and finally, and most importantly, from county cricket providing a proving ground for their young players.

But did this situation have to arise? What happened to the glowing dreams of the late 1960s that the introduction of immediate registration would herald a new golden age for county cricket while improving the quality of young English cricketers?

Like many ideas in the late 1960s, the introduction of immediate registration displayed an over-abundance of idealism. All that was good about the idea was championed and the problems left for the next generation to deal with. There were a few lone voices, such as Mike Turner's at Leicestershire sounding a warning in the late 1960s, but most counties were happy signing as many overseas players as the laws would allow.

The two main causes of today's problems with overseas players lay in not foreseeing how big an influence the presence of overseas players would be on English test cricket and in not restricting each county to one overseas player each. During the late 1960s concern centred around the domestic game, since the test team, if not doing as well as it had in the 1950s, was still relatively successful. Because of this, steps were taken (the introduction of overseas players and the expansion of one-day cricket) which were specifically aimed at helping county cricket regardless of the consequences to the national side. Largely because of these decisions we now face a situation in which changes have to be made to the domestic game (the introduction of 4-day county matches and 50 overs a side Sunday games), which have much more to do with helping improve the national side than increasing the attractiveness of the county game.

With the considerable benefit of hindsight it is clear that the rule changes of 1979 should have been introduced earlier and, where legally possible, with immediate effect. Action should have been taken as soon as it became obvious that the numbers of overseas players in county cricket were touching 15 per cent of the total number on the circuit, which it did in the early 1970s, rather than the 5 per cent originally envisaged. Immediate implementation might have caused some legal problems and probably would have created a serious imbalance in the strength of some counties for a short period, but it would have gone a long way towards remedying the drastic situation in which English cricket finds itself today. In an ideal world changes to legislation should be made in a way which answers the needs of domestic and test cricket equally, but this (admittedly tricky) balancing act nearly always seems to be beyond the game's administrators.

What of the future? What influence will overseas players have on English cricket over the next 25 years and what steps could be taken to make sure the influence is a positive one?

As demonstrated earlier, the influence of overseas players on English cricket is slowly declining, but that does not mean that the subject should now be swept under the carpet. Had the danger posed by the presence of overseas players been fully realized 15 years ago, it might have been possible (by the immediate introduction of the one player per county rule) to have greatly mitigated the resulting problems caused to the national team. Unfortunately, as too often in British life, the stable door has been closed after the horse has bolted. The amount of damage caused by the wholesale importation of overseas players in the 1970s and early 1980s means that radical action is still needed. If it is not taken, Bill Lawry's warning that English cricket will take decades to recover from the mistakes of the last 25 years is likely to come true.

The presence of overseas players (or, more importantly, the legacy of the massive influx of foreign talent during the late 1970s) is not the only cause of England's decline as a test power. More important, for example, is the fact that unlike most of its international rivals, Britain no longer has a sufficient number of people devoted to becoming high-class cricketers. The fact that more British people than ever now play cricket of their own accord (as against being coerced into schools games), does not necessarily mean that the ambition to achieve the highest honours in the game is as strong as it once was. For the great majority of its players, club cricket in the UK has become (like golf and tennis) simply a pleasant way of taking exercise. There are a few, of course, who aspire to first-class level, but as cricket's profile declines and those of other, rival, attractions increase, they are becoming fewer and fewer. Cricket is too complex (and too long) a game to attract much commitment from the districted citizens of the UK.

For West Indians cricket is, despite the counterattractions of basketball, still the major cause of national pride. In Australia, it is part of the country's highly successful and sophisticated sports industry, as well as occupying a much more central role in society. In India and Pakistan involvement in cricket at the highest level provides a way of defining class and background in countries which are still strongly divided along social lines. In South Africa, cricket is a way of shrugging off the apartheid past, as well as recapturing past glories. Only in New Zealand, because of the dominance of rugby; Zimbabwe, due to the failure of the majority black population to take an interest in the game; and in Sri Lanka, because of the civil war, does cricket occupy a lower position in the sporting and social hierarchy.

Set against this background of global attitudes towards sport, the influence of overseas players in county cricket may seem insignificant. But modifying the part that overseas cricketers play in the domestic game is one of the few ways in which English cricket can begin to counter the steadily worsening situation for itself.

The intention must be to maximize the advantages of employing overseas cricketers while minimizing the disadvantages. There are a number of ways in which this could be done, but the best starting point would be to prevent overseas players from taking part in county championship matches. This would have the advantage of increasing the opportunities for young English-qualified players in first-class games, while still supplying the extra revenue produced by overseas players drawing crowds to one-day matches. There would, of course, be a fall-off in the attendances of first-class matches, but as these are usually watched by those wanting to support their county rather than see an individual player, it should be minimal.

When not taking part in limited-overs matches, the overseas players should be responsible for coaching other members of the team. This requirement should be made clear in his contract and, if possible, the overseas player should divide his time equally between the second team and the younger members of the first XI. This may appear to be a radical departure from accepted practice, but it is really only a return to the role taken by club professionals the world over.

Freeing the overseas player from the demands of first-class cricket would also give him more time to make more appearances for potential sponsors or advertisers, thereby creating more revenue for the club (and player).

One final rule change would complete the new arrangements – a stipulation that all overseas professionals must have played at least 20 test matches. This would prevent the county circuit from being used as a finishing school for young overseas players, while ensuring that those foreign recruits signed on by the counties had sufficient experience to make good coaches. It would also return the regulations to its original intention of enabling 'eminent' overseas players to take part in county cricket.

However, it would not be fair to remove all chance of young overseas players benefiting from the English cricket system. England still has the largest domestic circuit among the test-playing nations and, as the sport's founding nation, it should provide some assistance to those countries with poorer facilities.

This could be achieved by returning to the 1960s for inspiration and creating a Young Cavaliers side, which would consist of players drawn equally from England's eight test rivals who had played less than 20 test matches and who were no more than 25 years of age. These regulations would enable the side's organizers to pick players with some international reputation, but who nevertheless were still relatively inexperienced, therefore making the team an attractive proposition for English cricket watchers.

The Young Cavaliers would play each county on the circuit, perhaps replacing Oxford and Cambridge in the fixture lists, in 18 4-day games. Played in the right spirit and marketed in the right way, the team should attract considerable sponsorship and provide sufficient prize money for the county sides to field a representative XI.

A Young Cavaliers side to tour England in 1994 might consist of Inzamam-ul-Haq and Ata-ur-Rehman from Pakistan; Jonty Rhodes and Richard Snell from South Africa; Grant and Andy Flower from Zimbabwe; Damien Martyn and Brendon Julian from Australia; Vinod Kambli and Rajesh Chauan from India; Muttiah Muralidharan and Hashan Tilekaratne from Sri Lanka; Junior Murray and Brian Lara from the West Indies; and Jeff Wilson and Michael Owens from New Zealand. The batting line-up with Kambli, Lara and Inzamam to the fore, would pull in the crowds (as would the fielding of Jonty Rhodes), while the bowling attack, dominated by fast–medium pacers, would be particularly useful in English conditions.

Each player would be restricted to spending two years as a member of the Young Cavaliers side and nominations for places would be put forward by the relative cricketing authorities of each county. During the English close season, test calls permitting, the Young Cavaliers could go on tour.

To make sure that young English players benefited equally from the new arrangements, each county that chose to employ an overseas player (and some might not choose to) would have to pay a levy to the Test and County Cricket Board. This levy, along with commercial sponsorship and fund-raising appeals, would be used to create a cricket academy along the lines of the Australian model for young English cricketers. One of the academy's jobs would be to try and ensure 'close season' positions for their charges with overseas clubs.

If these measures were adopted they might go some way towards remedying the damage to the English test team caused, in part, by the introduction of immediate registration and the resulting import boom in overseas talent. This is not to say that the employment of overseas cricketers in county cricket is an inherently bad thing; in fact handled in the right way from the start it could have been highly advantageous.

Furthermore, it would be wrong to suggest that overseas players in practice have caused nothing but harm. The preceding chapters have contained numerous examples of ways in which playing with or against overseas cricketers has helped an English cricketer to develop his game. And likewise the presence of their test players in English domestic cricket has not always been good for rival test nations. Ageing overseas test players have often been exhausted by county cricket and have seen their international form suffer as a result. The more sensitive of the younger players, such as Roger Harper and Lawrence Rowe, have also found the demands of the circuit too intense and gone into decline as a result. Most importantly of all we should never forget that overseas players were instrumental in helping save county cricket from the near terminal unpopularity and financial disaster towards which it was sliding during the 1960s. It might only be a temporary respite, but there is much to be grateful for.

It is hard to believe that any overseas player has arrived in county cricket with even a subconscious desire to harm English cricket. Most would have wanted to take advantage of the experience to improve their game and boost their chances of succeeding at test level. Many would also want to check out their likely international opponents (which would include other overseas players). If they did not undertake as much coaching as some would have liked, or if their salary upset their English team mates, then the fault lies mainly with the respective county authorities who drew up their contracts and failed to make sure that either it included a clause on coaching or that the overseas player failed to observe it. Overseas players are contracted by English counties to score runs and take wickets against other counties, and most do this job very well. If the end result of this essentially commercial relationship is that English test cricket is weakened then the fault lies with the employer and not the employee. If English test cricket has suffered because too many overseas players have played county cricket over the last 25 years, as this book has concluded, then the blame must lie with the counties who signed them and the cricketing authorities that sanctioned the regulations that made such wide-scale recruitment possible.

Graeme Wright sums up the position best in his book *Betrayal*. He writes:

The fact that Gloucestershire, for example, could field three players ineligible for England provides an illustration of how short-sighted the game's administrators can be. Indeed, however well intentioned, in retrospect cricket's planning seems ridiculously short-term, devised more for the moment than for the future, failing to take into account man's determination to advantage himself of any loophole, rather than close it.

It is the conclusion of this book that the large number of overseas players who have gained employment on the county circuit over the last 25 years has had an adverse effect on the quality and the results of the English test team. How great an effect is a moot point, but it would appear to rank only behind cricket's declining social importance and the spread of one-day cricket as a negative influence on English test cricket.

County supporters, players and officials have cheered the efforts of overseas players as they have helped bring home domestic honours for their sides. But how many of them had the feeling, as they watched Marshall demolish another set of stumps or Border launch another square cut, that they were fiddling while Rome burned?

Statistical commentary

Appearances (see Table 1)

The five overseas players with the most appearances in county cricket have all at one time in their career been classified as 'English qualified'. In each case the change in status was simply to let a long-serving county professional extend his career without his employers being prevented from fielding another overseas player and there was no thought of any of the five slipping on an England sweater.

The next six players in the list were able to enjoy extensive county careers for one of two reasons. Turner, Rice, McEwan and Procter were all able to concentrate on county cricket because they, voluntarily in Turner's case, did not play test cricket for the majority of their careers. Mushtaq and Greenidge racked up 250 plus appearances for their respective counties because they both made their English débuts at the age of 18.

It is not until we come to the next four players, Asif, Intikhab, Richards and Lloyd, that we find players who managed to maintain a wholly consecutive, lengthy test and county career.

As would be expected, most of the long-serving overseas players are batsmen. Fast bowlers, particularly, find it hard to slog round the county circuit year after year. This being the case, the records of Procter, Daniel and Marshall are particularly praiseworthy.

Of the entire list only Curran, who is now not considered as an overseas player by the Test and County Cricket Board (TCCB), has declared his intention to continue playing county cricket beyond 1993. His only competition as the circuit's most experienced overseas player comes from Franklyn Stephenson (109 matches), Donald (96) and Winston Benjamin (75). The steady decline in the number of first-class matches in an English season since the 1970s, means that the record of Younis is unlikely ever to be challenged.

Batting (see Tables 2 and 3)

One thing is immediately evident from the table of those overseas players with the highest batting average – that the late 1980s had proved an easy hunting ground for overseas batsmen. Eight of the ten overseas batsmen with the highest average made their debut in the mid-1980s. To this number could also be added the names of Salim Malik, Azharuddin and Steve Waugh, all of whom had county batting averages of around 60, but who did not score over 2,000 runs or play more than one season and are therefore excluded from the table.

Most astounding of all is Graeme Hick's record of 11,418 runs at an average of 66 – all made in the 7 seasons leading up to his 25th birthday. Almost as amazing is Jimmy Cook's feat of joining Somerset at the age of 36 (never having played first-class cricket outside South Africa before) and racking up over 7,000 runs in just 3 seasons. The fact that Cook could arrive from the talent-starved domestic cricket of South Africa and murder English bowling from the word go seems to reinforce Rod Marsh's claim that many county cricket bowlers are now no more than 'pie throwers'.

All the mid-1980s players have had the advantage of relatively short county careers and none have really played long enough to have a bad trot, although Hick soon experienced one when he became English qualified. As far as heavyweight run scoring over an extended period goes, it is a mixture of the world's leading batsmen and run-hungry Southern Africans who make up most of the leading group.

But at the top of the run-scoring table sits Pakistani batsman Younis Ahmed. Younis, of the 3 counties and the test career with a 20-year hole in the middle, might be one of county cricket's less well-known overseas stars but he certainly scored a lot of runs. Trailing Younis come the pick of modern test cricket's leading batsman, Turner, Greenidge, Kallicharran, Viv and Barry Richards, Zaheer Abbas and (somewhat surprisingly) Mushtaq Mohammad. Filling in the gaps come the forgotten generation of Southern African batsmen, Davison, McEwan and Rice.

Bowling (see Tables 4 and 5)

The bowling averages table is a testament to the complete mastery of Richard Hadlee. As far as his record in county cricket goes, the New Zealand paceman is head and shoulders above even great bowlers such as Marshall and Procter. His bowling average is three points lower than that of his nearest rival (Waqar Younis) and four lower than any of the other bowlers who have taken a similar number of wickets.

Behind Hadlee, the figures of Marshall, Roberts, Clarke, Procter and Daniel reflect the dominance that these five fast bowlers wielded over English batsmen. Following the introduction of immediate registration, English county players used to dealing with Snow and Willis once or twice a season, found themselves facing uninhibited fast bowling in almost every match, and it was the four West Indians and the ebullient South African who were the most feared.

In second place in the bowling averages list is Pakistani fast bowler Waqar Younis. Given a good fitness record and help from the bouncy Oval pitches, it is Waqar who poses the greatest threat to Hadlee's crown. The influence of the

Oval pitches appears to be significant, as even Surrey's second-string fast bowler, Tony Gray, has managed to haul himself up among the bowling greats. Surrey were no doubt right to choose Waqar over Gray, but the West Indian (like Australian batsman Tom Moody) was probably jettisoned from the county game too soon.

The three remaining players at the top of the list are Joel Garner, Terry Alderman and Ian Bishop. Garner's record is unquestionably impressive and, in this context, Somerset supporters might wonder what they gave up. However, the Big Bird's 94 games compares poorly with Hadlee's 148 over a similar period of time. Alderman could have become one of the English game's leading bowlers had he chosen to spend more than three seasons in county cricket. He didn't, and all that is left is the memory of some beautifully controlled swing bowling and the knowledge of what might have been. Ian Bishop still has the chance to become one of county cricket's leading bowlers, but persistent back problems seem to be stacking the odds against this.

Hadlee apart, perhaps the most outstanding bowling performance over a lengthy county career came from Indian left-arm spinner Bishan Bedi. No wonder Bedi was resentful when Northants sacked him. Had he not teased half of his 434 county wickets from the usually unresponsive Northampton pitches, a performance on par with that of fast bowling masters such as Imran Khan and Michael Holding?

Bedi, of course, was not the only spinner to make a success of county cricket. Mushtaq Mohammad captured 551 wickets at 24.00; Lance Gibbs 338 at 24.50; Armritt Latchman 481 at 2.94; Intikhab Alam 629 at 30.00; and Dilip Doshi 303 at 30.49. All of this goes to prove that class spinners can be a force in county cricket, although the presence of uncovered wickets certainly helped their cause. Perhaps the spread of four-day cricket will do the same for Mushtaq Ahmed, Carl Hooper and the modern breed of overseas spinner.

The bowling equivalent of Younis Ahmed is the former Kent and Gloucestershire all-rounder John Shepherd, the only overseas player to take more than 1,000 first-class wickets in county cricket.

All-rounders (see Table 6)

Who was the best county cricket all-rounder of the last 25 years? Well one thing is for certain, it was not an Englishman. Botham's county record does not compare with the four overseas players who clashed at county level in match after match during the late 1970s. The records of Richard Hadlee, Imran Khan, Mike Procter and Clive Rice tower over those of their contemporaries. True, Sobers showed flashes of genius, but his county career was not long enough to build a track record to compare with that of his four rivals.

Of the four leading all-rounders, it is hard to pick a clear winner. On figures alone it would seem that the number one spot would have to be contested by the Nottinghamshire pair of Hadlee and Rice. Due to a back injury, the South

African's bowling was the least feared of the four, but his batting was in turn the most dependable. But this said, the sheer weight of runs and wickets making up Procter's county cricket record is hard to ignore, and there are many who argue that Imran (when he felt like it) could be the most devastating performer of all.

Nottinghamshire in fact have employed four of county cricket's leading all-rounders, for after Sobers, Rice and Hadlee they signed Franklyn Stephenson who surprised everyone, including himself, by repeating Hadlee's feat of completing the double.

But despite the heroics of these high-profile players, it was a much more prosaic figure who reached the one milestone which all county cricket all-rounders seek to pass. Only John Shepherd, of Kent and Gloucestershire, has played long enough and well enough to record the 'maxi-double' of 10,000 runs and 1,000 wickets.

Finally the all-rounders' table reveals two further truths. The first is just how successful a player Mushtaq Mohammad was, despite his tender years and his role as an overseas pioneer, while the second underlines just how valuable the underrated Zimbabwean pair of Clift and Curran have been to their county employers.

First-class playing records for overseas county cricketers

Key to statistical tables: M = Matches; I = Innings; NO = Not out; R = Runs; Bat Av = Batting average; OV = Overs*; B R = Bowling Runs; W = Wickets; B Av = Bowling average

*I was surprised and concerned to discover that not all county statisticians keep records of the number of overs bowled. Where this figure was missing, I have (wherever possible) tried to do my own calculations.

Table 1 **Number of appearances** (150 plus)

Surname	Initials	M	Surname	Initials	M
Younis Ahmed		405	Boyce	K.D.	211
Shepherd	J.N.	374	Zaheer Abbas		206
Davison	B.F.	327	Moseley	H.R.	205
Cordle	A.E.	312	Richards	B.A.	204
Kallicharran	A.I.	285	Marshall	M.D.	197
Turner	G.M.	284	Sadiq Mohammad		193
Rice	C.E.B.	283	Howarth	G.P.	186
McEwan	K.S.	282	Holder	V.A.	181
Greenidge	C.G.	275	Curran	K.M.	177
Mushtaq Mohammad		262	Engineer	F.M.	175
Procter	M.J.	259	Kanhai	R.	173
Asif Iqbal		243	Imran Khan		171
Intikhab Alam		232	Clarke	S.T.	160
Richards	I.V.A.	223	Wright	J.G.	156
Clift	P.B.	219	Murray	D.L.	155
Lloyd	C.H.	219	Majid Khan		154
Featherstone	N.G.	216	Sarfraz Nawaz		151
Daniel	W.W.	214	McKenzie	G.D.	151
Latchman	A.H.	214			

Table 2
Batting Average (two seasons and 2,000 runs plus)

Surname	Initials	M	I	NO	R	Bat Av
Cook	S.J.	71	124	19	7,604	72.41
Hick	G.A.	129	200	27	11,418	66.00
Moody	T.M.	38	64	7	3,557	62.40
Waugh	M.E.	59	92	16	4,611	60.67
Lamb	A.J.	92	149	38	6,679	60.17
Crowe	M.D.	48	79	12	3,984	59.46
Border	A.R.	39	62	11	2,746	53.84
Haynes	D.L.	63	111	12	5,305	53.59
Javed Miandad		123	202	33	9,042	53.50
Wessels	K.C.	53	94	11	4,329	52.16
Turner	G.M.	284	493	65	22,298	52.09
Kanhai	R.	173	272	47	11,615	51.62
Richards	B.A.	204	342	33	15,607	50.50
Zaheer Abbas		206	360	37	16,083	49.79
Kirsten	P.N.	106	181	25	7,722	49.50
Sobers	G.St.A.	107	174	30	7,041	48.89
Richards	I.V.A.	223	369	23	16,845	48.68
Greenidge	G.G.	275	472	35	19,840	45.40
Lloyd	C.H.	219	326	42	12,764	44.94
Rice	C.E.B.	283	450	65	17,053	44.29
Wright	J.G.	156	265	24	10,638	44.14
Kallicharran	A.I.	285	471	56	18,157	43.73
Pienaar	R.F.	45	72	6	2,876	43.57
McEwan	K.S.	282	458	41	18,088	43.47
Kapil Dev		40	64	10	2,312	42.81
Davison	B.F.	327	518	60	19,521	42.62
Shastri	R.J.	62	98	18	3,402	42.53
Fredericks	R.C.	45	80	8	2,991	41.54
Younis Ahmed		405	669	107	23,233	41.34

Table 3

Run aggregate (6,500 runs plus)

Surname	Initials	M	I	NO	R	Bat Av
Younis Ahmed		405	669	107	23,233	41.34
Turner	G.M.	284	493	65	22,298	52.09
Greenidge	G.G.	275	472	35	19,840	45.40
Davison	B.F.	327	518	60	19,521	42.62
Kallicharran	A.I.	285	471	56	18,157	43.75
McEwan	K.S.	282	458	41	18,088	43.47
Rice	C.E.B.	283	450	65	17,053	44.29
Richards	I.V.A.	223	369	23	16,845	48.68
Zaheer Abbas		206	360	37	16,083	49.79
Mushtaq Mohammad		262	454	46	15,961	39.12
Richards	B.A.	204	342	33	15,607	50.50
Procter	M.J.	259	437	38	14,441	36.19
Asif Iqbal		243	399	42	13,231	37.06
Lloyd	C.H.	219	326	42	12,764	44.94
Sadiq Mohammad		193	346	19	12,012	36.73
Shepherd	J.N.	374	540	96	11,907	26.82
Kanhai	R.	173	272	47	11,615	51.62
Hick	G.A.	129	200	27	11,418	66.00
Wright	J.G.	156	265	24	10,638	44.14
Majid Khan		154	270	17	9,610	37.98
Howarth	G.P.	186	323	25	9,284	31.15
Javed Miandad		123	202	33	9,042	53.50
Featherstone	N.G.	216	344	34	8,882	28.69
Imran Khan		171	277	47	8,734	37.97
Curran	K.M.	177	269	44	8,193	36.41
Kirsten	P.N.	106	181	25	7,722	49.50
Cook	S.J.	71	124	19	7,604	72.41
Sobers	G.St.A.	107	174	30	7,041	48.89
Boyce	K.D.	211	319	18	6,848	22.75
Lamb	A.J.	92	149	38	6,679	60.17

Table 4
Bowling average (150 wickets plus)

Surname	Initials	M	OV	B R	W	B Av
Hadlee	R.J.	148	4,162.2	9,031	622	14.51
Waqar Younis		31	992.1	2,980	170	17.53
Garner	J.	94		6,121	338	18.11
Marshall	M.D.	197		14,542	798	18.22
Alderman	T.M.	60	1,770.4	4,618	249	18.54
Roberts	A.M.E.	94		7,143	385	18.55
Clarke	S.T.	160		11,226	591	18.99
Bishop	I.R.	45	1,227.3	3,162	164	19.28
Procter	M.J.	259		16,299	833	19.56
Gray	A.H.	39	1,183.4	3,568	180	19.82
Daniel	W.W.	214	8,004.0	15,088	685	20.02
Bedi	B.S.	110	3,916.3	9,067	434	20.89
Walsh	C.A.	122	3,847.2	11,011	523	21.05
Imran Khan		171		11,269	535	21.06
Donald	A.A.	96	2,509.2	7,314	337	21.70
McKenzie	G.D.	151		10,337	465	22.23
Holding	M.A.	63		5,356	236	22.69
Holder	V.A.	181	5,309.5	13,530	586	23.08
Wasim Akram		44	1,931.2	3,606	156	23.11
Le Roux	G.	136		9,114	393	23.19
Sarfraz Nawaz		151	4,408.3	11,962	511	23.41
Rice	C.E.B.	283		11,227	476	23.58
Boyce	K.D.	211	5,578.3	15,704	662	23.72
Clift	P.B.	219		14,010	586	23.90
Stephenson	F.D.	109		10,181	425	23.96
Mushtaq Mohammad		262	4,681.0	13,224	551	24.00
Moseley	H.R.	205		13,184	547	24.10
Gibbs	L.R.	109		8,281	338	24.50

Table 5
Wicket aggregate (300 wickets plus)

Surname	Initials	M	OV	B R	W	B Av
Shepherd	J.N.	374		28,537	1,036	27.55
Procter	M.J.	259		16,299	833	19.56
Marshall	M.D.	197		14,542	798	18.22
Cordle	A.E.	312	7,013.5	19,281	701	27.50
Daniel	W.W.	214	8,004.0	15,088	685	20.02
Boyce	K.D.	211	5,578.3	15,704	662	23.72
Intikhab Alam		232		18,871	629	30.00
Hadlee	R.J.	148	4,162.2	9,031	622	14.51
Clarke	S.T.	160		11,226	591	18.99
Holder	V.A.	181	5,309.5	13,530	586	23.08
Clift	P.B.	219		14,010	586	23.90
Mushtaq Mohammad		262	4,681.0	13,224	551	24.00
Moseley	H.R.	205		13,184	547	24.10
Imran Khan		171		11,269	535	21.06
Walsh	C.A.	122	3,847.2	11,011	523	21.05
Sarfraz Nawaz		151	4,408.3	11,962	511	23.41
Latchman	A.H.	214		13,438	481	27.94
Rice	C.E.B.	283		11,227	476	23.58
McKenzie	G.D.	151		10,337	465	22.23
Bedi	B.S.	110	3,916.3	9,067	434	20.89
Stephenson	F.D.	109		10,181	425	23.96
Phillip	N.	144	3,477.1	10,638	423	25.14
Le Roux	G.	136		9,114	393	23.19
Roberts	A.M.E.	94		7,143	385	18.55
Davis	W.W.	102	3,122.4	9,987	350	28.53
Gibbs	L.R.	109		8,281	338	24.50
Garner	J.	94		6,121	338	18.11
Donald	A.A.	96	2,509.2	7,314		21.70
Ferreira	A.M.	138		10,891	335	32.51
Curran	K.M.	177	2,868.3	8,633	328	26.32
Doshi	D.R.	87		9,238	303	30.49

Table 6
All-rounders (3,000 runs at 25 plus, 200 wickets at less than 30)

Surname	Initials	M	Runs	Bat Av	W	B Av
Baptiste	E.A.E.	100	3,563	26.79	257	28.80
Clift	P.B.	219	5,825	25.77	586	23.90
Curran	K.M.	177	8,193	36.41	328	26.32
Hadlee	R.J.	148	5,854	38.76	622	14.51
Imran Khan		171	8,734	37.97	535	21.06
Le Roux	G.	136	3,341	28.55	393	23.19
Marhshall	M.D.	197	5,597	25.79	798	18.22
Mushtaq Mohammad		262	15,961	39.12	551	24.00
Procter	M.J.	259	14,441	36.19	833	19.56
Rice	C.E.B.	283	17,053	44.29	476	23.58
Shepherd	J.N.	374	11,907	26.82	1,036	27.55
Sobers	G.St.A.	107	7,041	48.89	281	25.62
Stephenson	F.D.	109	3,588	25.63	425	23.96

Table 7
Playing records (alphabetical order)

Surname	Initials	M	I	NO	R	Bat Av	OV	B R	W	B Av
Ackerman	H.M.	97	174	10	5,182	31.60	31	103	4	25.75
Alderman	T.M.	60	70	32	457	12.03	1,770.4	4,618	249	18.54
Alleyne	H.L.	47	56	12	470	10.68	1,170.5	3,656	128	28.56
Ambrose	C.E.L.	42	52	20	530	16.56	1,328.2	3,515	139	25.29
Aquib Javed		18	12	8	25	6.25	510.1	1,656	53	31.24
Armstrong	G.D.	30	42	11	426	13.74	655.3	2,423	72	33.65
Asif Iqbal		243	399	42	13,231	37.06		2,996	73	28.71
Azharuddin	M.	22	39	5	2,016	59.29	86.4	252	3	84.00
Baptiste	E.A.E	100	143	10	3,563	26.79		7,402	257	28.80
Barlow	E.J.	60	98	8	2,813	31.26		2,108	98	21.51
Bedi	B.S.	110	123	33	1,002	11.13	3,916.3	9,067	434	20.89
Benjamin	W.K.M.	75	88	18	1,636	23.37	1,930.3	5,660	205	27.61
Bishop	I.R.	45	57	8	901	18.39	1,227.3	3,162	164	19.28
Border	A.R.	39	62	11	2,746	53.84				
Bourne	W.A.	59	76	13	1,300	20.63		4,074	126	32.33
Boyce	K.D.	211	319	18	6,848	22.75	5,578.3	15,704	662	23.72
Bryson	R.E.	11	13	2	257	23.26	333.4	1,256	23	54.60
Cairns	C.L.	30	42	8	1,229	36.15	580.5	2,762	82	33.68
Carse	J.A.	11	10	8	129	64.50	238.5	722	22	32.82
Chappell	G.S.	52	92	9	2,493	30.04		1,967	71	27.70
Clarke	S.T.	160	155	18	2,130	15.54		11,226	591	18.99
Clift	P.B.	219	284	58	5,825	25.77		14,010	586	23.90
Connolly	A.N.	44	44	14	180	6.00	1,252.4	3,340	126	26.43
Cook	S.J.	71	124	19	7,604	72.41		68	2	34.00
Cordle	A.E.	312	433	73	5,239	14.67	7,013.5	19,281	701	27.50
Croft	C.E.H.	49	50	10	433	10.82		3,604	136	26.50
Crowe	M.D.	48	79	12	3,984	59.46		1,453	44	33.02
Curran	K.M.	177	269	44	8,193	36.41	2,863.3	8,633	328	26.32
Daniel	W.W.	214	187	86	1,043	10.32	8,004.0	15,088	685	20.02
Davis	B.A.	60	103	8	2,848	29.87	74.00	229	4	57.25
Davis	W.W.	102	113	34	1,230	15.57	3,122.4	9,987	350	28.53
Davison	B.F.	327	518	60	19,521	42.62				
De Villiers	F.	12	15	3	264	22.00		992	25	39.68
Dodemaide	A.I.C.	61	93	24	2,118	30.70	1,908.2	5,760	173	33.29
Donald	A.A.	96	107	37	876	12.51	2,509.2	7,314	337	21.70
Doshi	D.R.	87	92	30	387	6.24		9,238	303	30.49
Ellcock	R.M.	26	31	10	308	14.56	561.3	2,012	62	32.45
Engineer	F.M.	175	262	39	5,942	26.64				
Featherstone	N.G.	216	344	34	8,882	28.69	1,217.1	3,477	137	25.38
Ferreira	A.M.	138	194	53	4,088	28.99		10,891	335	32.51
Ferris	G.J.F.	71	76	26	550	11.00	1,790.2	5,802	224	25.90
Francis	B.C.	47	84	7	2,962	38.46				
Fredericks	R.C.	45	80	8	2,991	41.54	207.1	667	20	33.35
Garner	J.	94	92	27	1,170	18.00		6,121	338	18.11
Gavaskar	S.M.	15	23	3	686	34.30		69	0	0
Gibbs	L.R.	109	96	48	370	7.70		8,281	338	24.50
Gilbert	D.R.	20	26	6	292	14.60	602.2	1,695	55	30.81
Goldstein	F.S.	10	18	1	437	25.71				
Gomes	H.A.M.L.	42	63	9	1,199	22.20	333.5	923	23	40.13
Gore	H.E.I.	11	11	5	48	8.00		669	14	47.79
Gray	A.H.	39	32	6	223	8.57	1,183.4	3,568	180	19.82

Surname	Initials	M	I	NO	R	Bat Av	OV	B R	W	B Av
Greene	V.S.	16	21	4	218	12.82	449.0	1,484	52	27.48
Greenidge	C.G.	275	472	35	19,840	45.40		387	16	24.18
Hadlee	R.J.	148	196	45	5,854	38.76	4,162.2	9,031	622	14.51
Hanley	R.A.	17	21	7	131	9.36	399.1	1,182	37	31.95
Harper	R.A.	54	63	14	1,834	37.43	1,776.0	4,188	137	30.57
Haynes	D.L.	63	111	12	5,305	53.59	43.4	131	3	43.67
Hick	G.A.	129	200	27	11,418	66.00	1,047.3	3,249	100	32.49
Hickey	D.J.	13	9	5	19	4.75	281.5	1,102	24	45.91
Holder	V.A.	181	196	51	1,553	10.71	5,309.5	13,530	586	23.08
Holding	M.A.	63	82	10	1,271	17.65		5,356	236	22.69
Howarth	G.P.	186	323	25	9,284	31.15				
Imran Khan		171	277	47	8,734	37.97		11,269	535	21.06
Intikhab Alam		232	338	45	5,707	19.47		18,871	629	30.00
Irvine	B.L.	54	89	12	2,674	34.72				
Javed Miandad		123	202	33	9,042	53.5				
Jefferies	S.T.	55	81	19	1,888	30.45	1,428.0	4,595	138	33.30
Jones	D.M.	14	23	7	1,179	73.68	18.1	71	1	71.00
Joshi	U.C.	76	92	35	514	9.02		5,984	177	33.81
Julien	B.D.	80	109	15	2,057	21.88		5,256	198	26.54
Kallicharran	A.I.	285	471	56	18,157	43.75		2,352	49	48.00
Kanhai	R.	173	272	47	11,615	51.62		211	4	52.75
Kapil Dev		40	64	10	2,312	42.81	998.0	2,729	103	26.50
King	C.L.	18	30	1	969	33.41	274.1	769	21	36.62
Kirsten	P.N.	106	181	25	7,722	49.50		1,896	49	38.14
Kuiper	A.P.	12	17	0	407	23.94	125.3	393	12	32.75
Lamb	A.J.	92	149	38	6.679	60.17				
Latchman	A.H.	214	236	63	2,313	13.37		13,438	481	27.94
Le Roux	G.	136	156	39	3,341	28.55		9,114	393	23.19
Lloyd	C.H.	219	326	42	12,764	44.94		1,809	55	32.89
Maguire	J.N.	24	24	7	237	13.94	786.0	2,437	77	31.64
Majid Khan		154	270	17	9,610	37.98	723.3	1,674	51	32.82
Marshall	M.D.	197	253	35	5,597	25.79		14,542	798	18.22
McEwan	K.S.	282	458	41	18,088	43.47				
McKenzie	G.D.	151	161	40	1,830	15.12		10,337	465	22.23
McMillan	B.M.	12	21	4	999	58.76		808	17	47.52
Merrick	T.A.	57	72	16	774	13.82		5,260	205	25.66
Moody	T.M.	38	64	7	3,557	62.40				
Moseley	E.A.	35	43	10	655	19.85	910.1	2,729	114	23.94
Moseley	H.R.	205	207	86	1,502	12.41		13,184	547	24.10
Murray	D.L.	155	235	36	5,646	28.37				
Mushtaq Mohammad		262	454	46	15,961	39.12	4,681.0	13,224	551	24.00
Nanan	N.	32	58	5	846	15.96		257	7	36.71
O'Keeffe	K.J.	46	57	17	830	20.75		2,867	93	30.83
Ontong	R.C.	76	123	15	2,898	26.83	990.0	3,309	193	36.36
O'Sullivan	D.R.	26	31	9	347	15.77		2,001	84	23.82
Page	H.A.	12	16	4	201	16.75	240.2	839	25	33.56
Parker	J.M.	61	103	9	3,315	35.26	36.0	188	4	47.00
Patterson	B.P.	70	61	24	187	5.05		5,496	202	27.20
Phillip	N.	144	201	22	3,784	21.13	3,477.1	10,638	423	25.14
Phillips	R.W.	16	25	0	431	17.24				
Pienaar	R.F.	45	72	6	2,876	43.57	551.0	1,632	51	32.00
Procter	M.J.	259	437	38	14,441	36.19		16,299	833	19.56
Reifer	E.L.	20	26	8	357	19.83		1,761	49	35.93
Rice	C.E.B.	283	450	65	17,053	44.29		11,227	476	23.58

Surname	Initials	M	I	NO	R	Bat Av	OV	B R	W	B Av
Richards	B.A.	204	342	33	15,607	50.50		1,675	46	36.41
Richards	I.V.A.	223	369	23	16,845	48.68		4,699	101	46.52
Roberts	A.M.E.	94	117	32	1,478	17.39		7,143	385	18.55
Rowe	L.G.	17	30	1	1,059	36.52		84	1	84.00
Sadiq Mohammad		193	346	19	12,012	36.73		4,666	138	33.81
Salim Malik		22	33	9	1,891	78.76				
Sarfraz Nawaz		151	198	44	3,212	20.86	4,408.3	11,962	511	23.41
Shastri	R.J.	62	98	18	3,402	42.53	1,307.4	3,228	95	33.98
Shepherd	J.N.	374	540	96	11,907	26.82		28,537	1,036	27.55
Smith	R.A.	15	27	6	926	44.09		19	0	
Smith	C.L.	29	51	4	1,547	32.91		210	2	105
Sobers	G.St.A.	107	174	30	7,041	48.89		7,202	281	25.62
Stephenson	F.D.	109	162	22	3,588	25.63		10,181	425	23.96
Swart	P.D.	44	73	8	1,996	30.70	512.3	1,785	64	27.89
Tendulkar	S.R.	16	25	2	1,070	46.52	62.3	195	4	48.75
Turner	G.M.	284	493	65	22,298	52.09	33.0	114	5	22.80
Van Der Bijl	V.A.	21	16	3	331	25.46	671.3	1,290	86	15.00
Van Zyl	C.J.P.G.	12	10	1	115	12.78	286.1	850	17	50.00
Venkataraghavan	S.	46	71	20	988	19.37		4,767	171	27.88
Walsh	C.A.	122	144	25	1,776	14.92	3,847.2	11,011	523	21.05
Waqar Younis		31	29	15	233	16.64	992.1	2,980	170	17.53
Wasim Akram		44	67	6	1,438	25.22	1,931.2	3,606	156	23.11
Watson	W.K.	22	24	11	234	18.00		1,623	58	27.98
Waugh	M.E.	59	92	16	4,611	60.67	438.0	1,672	43	38.88
Waugh	S.R.	19	30	9	1,654	78.76		408	14	29.14
Wessels	K.C.	53	94	11	4,329	52.16		11	0	
Wilkins	C.P.	71	126	12	4,060	35.61		1,615	47	34.36
Wright	J.G.	156	265	24	10,638	44.14		193	2	96.50
Younis Ahmed		405	669	107	23,233	41.34				
Zaheer Abbas		206	360	37	16,083	49.79				

Bibliography

Bailey, Trevor: *Sir Gary*, Collins, 1976
Brearley, Mike: *The Art of Captaincy*, Hodder & Stoughton, 1985
Crace, John: *Wasim and Waqar*, Boxtree Ltd, 1992
Edmundson, David: *See the Conquering Hero*, Mike McLeod Litho Ltd, 1992
Engel, Matthew: *Sportswriter's Eye*, Stanley Paul, 1992
Foot, David: *Sunshine, Sixes and Cider*, David & Charles, 1986
Garner, Joel: *Big Bird, Flying High*, Weidenfeld & Nicolson Ltd, 1988
Gooch, Graham with Murphy, Patrick: *Captaincy*, Stanley Paul, 1992
Green, Benny: *A History of Cricket*, Guild Publishing, 1988
Green, David: *The History of Gloucestershire County Cricket Club*, Christopher Helm, 1990
Greenidge, Gordon with Symes, Patrick: *The Man in the Middle*, David & Charles, 1980
Hadlee, Richard with Becht, Richard: *Rhythm and Swing*, MDA Publications, 1989
Hignell, Andrew: *The History of Glamorgan County Cricket Club*, Christopher Helm, 1988
Khan, Imran: *All Round View*, Chatto & Windus, 1988
Lee, Christopher: *From the Sea End*, Partridge Press, 1989
Lemmon, David: *Cricket Mercenaries*, Pavilion, 1987
Lemmon, David: *The History of Surrey County Cricket Club*, Christopher Helm, 1989
Lemmon, David: *The History of Worcestershire County Cricket Club*, Christopher Helm, 1989
McGregor, Adrian: *Greg Chappell*, Collins, 1985
Moore, Dudley: *The History of Kent County Cricket Club*, Christopher Helm, 1988
Procter, Mike: *And Cricket*, Pelham Books, 1981
Richards, Viv: *Hitting Across the Line*, Headline Book Publishing, 1991
Roebuck, Peter: *From Sammy to Jimmy*, Partridge Press, 1991
Shawcroft, John: *The History of Derbyshire County Cricket Club*, Christopher Helm, 1989
Sobers, Sir Garfield with Scovell, Brian: *Sobers*, Macmillan, 1988
Sproat, Ian: *The Cricketer's Who's Who*, Lennard Publishing, 1992
Steen, Rob: *Spring, Summer, Autumn*, The Kingswood Press, 1991
Wooldridge, Ian and Dexter, Ted: *The International Cavaliers' World of Cricket*, Purnell, 1970
Wright, Graeme: *Betrayal*, H.F. & G. Witherby, 1993

Journals and magazines

The Cricketer
Cricket Life International
The Guardian
The Independent

Johnny Miller 96 Not Out
Sticky Wicket
Wisden Cricketers Almanack
Wisden Cricket Monthly

Index of names